bristol museum & art gallery

Guide to the art collection

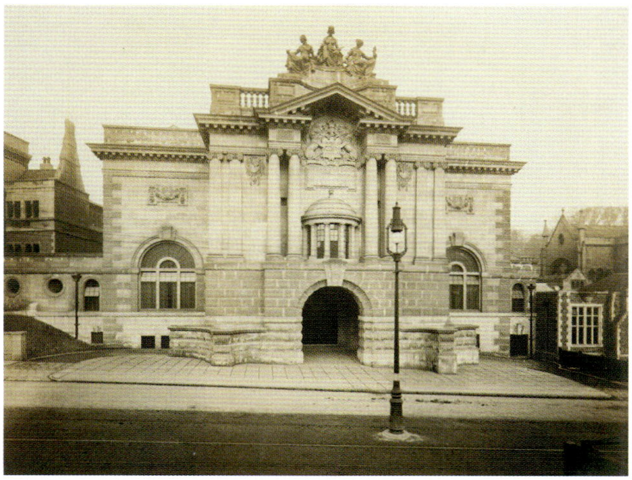

by Julia Carver

BRISTOL BOOKS

Bristol Books CIC, 1 Lyons Court, Long Ashton Business Park,
Yanley Lane, Long Ashton, Bristol BS41 9LB

ISBN 9781909446120

Bristol Museum & Art Gallery: Guide to the art collection
by Julia Carver

First published in 2017 by Bristol Books

Design: Joe Burt (joe@wildsparkdesign.com)

A CIP record for this book is available from the British Library

Front cover: Sir Lawrence Alma-Tadema, **Unconscious rivals** (see page 47)
Inside front cover: Jan Griffier the Elder, **Noah's Ark** (see page 19)
Inside back cover: John Craxton, **Four figures in a mountain landscape** (see page 74)
Back cover: Sir Howard Hodgkin, **Robyn Denny and Katherine Reid** (see page 78)

A brief history of the art collection

The art collection at Bristol Museum & Art Gallery tells the story of Western art, from the Old Masters to young artists emerging on the global art scene today.

Bristol Art Gallery and Museum of Antiquities opened in 1905 with the help of a grant of £60,000 (which would be worth over £6,000,000 today) from the tobacco magnate and Liberal politician, Sir William Henry Wills, later Lord Winterstoke. The gallery was sited next door to the Museum of Natural History and was originally conceived as a separate institution to the Museum, which had opened in 1823 as the Bristol Institution for the Advancement of Science and Art. The new building was designed in a decorative Edwardian Baroque style by Lord Winterstoke's cousin, the architect Sir Frank William Wills. The artist Sir Hubert von Herkomer opened the Gallery with a plea to 'keep the collection British!' However the names of the artists in plasterwork relief on the walls reveal aspirations for an international collection that included Van Dyck and Murillo along with Turner and Gainsborough. Important early gifts of paintings by major European artists such as Marieschi, Bellini, and Jacob van Ruisdael set the international ambitions for the collection.

The Museum purchased its first work of art in 1826, well before the opening of the Art Gallery. *Eve at the fountain,* a marble sculpture carved by the Bristol artist Edward Hodges Baily, illustrates the moment in Milton's 'Paradise Lost' when Eve is seduced by her own image seen reflected in a pool. Baily is best known for his figure of Nelson atop the column in Trafalgar Square. He also carved the frieze on the original Museum building lower down on Park Street.

The first Superintendent of the Gallery was Richard Quick, formerly of Wolverhampton Museum and Art Gallery, who occupied the post from 1905 until 1921. The Gallery was a success from the outset, attracting more than 200,000 visitors a year, and it soon became clear that an extension was needed. Planning for this was halted by World War I when parts of the building were requisitioned by the Army and it was not until after the war that the extension was built. In 1930 Wills family funding enabled the creation of the rear hall and more galleries.

World War II brought further devastation to the city, and the Museum and Art Gallery were no exceptions. During the Blitz of 24-25th November 1940, an incendiary bomb destroyed the interior of the Museum – along with many natural history specimens. The rear hall of the Art Gallery was also hit, although the damage there was less severe. The Museum's collections were moved into the Art Gallery with the desire that a new building would follow after the end of the war.

In the 1950s the Hong Kong-born German émigré director Hans Schubart planned for a new modernist building on Wine Street, but because of a lack of funds the development was never realised. Frustrating though this must have been, it meant that Sir Frank Wills's building

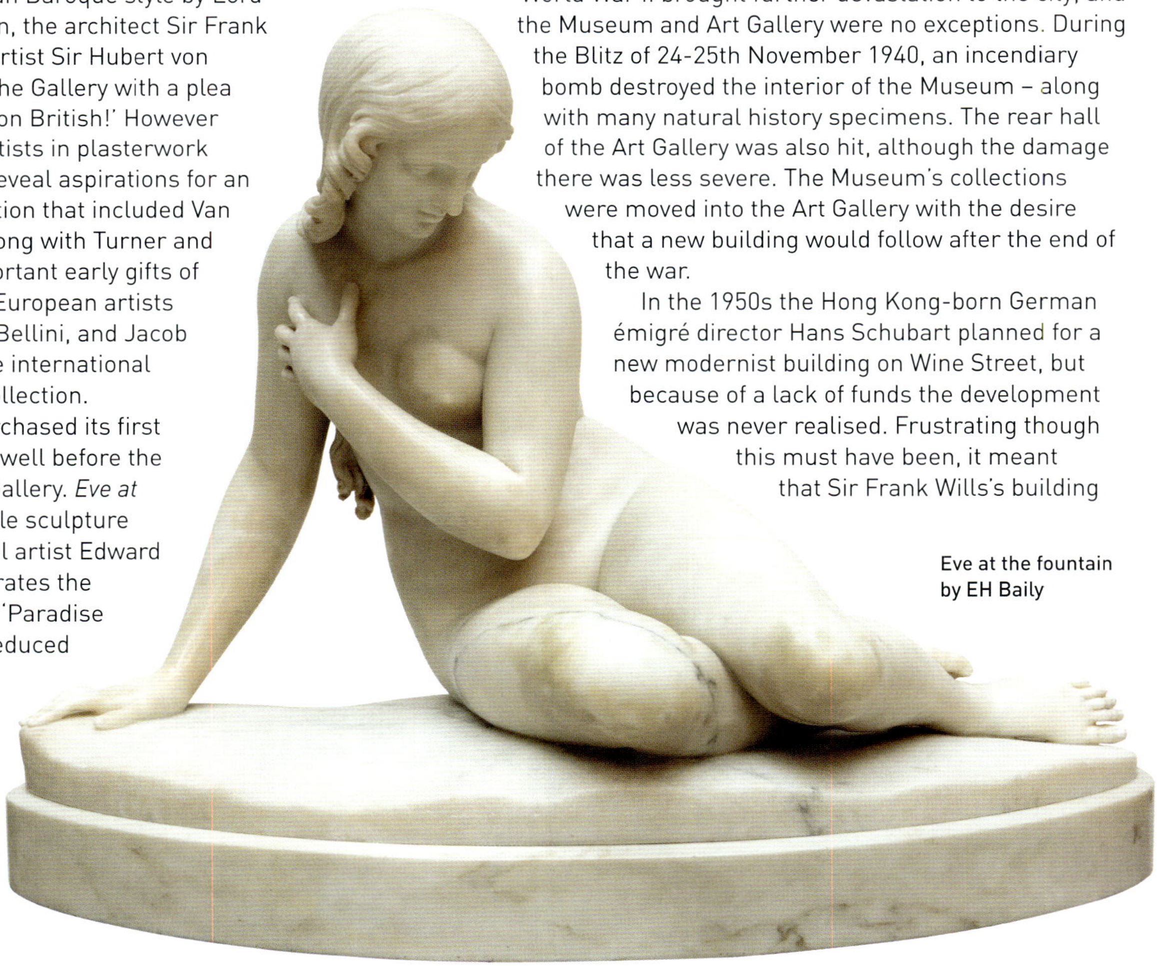

Eve at the fountain by EH Baily

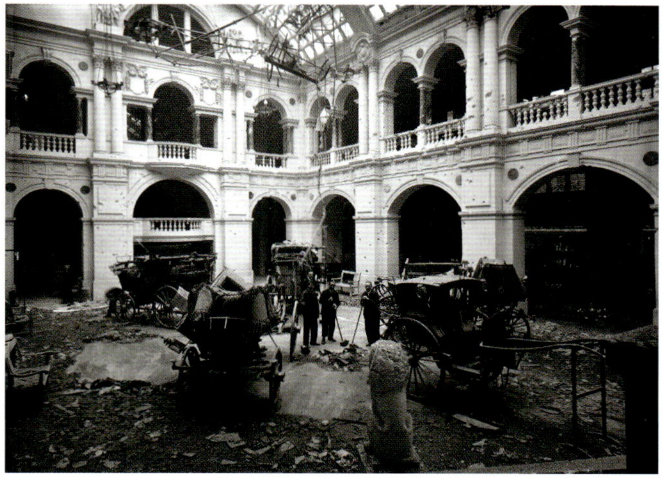

Blast damage following the blitz on Bristol on 24-25th November 1940

was preserved and later became Grade II* listed. The dynamic Schubart, who originally trained as a paintings conservator, became curator of the Art Gallery in 1946 and then director in 1953. He put his cosmopolitan stamp on the art collection, building on earlier gifts to acquire modern French paintings by Delacroix, Seurat, Courbet and Vuillard, along with German Expressionist drawings, often in the face of opposition from the local press. His confidence inspired the curators who followed to continue the spirit of his collecting.

Utilising funding from public bodies such as the Victoria & Albert Museum Purchase Grant Fund and the Art Fund, as well as funding schemes such as the government's gifts in lieu of tax, and private gifts and bequests, the collection grew to include Jacobean portraits, Venetian scenes and the monumental *Noah's Ark*. The early acquisition of Old and Modern Masters informed a wide-ranging collecting policy. In 1948 the Friends of the Art Gallery formed to assist with acquisitions, and they continue to run a lecture programme named after Schubart to the present day. Research was developed around the landscape paintings of the Bristol School artists that secured their reputation in the history of British art. In turn, gifts such as the Dyer Bequest (1961) and initiatives such as the Gulbenkian Fund (1976-80) and Art Fund International (2007-12) boosted modern and contemporary collecting.

Chronologically, the collection begins with the Northern and Italian Renaissance and moves on from Baroque painting to the Grand Tour. As new aristocratic patrons replaced the Church, artists began to explore new subjects such as still life and landscape painting. Pioneering British art in the 19th century is represented by the Bristol School of artists, the early artist travellers to the Middle East, the Pre-Raphaelites and the Aesthetes. The artistic ferment in 19th-century France is also represented, with examples of Impressionism and Symbolism. The influence of Modernism in 20th-century Britain can be seen in the work of David Bomberg, the St Ives School and mid-century Abstraction through to Pop Art. The work of Richard Long offers a contemporary approach to landscape art, and Bristol Museum & Art Gallery has a growing collection of artists' film and video. The acquisition of work by Ai Weiwei and Do Ho Suh has kick-started the collection of international contemporary art.

Today, Bristol Museum & Art Gallery continues to collect both historic and contemporary art. Examples of recent acquisitions include a 'lost' early watercolour of the Avon Gorge by JMW Turner, painted on a visit to family friends in Bristol when he was a teenager, and a live digital work by Alison Craighead and Jon Thomson that streams images from all the 25 time-zones of the world.

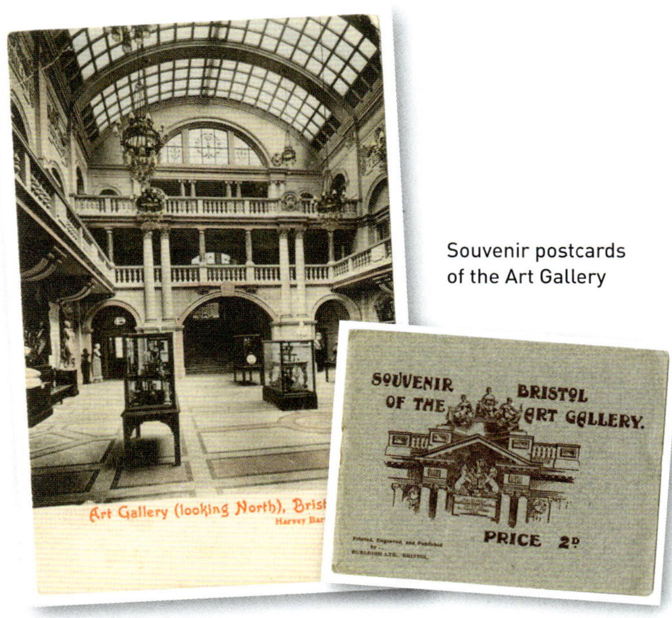

Souvenir postcards of the Art Gallery

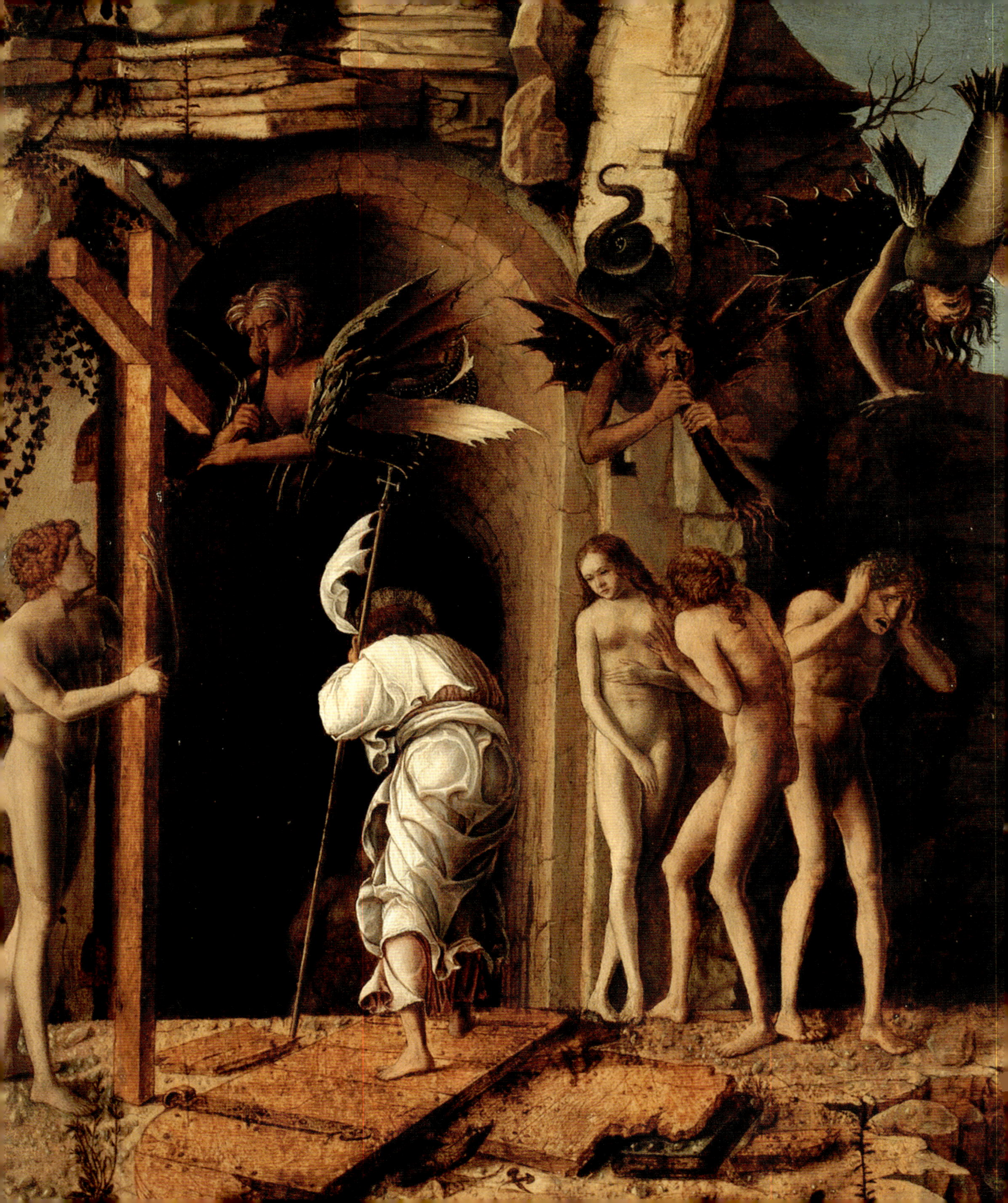

Old Masters: Renaissance, the Reformation and a changing world

The term 'renaissance' means 'rebirth', and is taken to refer to a combination of intellectual and cultural trends that originated in Italy in the 14th century and then spread throughout Europe. These trends affected everything from science and art to political thought. In Italy, the focus was on a return to classical learning from Roman and Greek antiquity. This was a period of rediscovery through the archaeological finds that revealed the glories of pre-Christian history and culture. In northern Europe, the cosmopolitan influence of the International Gothic was retained alongside the innovations of the Italians.

The Renaissance is where our understanding of the history of art in the West begins. During this period the realistic and monumental sculptures of ancient Rome inspired a visual language exemplified by the illusionistic, three-dimensional forms of the Florentine artist Giotto di Bondone (about 1267-1337). One of the earliest paintings in Bristol's collection is *The Crucifixion and Lamentation* (about 1335) by Taddeo Gaddi, who worked in Giotto's studio for 24 years. The shaded contours of Christ's body and the naturalistic arrangement of the figures mark a break with the stylised expression of Byzantine and Gothic art. The Renaissance combined scientific curiosity about the world and a desire for harmony and symmetry to produce an art that fused naturalism, humanism and innovation.

Portraiture from the period reveals the changing priorities: the solemn child duke clutching a goldfinch in Marco d'Oggiono's *Il Duchetto* is painted in the smoky (*sfumato*) style of Leonardo da Vinci, in whose studio d'Oggiono was employed. The Renaissance was a time of prosperity in Western Europe which, in England, saw the gradual replacement of feudalism by nascent capitalism and the forging of international trading links.

Cultural links soon followed. The English member of parliament Paul Withypool commissioned the Italian artist Antonio da Solario to incorporate his likeness into the nativity scene. To modern eyes, the appearance of the 16th-century figure of Withypool at the birth of Christ may seem jarring, but donor portraits were common at this time as a kind of promissory insurance for the afterlife of the donor.

Theology was changing too and art reflected this. Nearly two centuries after Gaddi's *Crucifixion*, the Protestant Reformer Martin Luther was portrayed in 1525 by Lucas Cranach the Elder as a shrewd and thoughtful figure. The individualistic style of Cranach's portrait anticipates the changes set in motion by Luther's Protestant Reformation.

While British art retained the angular emblematic qualities of the earlier International Gothic or mediaeval period, a monumental physicality can be seen in 17th-century Italian painting such as the Baroque *Flight into Egypt* by Il Cerano. The massive figures loom out of the picture and almost into the space of the viewer – an effect achieved using foreshortening and the skilful play of light and shadow (*chiaroscuro*). The Flemish artist Jacob Jordaens assisted in the studio of Peter Paul Rubens, where he learnt to create complex compositions. Numerous small group scenes in his *Nativity* (1653) unfurl rhythmically around the panel.

Around this time, the traditional patrons of art – the Church and the aristocracy – were joined by the gentry and merchant class. Rapidly developing trade increased the spending power of this class, who stimulated new styles and subject matter beside those of devotion and power. Artists began to paint secular subjects, such as Pieter Codde's scene of lords and ladies at play. The luxuriant display of fine fabrics underlined Dutch prosperity. The heavy clouded skies of Jacob van Ruisdael's portrayals of the Dutch landscape would have an important influence on later British art.

It is believed that Ruisdael's pupil Jan Griffier was commissioned to paint *Noah's Ark* by Sir John Trevelyan of Nettlecombe in Somerset. The artist used the traditional biblical subject of the Flood to paint a menagerie of animals. Natural history takes centre stage in this painting (along with a pair of mythical unicorns).

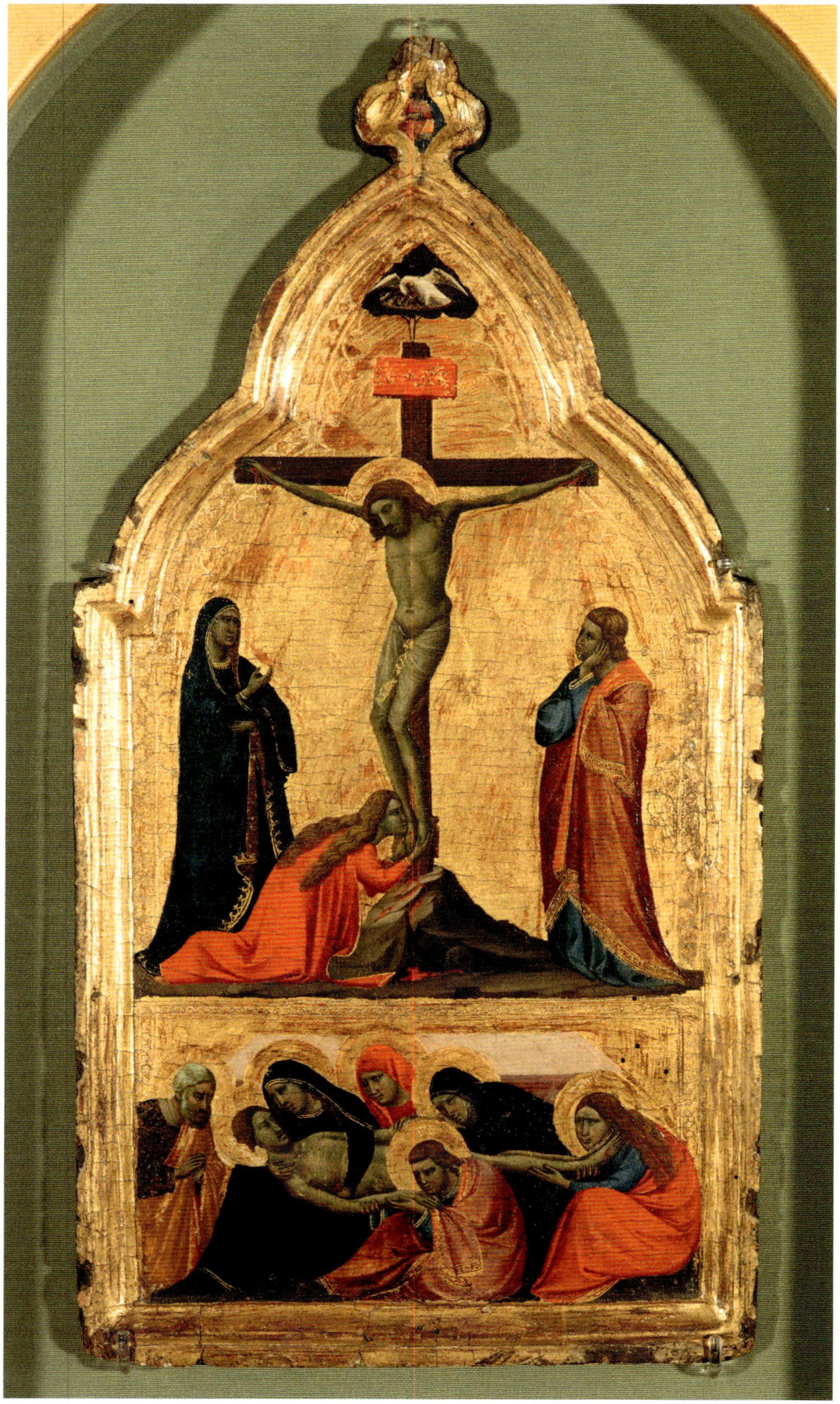

Taddeo Gaddi (about 1300 -1366)
Crucifixion and Lamentation
tempera and gilding on panel, about 1335
52.4 x 26.7 cm
Purchased with the assistance of the Victoria & Albert Museum Purchase Grant Fund, 1959
K2771

This panel shows the Crucifixion with the Virgin, St John the Evangelist and Mary Magdalene. The pelican above the Crucifixion is a symbol of Christ's sacrifice (as the pelican was supposed to draw blood from her chest to feed her young). In the lower portion the same figures are seen lamenting over the body of the dead Christ.

Taddeo Gaddi was a pupil and collaborator of Giotto, the most influential artist of the Italian Renaissance. Giotto brought a new humanity to art, replacing the flat formalism of Byzantine religious painting with a radical naturalism. Gaddi, who was described by Giorgio Vasari, the biographer and contemporary of the High Renaissance artists, as Giotto's most talented pupil, continued Giotto's innovations after the older artist's death, becoming one of the leading painters in Florence.

Gaddi used a limited range of colours. The gold background enhances the expressive outline of the figures. There is a striking naturalism and poignancy in the way that Mary embraces her dead son and the assembled saints support his body.

The panel is a variation on the subject painted by Gaddi in the right wing of an altarpiece which is now at the Gemäldegalerie in Berlin. It is smaller and was probably made for private devotion.

Giovanni Bellini (about 1430-1516)
The descent of Christ into Limbo
oil on vellum on panel, about 1475-80
51.8 x 37.3 cm
Bequest, FPM Schiller, 1946
K1654

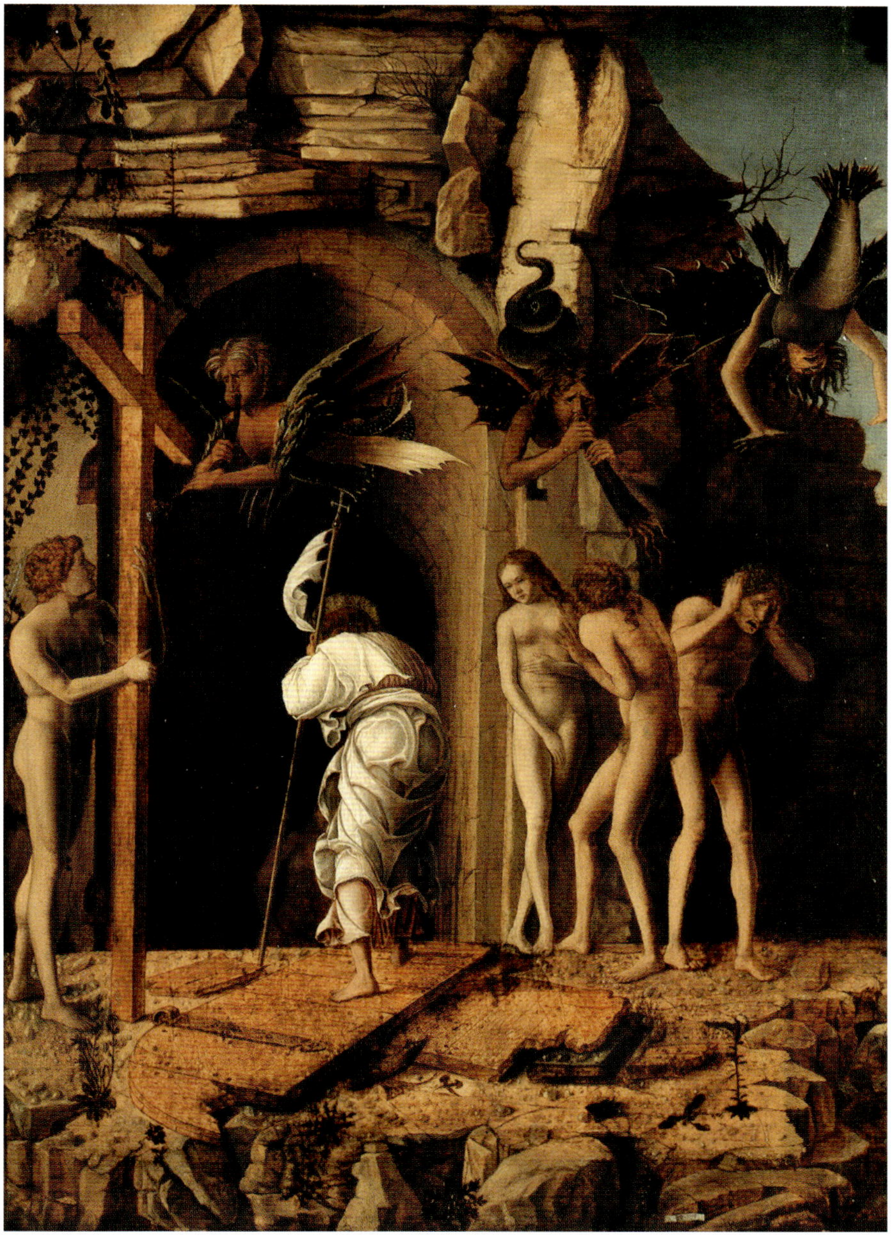

The Bible has only brief references to Christ's descent into Limbo, which took place after his crucifixion and before the resurrection. The story is told in full in the *Golden Legend* compiled in the 13th century. Limbo refers to the edge of Hell, a state of the afterlife for those souls not yet assigned to damnation or Heaven.

Giovanni Bellini came from a family of artists and his brother-in-law was Andrea Mantegna, with whom this painting is closely connected. *The descent of Christ into Limbo* was also painted by Bellini's father, Jacopo Bellini in 1459-60, but Giovanni's portrayal is very close to a drawing and an engraving made by Mantegna. It is highly naturalistic: Christ is depicted with his back to the viewer looking into the mouth of Limbo as humans and demons emerge. Adam and Eve are shown naked, underlining Christ's atonement for their Original Sin. Dismas, the Good Thief crucified alongside Christ, seems to stand on guard with his cross beside the abyss. Another man cringes at the cacophony made by the trumpeting demons, the defeated forces of Satan.

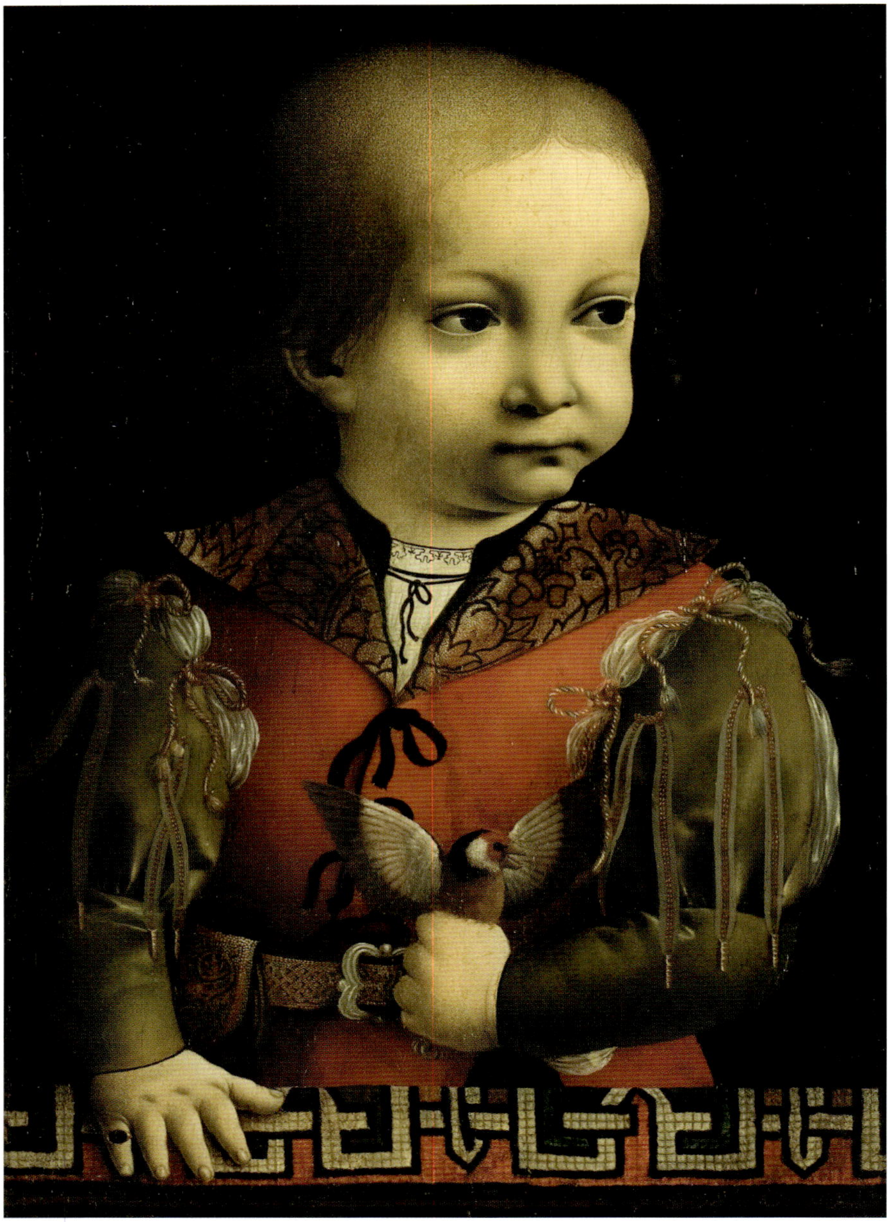

Marco D'Oggiono (about 1467-1524)
Portrait of Francesco Maria Sforza, known as Il Duchetto
oil on canvas, transferred from panel, about 1493
26.6 x 36.8 cm
Bequest of FPM Schiller, 1946
K1653

This smart young boy is Francesco Maria Sforza (1491-1512), son of Gian Galeazzo and Isabella d'Aragona. He was nicknamed *'il duchetto'* ('the little duke') as he became titular Duke of Milan in 1494 when he was only three.

The fine clothing, signet ring and belt-purse the child is wearing indicate his high status, but the way he clasps the goldfinch betrays a childlike lack of awareness of the pain inflicted on the bird. Children often kept birds as pets but the goldfinch, with the red spot on its head, doubles as a symbol of the events leading up to Christ's crucifixion ('the Passion') and a talisman against evil. The artist was originally thought to be Giovanni Ambrogio de Predis (about 1455-after 1508), the court painter to the Duke of Milan, Ludovico Sforza. In 2011, it was reattributed to Marco D'Oggiono who worked with Leonardo da Vinci (1452–1519).

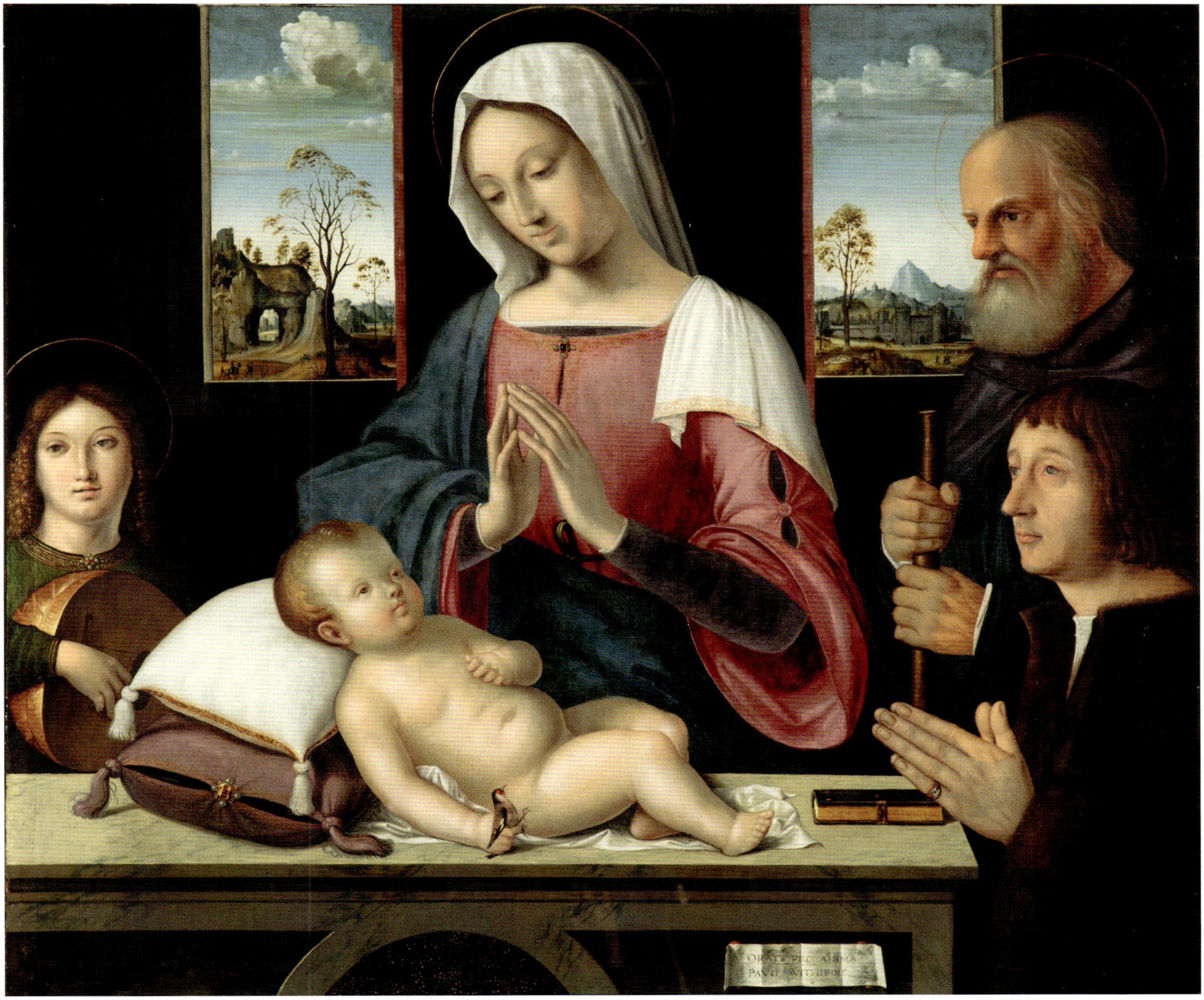

Antonio da Solario
(probably active 1502-1518)
The Virgin and Child with Saint Joseph and donor
oil on canvas on panel, 1514
78.7 x 91.5 cm
Purchased with the assistance of the Art Fund, 1937
K1394

The Holy Family is shown inside a chamber with a view of a distant landscape. Clutching a goldfinch, symbolic of the Passion, the Christ Child lies on a marble slab reminiscent of both a tomb and an altar. The English merchant Paul Withypool (died 1547), who commissioned the painting, kneels to the right. During the 15th and 16th centuries it was common for donors to have their portraits included in the religious paintings they commissioned. A painted piece of parchment (*cartellino*) implores the Virgin to intercede for Withypool's soul.

Withypool was a member of parliament for the City of London in the Reformation Parliament from 1529 to 1536, and moved in the circle of Henry VIII. He may have commissioned this work from the Venetian Antonio da Solario (known as *'Lo Zingaro'*, the Gypsy) when he was in Italy.

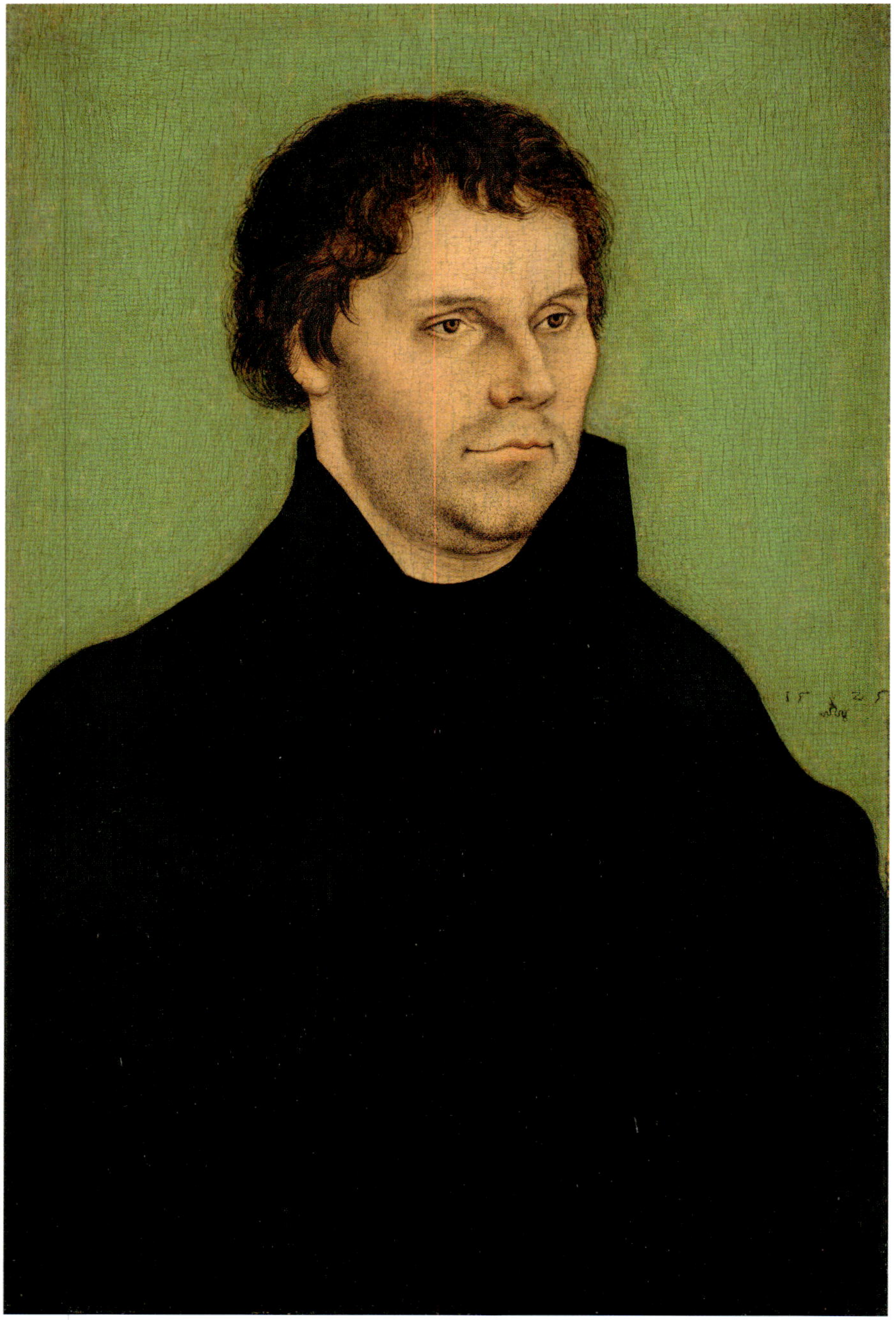

Lucas Cranach the Elder (1472-1553)
Portrait of Martin Luther
oil on panel, 1525
40 x 26.6 cm
Bequest of FPM Schiller, 1946
K1650

This highly individualistic portrait is remarkably informal, lacking any of the devices of Renaissance portraiture that would usually tell a viewer something about the sitter. Instead the artist presents what appears to be an unmediated vision, wholly focused on the face, with its soft, fleshy jaw and half-smiling mouth, as Luther gazes into the middle distance.

Lucas Cranach the Elder has been described as the 'painter of the Reformation'. He worked for 49 years in Wittenberg where he was at the centre of the Protestant movement. Through his paintings and prints of the Protestant reformer Martin Luther, Cranach helped to popularise the Protestant cause.

This portrait was painted in 1525, the year of Luther's marriage to the nun Katharina von Bora, possibly as part of a pair to mark the marriage. It was three years after Luther had begun to translate the Bible into German and eight years after his controversial 95 Theses attacking corruption in the Catholic Church, which led to his excommunication. Luther was forced into hiding, but the recent invention of the printing press ensured his ideas circulated around Germany and Europe and changed the course of history.

Giovanni Battista Crespi, called 'Il Cerano' (about 1575-1632)
The flight into Egypt
oil on canvas, about 1610-20
113.3 x 146.5 cm
Purchased with the assistance of the Art Fund, 1958
K2755

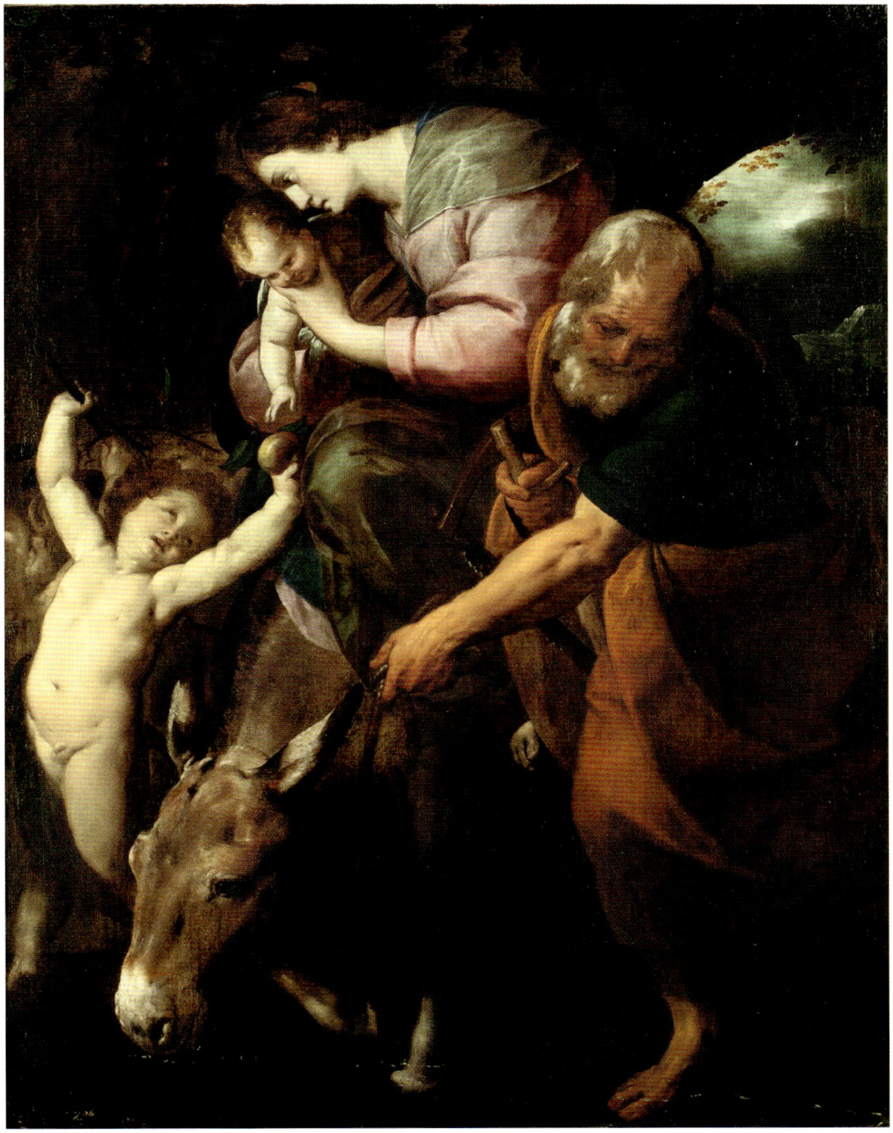

According to the biblical story, the Holy Family fled from Bethlehem to Egypt fearing that the infant Christ would be murdered by King Herod's soldiers. In this composition Joseph leads the donkey and Mary shields the child. A cherub holds out an apple, a reference to the Tree of Life in the Garden of Eden, indicating Christ's role as the new Adam. The extreme contrasts of light and dark (*chiaroscuro*) add to the claustrophobia of the scene, as the figures and donkey appear to project out from the canvas into the viewer's space. But there is also a subtle rhythm to the composition, as Joseph's posture echoes the forms of the donkey and the cherub, moving in the opposite direction to Mary. It is a complex and yet harmonious composition where the realism is emphasised by the solidity of the figures and the dark shadows they cast. This is characteristic of Baroque painting, the style that shaped the 17th century.

Il Cerano was named after his native village in northern Italy. He served his apprenticeship in Rome and then settled in Milan, where he became one of the greatest Baroque painters of his generation.

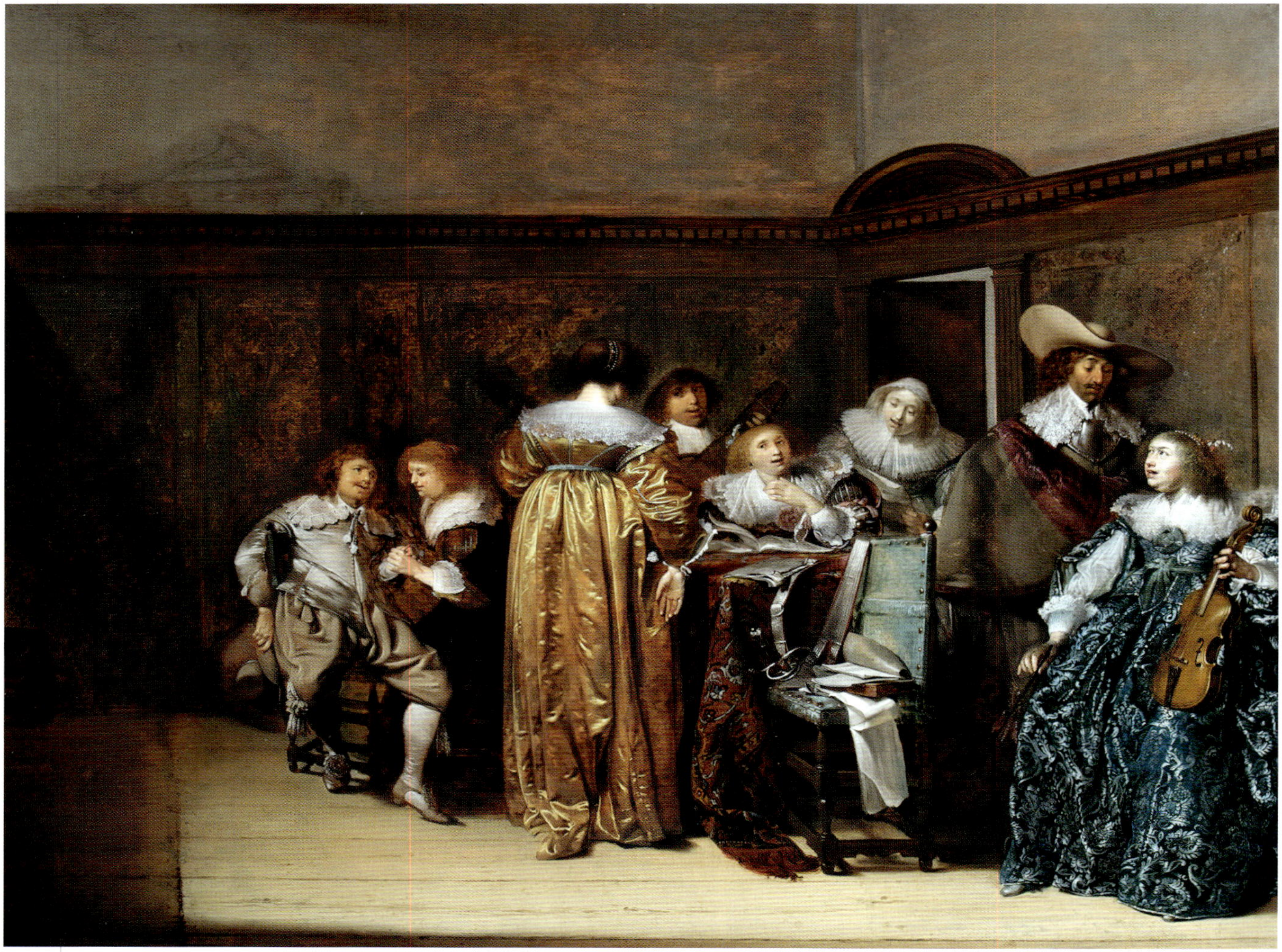

Pieter Jacobsz Codde (1599-1678)
Dutch cavaliers and their ladies making music
oil on oak panel, 1631
47.2 x 62.5 cm
Bequest of FPM Schiller, 1946
K1644

Elegant or Gallant Company scenes were popular in the Netherlands from 1620-1670, along with the more bawdy or moralistic Merry Company scenes of drinking peasants. This scene is distinct from a moralising genre painting, showing instead a group of fashionably-dressed upper-class men and women pausing between playing music.

The Amsterdam artist Pieter Codde, who was active in music and literary circles, was well known for his genre interiors. Often these contained coded references to romance, such as his painting *After the hunt* in the Rijksmuseum in Amsterdam, where the quarry is love. Likewise, the musical theme in *Dutch cavaliers and their ladies* seems suggestive of lovemaking. This is hinted at in the voluptuous curves of the violin resting on the knee of the lady on the right, and more overtly by the physical contact between the couple on the left. This aspect of sensual pleasure is emphasised by the exquisite attention given to the gleaming textures of the silk dresses that seem to rustle as we watch.

William Larkin (about 1585-1619)
Portrait of an unknown lady
oil on panel, about 1615
57.1 x 44.4 cm
Purchased, 1969
K3046

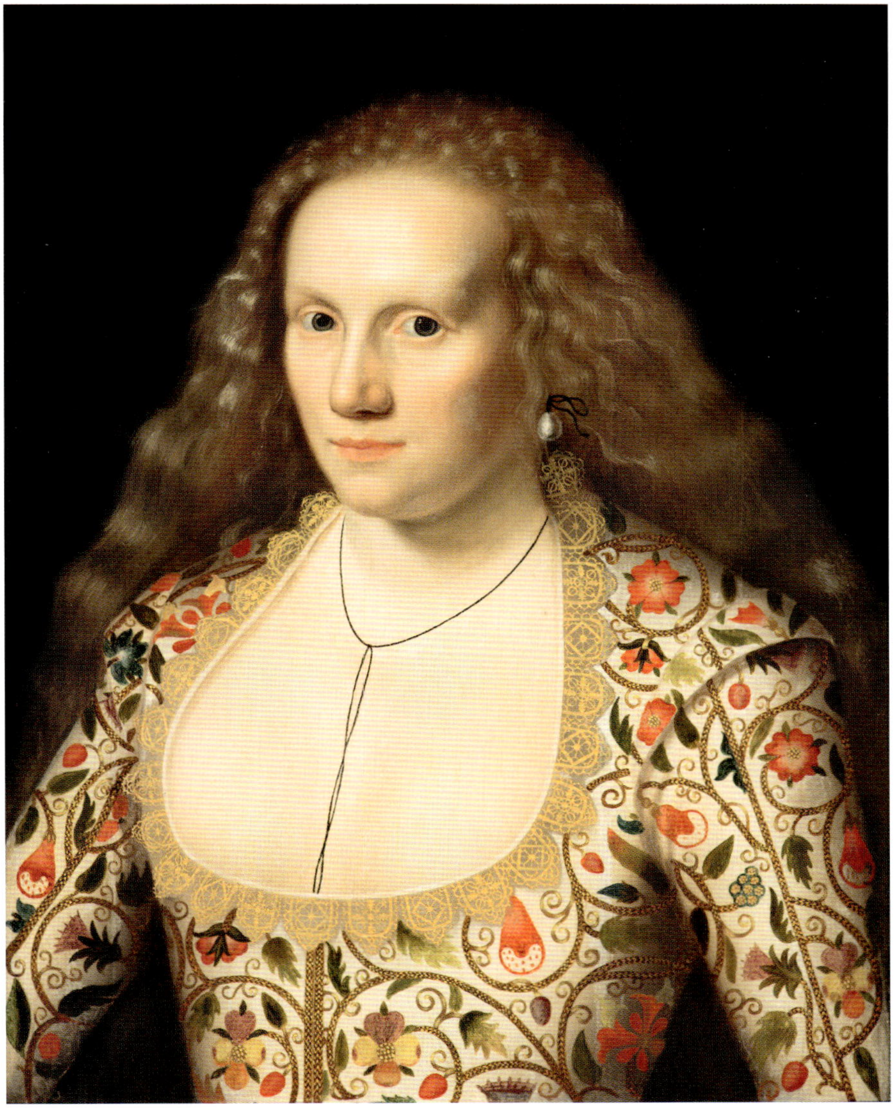

The unknown sitter in this portrait looks straight out at the viewer, confidently holding our gaze. Her low-cut embroidered bodice, high forehead and loose flowing hair were highly fashionable in 1615 when this portrait was painted.

After the Reformation, portraiture in England returned to the symbolic style of mediaeval illuminated manuscripts. Surface decoration was favoured over individualised facial features. A small circle of artists: Robert Peake, Marcus Gheeraerts, John de Critz, Nicholas Hilliard and Isaac Oliver established the richly embellished Jacobean style, in miniature, bust and life-size formats, on ivory, wooden panels and canvas. In some studios different artists took responsibility for the faces and the costume in a portrait. For example, the face in this portrait might have been painted by a different hand to the bodice. The clear pale complexion is modelled with subtle highlighting along the nose, cheekbones and on the forehead and chin. In contrast, the embroidery and lace are rendered in a flatter, more two-dimensional style that focuses on the design. The flowers include heartsease, roses and thistles; the tendrils that link them are plaited braid stitches in metallic thread. The lace is Italian needlepoint and originally formed part of a chemise worn under the bodice.

William Larkin died tragically young in 1619. Little is known of his life. The only evidence for the date of his death is his will which was signed on 10th April and proved on 14th May 1619. He is believed to have been the son of an inn keeper, also William, who introduced him to his neighbour, Robert Peake, the court artist who painted Henry, Prince of Wales and Charles I. Under the patronage of James I's cousin, Lady Arabella Stuart, Larkin became a Freeman of the Worshipful Painter-Stainers of London. It was only in the 20th century that a major series of large-format aristocratic portraits, now at Kenwood House in London, were attributed to Larkin, owing to their precise rendering of magnificent draperies, textiles, lace, and Turkish carpets.

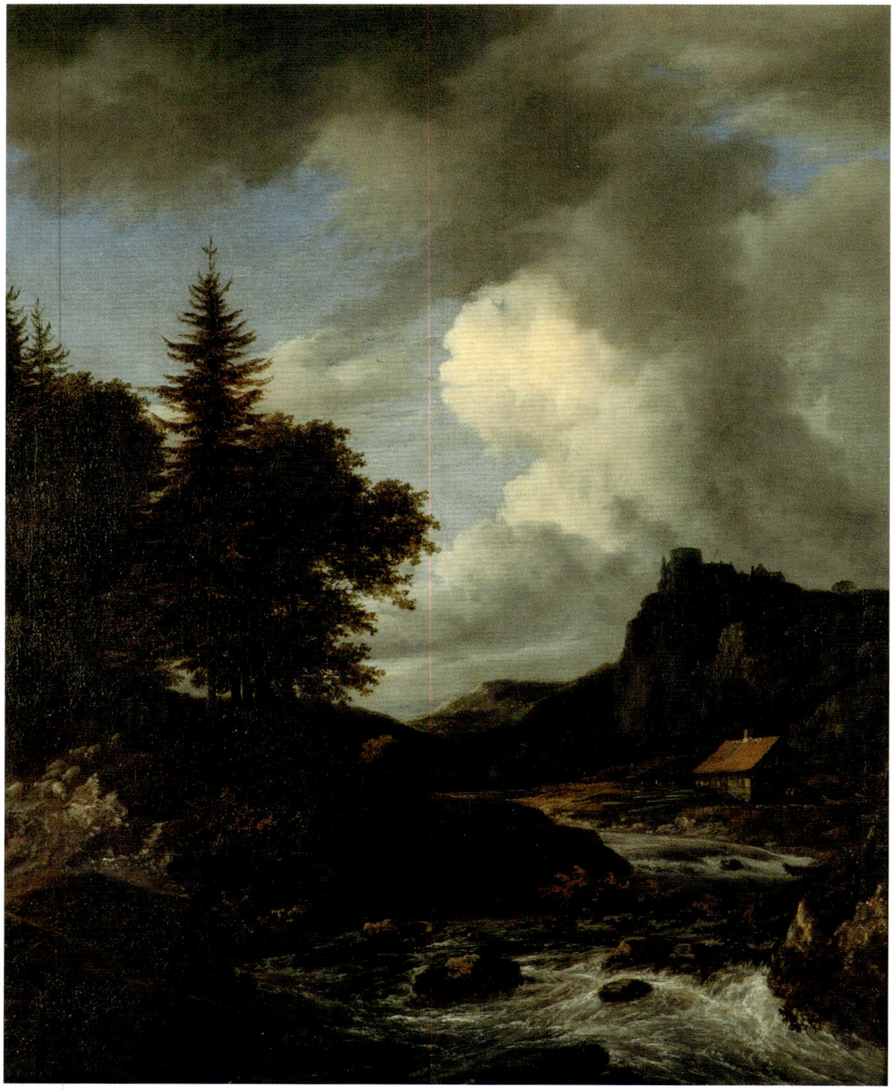

Jacob van Ruisdael (1628/29-1682)
River in spate
oil on canvas, about 1640
66 x 54 cm
Bequest of Ernest Cook through the Art Fund, 1955
K2421

In the portrait format of Jacob van Ruisdael's painting the dark greens and dense browns of the tall trees are set against the heavy white and pewter clouds whose greys are reflected and repeated in the rushing water below. The distant clifftop echoes the dark silhouette of the woody foreground.

The paintings of Jacob van Ruisdael helped to shape landscape art in its early years. He was born in Haarlem, the son of the painter and frame-maker Isaack Jacobsz van Ruysdael and the nephew of another artist, Salomon Jacobsz Ruysdael. In 1657 he settled in Amsterdam where he consolidated his mature style focused on pure landscape. The writer and painter Eugène Fromentin claimed that Ruisdael never painted a sunny day, concentrating instead on the effects of rain and cloud, which gives his landscapes a melancholy atmosphere. His precise recording of nature was highly influential to landscape artists in the 18th and 19th centuries, including Gainsborough and Constable.

It is not known if this painting was based on a specific place. Ruisdael frequently painted mountain scenery and travelled across the border to Bentheim in 1647, where he painted the castle. Alternatively, it has been suggested that the view may have been inspired by the Scandinavian mountain studies of the Amsterdam landscape painter Allart van Everdingen.

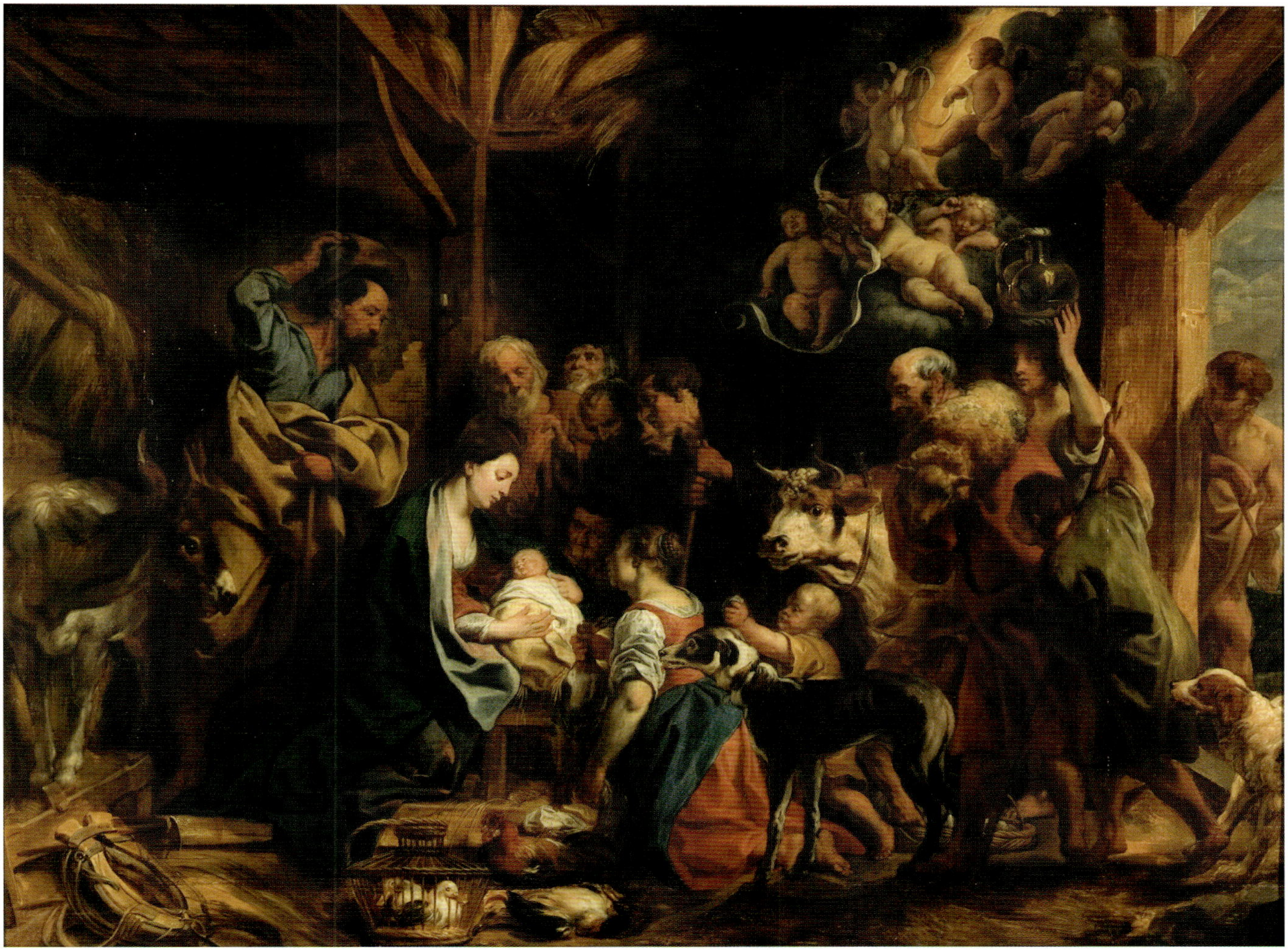

Jacob Jordaens the Elder (1593-1678)
The Nativity
oil on panel, about 1653
126.3 x 166.3 cm
Purchased, 1931
K1093

A throng of peasants and their animals crowd into the stable to greet the new-born Christ cradled in Mary's arms. Watched over by cherubs hovering above, these earthy figures have been arranged by Jordaens to give the viewer the impression of being part of the adoring crowd. Notice the way the water-carrier looks out and holds our gaze.

Jacob Jordaens was born in Antwerp and worked for Peter Paul Rubens on his later commissions in 1636-37. After the deaths of Rubens and Van Dyck he became the leading Flemish painter of his day. Catholicism was the official religion in Spanish-occupied Antwerp, but the Eighty Years' War (fought over the religious divisions between the Protestant north and the Catholic south) ended with the independence of the Netherlands in 1648. Jordaens converted to Protestantism in around 1650, before this painting was made. His Calvinist teaching is expressed in the naturally painted human figures in his religious scenes. He painted *The Adoration of the shepherds* at least three times in the early 1650s.

This rendering is painted over fifteen joined oak panels. X-ray examination has revealed a smaller composition, *The return from Egypt*, underneath, which Jordaens may have painted up to 30 years earlier.

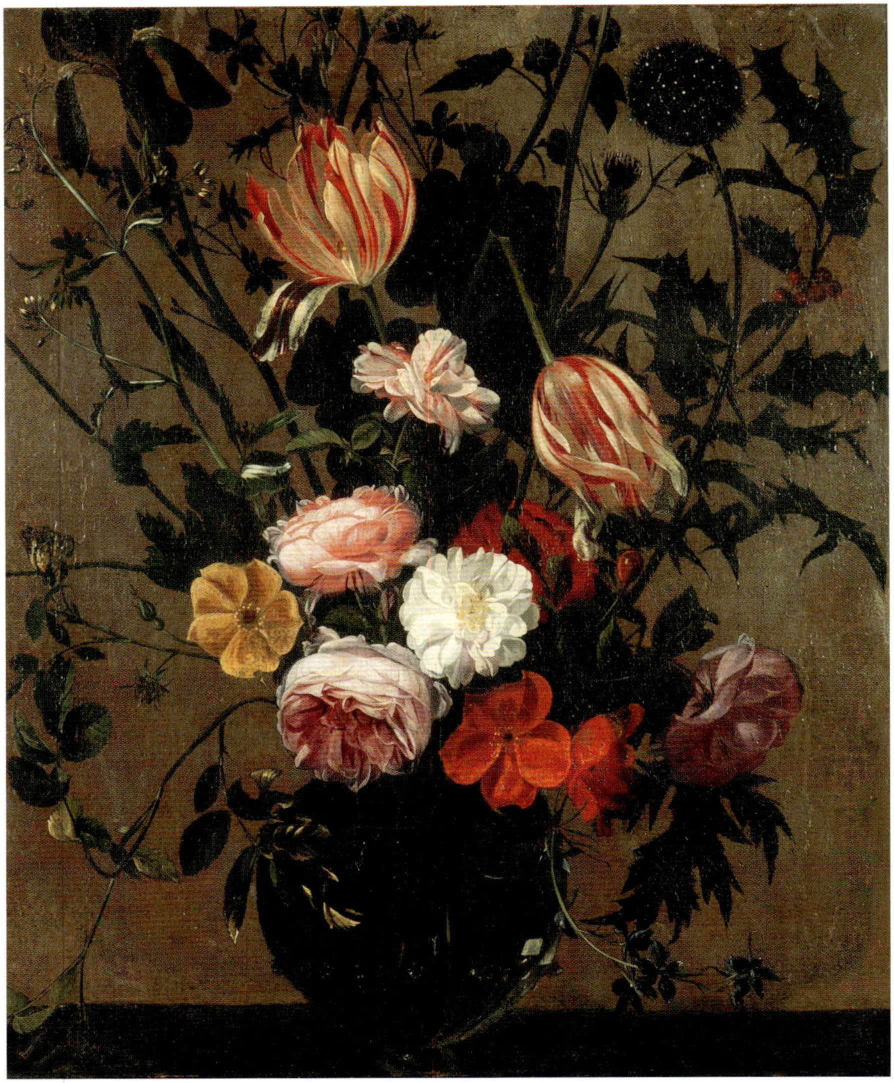

17th-century Flemish School
Flowerpiece
oil on canvas,
between 1675-1700
58.5 x 48.5 cm
Bequest of Alan Frederick Penraven, 1922
K711

The fashion for flower painting in the 17th century coincided with an interest in horticulture and with recording plant species in beautifully illustrated botanical guides. Flowers represented luxury since flower gardens were the preserve of the wealthy. Tulips, first introduced into Europe from Turkey, were particularly prized. The roses and irises in this painting would not have bloomed at the same time as tulips, but Dutch and Flemish artists often combined plants from several seasons.

There is also a sombre aspect to the painting. The tulip's broken stem hints at the fleeting beauty of the flowers and invites reflection on the transience of life. In contrast with the bright flowers, the dark prickly holly leaves allude to the crown of thorns worn by Christ on the cross.

The unknown painter of this flower piece was probably influenced by Jan Davidsz de Heem, one of the best known of the 17th-century still-life painters whose paintings were purchased by the new merchant class of art collectors for display in their homes.

Jan Griffier the Elder
(about 1646-1718)
Noah's Ark
oil on canvas, about 1710
374 x 374 cm
Purchased with assistance from the Victoria & Albert Museum Purchase Grant Fund, the GWS Melhuish Bequest, the Art Fund, the Wills Art Fund, the Peter John Blyth Art Fund, a private trust fund and the Friends of Bristol Art Gallery, 1992
K5531

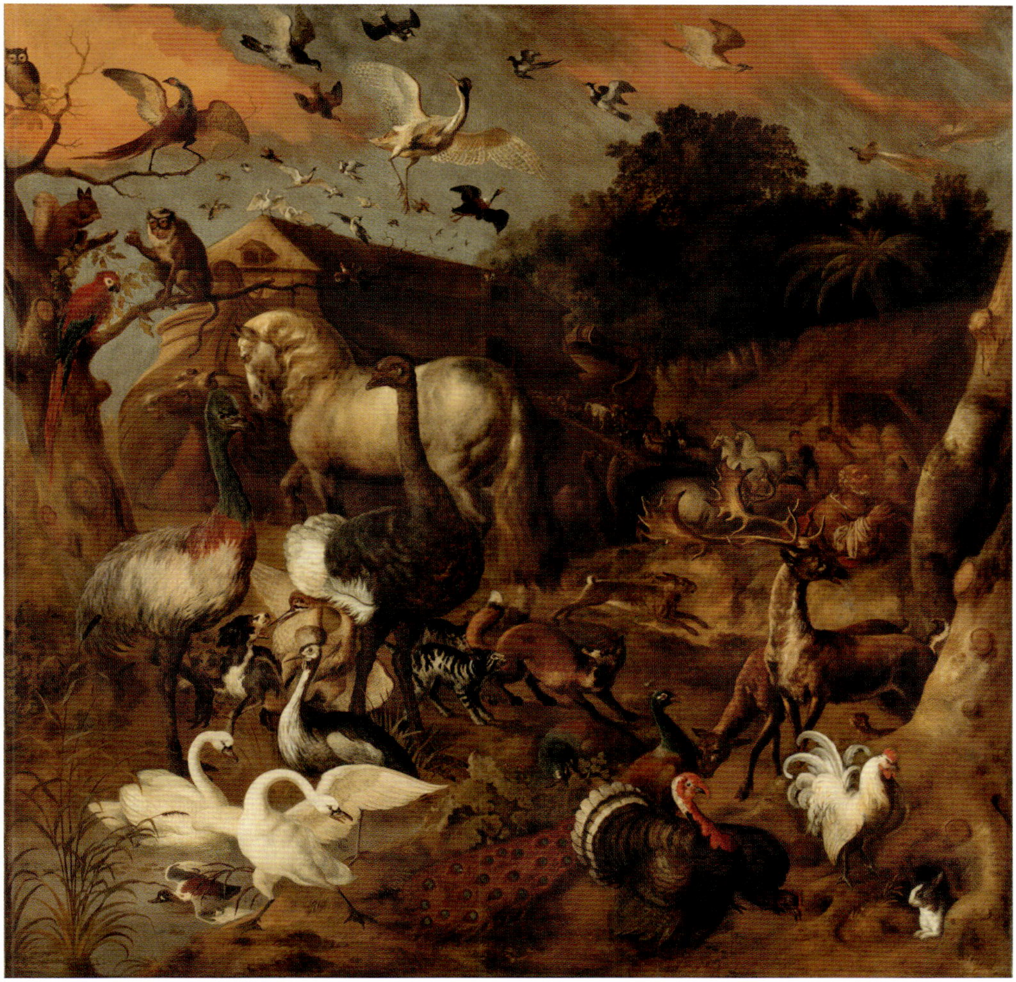

In the Old Testament God instructed Noah to build a vessel large enough to save his family and preserve a pair of all the world's animals from the Great Flood. In depicting the gathering of all the animals onto the Ark on a grand scale, Jan Griffier shows his skill as an animal painter. The interplay between the various birds and beasts is dynamically observed in a composition that spirals out from the centre where a fox and two cats bark and hiss at each other. In the foreground, a swan rears up and there is a flurry in the sky as assorted birds come to land on the Ark.

In a departure from the biblical tale, not all the animals in the painting have a partner. Some pairs, like the swans, appear twice, and Griffier also included the mythical unicorns trotting up the ramp.

Griffier trained with Roelart Roghman and Jacob van Ruisdael in Amsterdam before coming to England after the Great Fire of London in 1666 (which he painted). In the 1680s he studied with the animal painter Francis Barker. The contemporary taste for animal paintings was partly inspired by a growing interest in the animal world and the private menageries that Griffier and Barker would have visited to make their studies.

This immense painting was probably commissioned by Sir John Trevelyan of Nettlecombe Court, Somerset, where it hung in the Great Hall for almost 300 years. The biblical scene is an unusual choice for a country house, where sporting pictures were the usual fare. Sport was not out of favour entirely, however. Circular cracks all over the picture's surface are the result of impact from ball games and there is even evidence of the painting having been hit by gunshot.

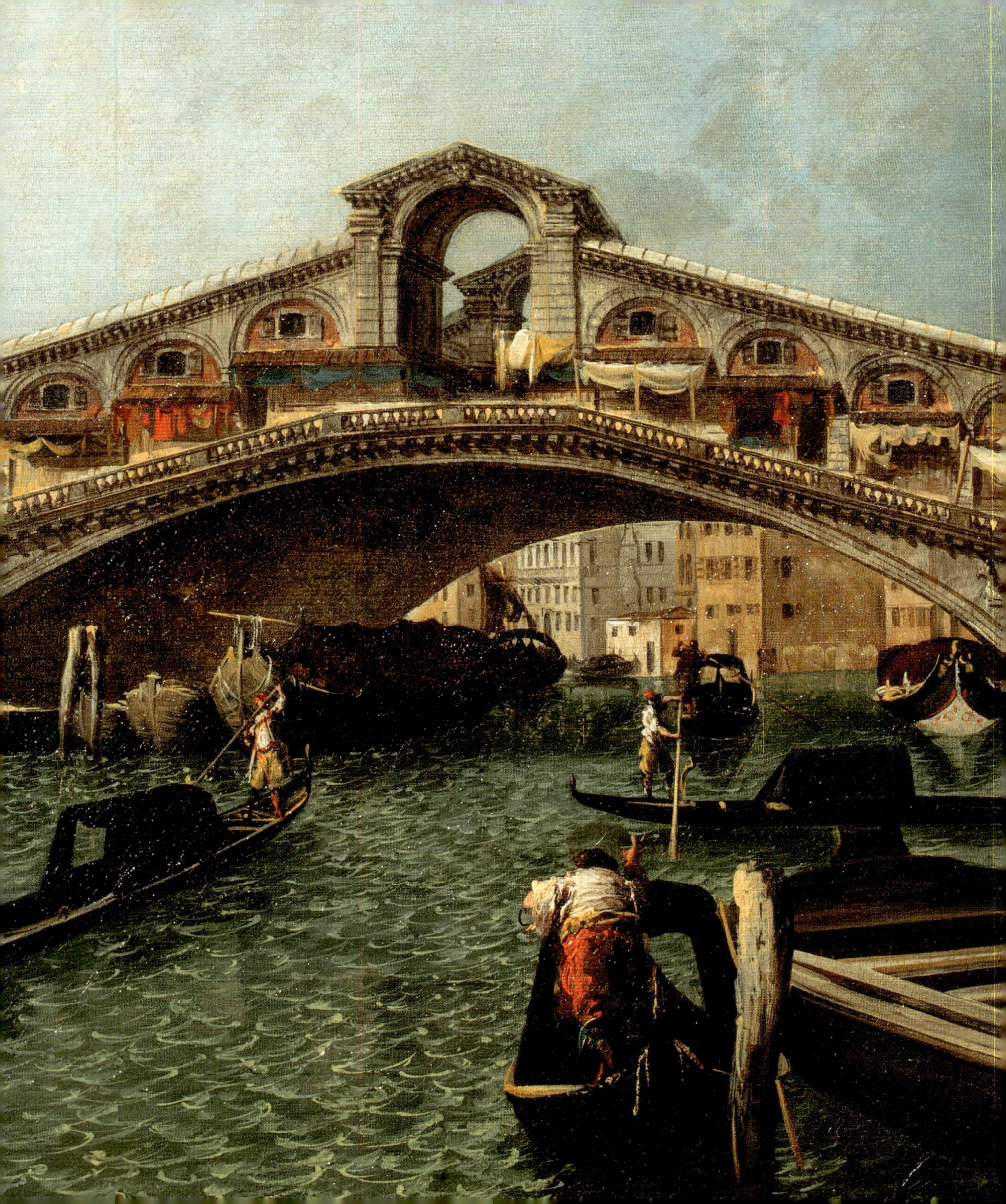

The Grand Tour and the Enlightenment

The expansion of art patronage in the 17th century widened the pictorial possibilities of art. In the 18th century the 'Grand Tour' of Europe was, among other things, an art education. It introduced young British and French aristocrats to classical civilisation and art, as well as to artists and fellow collectors. Wealthy young men would travel across Europe and return with an art collection, often having had their portraits painted by ambitious artists also on the Tour.

The member of parliament, collector and antiquarian Horace Walpole, who commissioned *The 'out of town' party* by Sir Joshua Reynolds, travelled to Reims, Dijon and Lyon, and then on to Geneva and Italy with the Romantic poet Thomas Gray. The 'Conversation Piece' portrait of his friends, George Selwyn, 'Gilly' Williams and Lord Edgcumbe, expresses the ideals of the Grand Tour, notably the sharing of ideas amongst learned men. Not for nothing was the painting once known as *The committee of taste*.

The Grand Tour was a manifestation of the belief in the formative power of knowledge and reason that was central to the Enlightenment as formulated in the philosophy and writing of René Descartes, Denis Diderot, Sir Isaac Newton and Immanuel Kant. In parallel with Diderot's encyclopaedia (published in 1751), the first museums were a material embodiment of the desire to gather and classify knowledge. The Enlightenment philosophers also questioned religious dogma and the absolute power of the monarchy. Such questioning of received truths would lead to liberal and emancipatory political debate, such as the campaign to abolish the transatlantic slave trade.

Port cities such as Bristol profited from the slave trade. Edward Colston is probably the best known of the Bristol merchants who benefited, in equal parts due to his role in the Royal African Slave Company and his philanthropy to Bristol. In 1726 the sculptor Michael Rysbrack created a posthumous portrait in terracotta for a memorial to commemorate the merchant. Based on an earlier portrait, the bust represents a dynamic Rococo style characteristic of which is the long curled periwig worn by Colston. In 1788 the city's first petition against slavery was signed by 800 people. The Abolition campaigner William Wilberforce visited Bristol in 1791 and the Methodist John Wesley preached against the slave trade in the New Rooms on Broadmead. The parliamentary campaign to end the trade succeeded in 1807, although trade from the West Indies remained important to Bristol. Colston remains a contentious figure in Bristol's history.

Enlightenment thinking underlined the importance of formal education, which included art. Art academies already flourished in continental Europe, but it wasn't until 1768 that the Royal Academy was founded in England with Sir Joshua Reynolds as its President. The Academy instituted a hierarchy of subject matter, with history painting, genre and portraiture at the top, and landscape and still life at the bottom. Despite this, some artists found other ways to explore the genres that interested them. The Welsh painter Richard Wilson (also a founder member of the RA) was in Italy between 1750-57, where the artist Francesco Zuccarelli urged him to concentrate on landscape painting. Is *Diana and Callisto* a classical history scene or a landscape or both? Wilson paints in the harmonious Neo-Classical style of Poussin and Claude Lorrain, as can be seen from the way the tree foliage gently frames the scene.

British artists influenced by Wilson developed their own approach to landscape. *Sunset at sea after a storm* by Francis Danby was purchased from the Royal Academy exhibition in 1824 by Sir Thomas Lawrence, the Academy's President at the time. It is said that Danby's early masterpiece of the aftermath of a shipwreck was inspired by an account of Théodore Géricault's painting, *The raft of the Medusa*. Note how the muscular forms of the survivors are almost hidden in the darkening seascape.

Danby's painting is an example of the way ideas then current filtered through to art. Immanuel Kant and Sir Edmund Burke both explored the Sublime in their philosophy as a way of understanding the precarious position of humanity in the vastness of the universe. For Burke, the Sublime was a dreadful phenomenon likely to fill the onlooker with fear and awe. It was a philosophy that gave substance to Romantic painting in the 19th century.

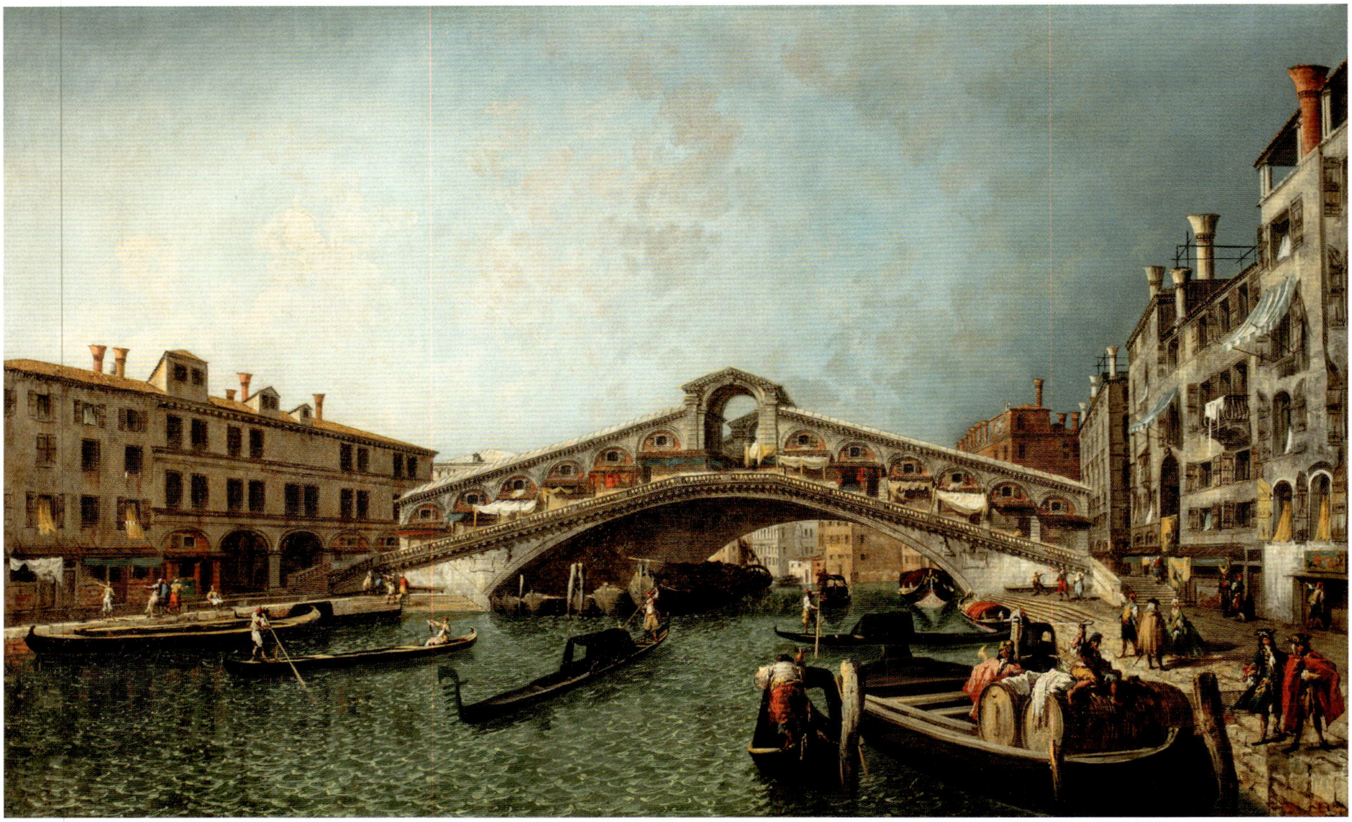

Michele Marieschi (1710-1743)
The Rialto Bridge
oil on canvas, about 1740
62.2 x 96.6 cm
Gift, Aaron de Pass, 1936
K1356

This quintessential Venetian scene, showing the Rialto Bridge spanning the Grand Canal with gondolas in the foreground, exemplifies the kind of painting purchased by English visitors to Venice on the Grand Tour in the 18th century. The success of Canaletto had already shown the demand for such mementoes and it has been suggested that Michele Marieschi began his career, like Canaletto, designing stage scenery.

Marieschi was the son of a craftsman who died when Michele was just ten years old. He was known for his Venetian cityscapes (*vedutisti*). In his short life Marieschi's output was small compared with Canaletto's, but he followed his more successful compatriot in publishing a series of engravings of Venice – although Marieschi actually engraved the views himself.

The Rialto Bridge, a famous landmark in Venice, provided the only foot passage across the Grand Canal. In Marieschi's painting the bridge seems to widen the view, showing activity on both sides of the quay. Loosely-worked figures pilot gondolas under the bridge, while in the foreground two merchants on the steps of the quay appear to inspect the wine barrels about to be unloaded.

The picture is a rare example of a signed work by the artist whose monogram appears on one of the wine barrels. The signature has helped with the reconstruction of Marieschi's career, aspects of which remain mysterious or controversial because of the similarities between his painting and that of his student, Francesco Albotto (1721-1757), who married Marieschi's widow, Angela Fontana.

Bernardo Bellotto (1722-1780)
Capriccio: the lagoon, Venice
oil on canvas, about 1743-44
37.5 x 62.2 cm
Accepted by Her Majesty's Government in lieu of tax and presented to Bristol City Art Gallery, 1988
K5270

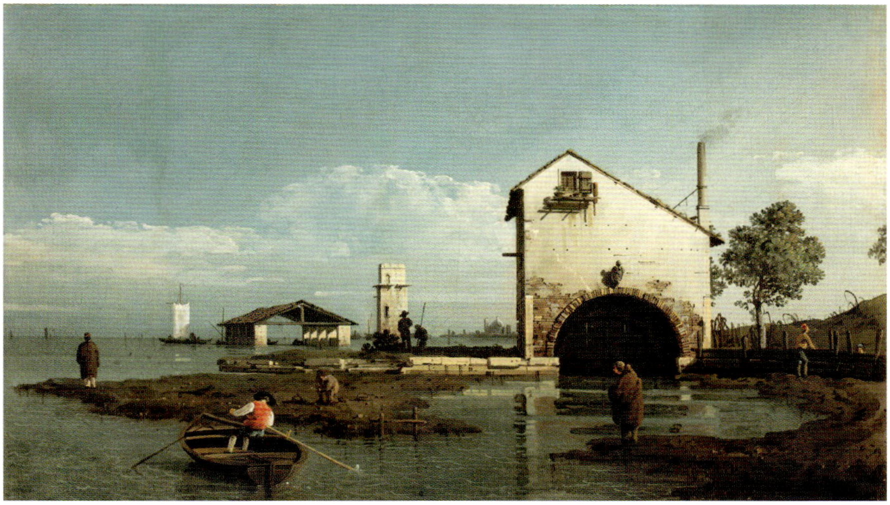

A *capriccio* is a view that combines the real with the imagined. This scene shows the view from the Venetian Lagoon and incorporates buildings on the shore with figures in the marshes and on the water in the foreground. Although the distant church suggests the Venice skyline, it is not an accurate depiction of Santa Maria della Salute.

Bernardo Bellotto was the nephew of Giovanni Antonio Canal (1697-1768), commonly called Canaletto, and entered his uncle's studio at about the age of fifteen. Canaletto was probably at his busiest in the mid-1730s, so the assistance of his talented nephew must have been welcome. Bellotto's earliest Venetian views are virtually indistinguishable from his uncle's work, but in this painting and its companion, made towards the end of his apprenticeship, characteristics of his own mature style are becoming apparent. Although they are very closely based on known compositional views by Canaletto, the cooler and more atmospheric colour and the almost calligraphic marks used for vegetation on the right are distinctively the work of Bellotto. Bellotto left Venice in 1747 and worked as a court painter in Dresden, Vienna and Warsaw, where he painted dazzling views often considered to rival the work of his uncle.

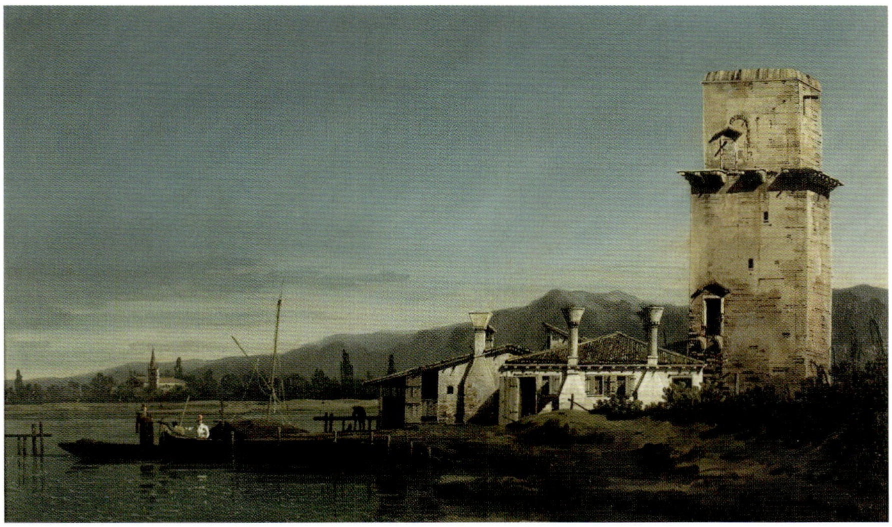

Capriccio: the tower of Malghera
oil on canvas, about 1743-44
37.3 x 62.2 cm
K5269

A disused mediaeval watchtower stands above a row of humble dwellings with distinctive Venetian funnel-shaped chimneys. Local fishermen work from the rickety jetty and in the distance are the Euganean Hills. Bellotto and Canaletto travelled along the Brenta Canal towards Padua in around 1741, setting out from Venice and passing through the Lagoon towards Malghera.

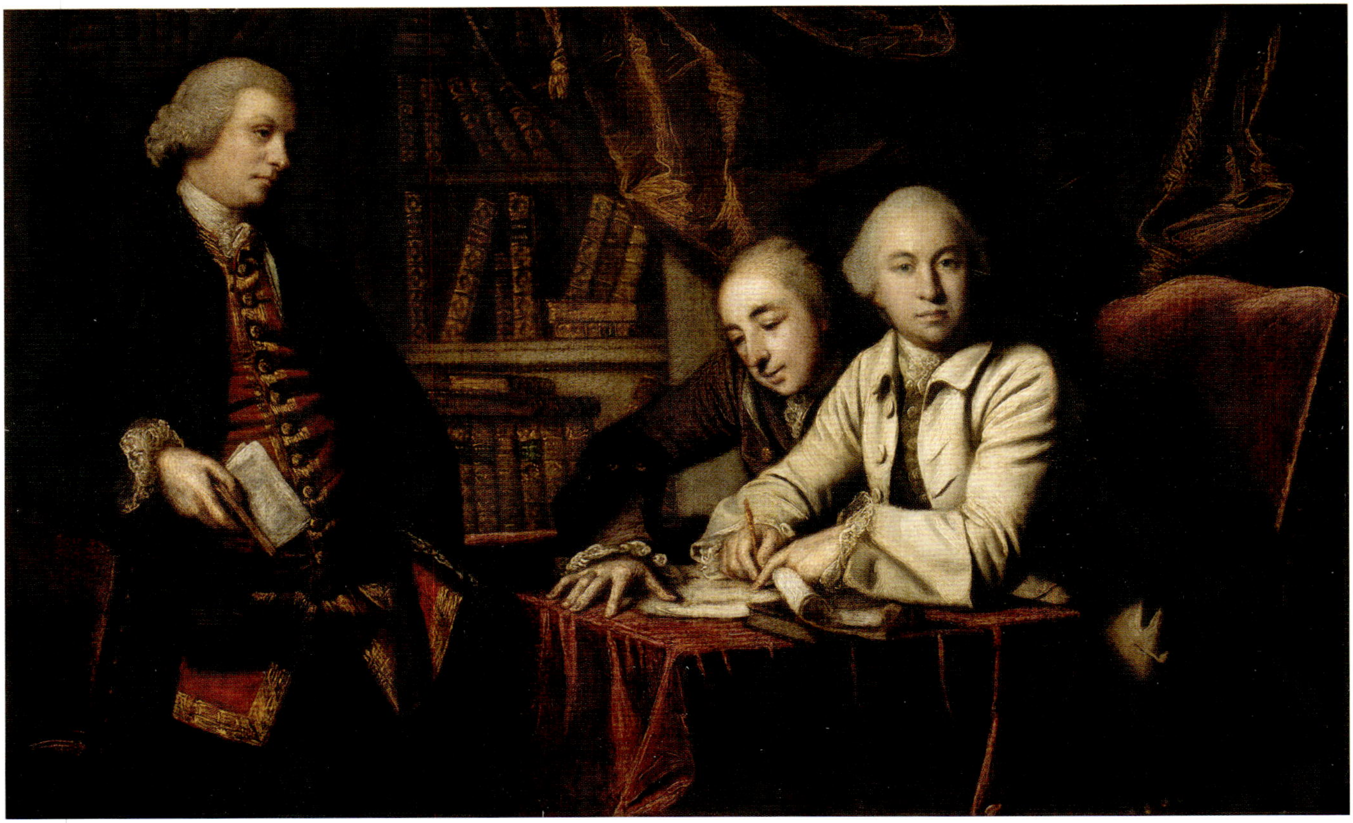

Sir Joshua Reynolds (1723-1792)
The 'out of town' party
oil on canvas, about 1759-61
53.3 x 82.5 cm
Bequest of FPM Schiller, 1946
K1589

Sir Joshua Reynolds was the first President of the Royal Academy from 1768 and had a pervasive influence on art teaching in England in the 18th century through his *Discourses on art*, which set out a hierarchy of painting styles. Reynolds was primarily a painter of portraits but he incorporated the grand style he prized in painting into his portraits, often depicting his sitters as muses and heroic figures in classical settings.

The small scale of this portrait and the relaxed intimacy of the sitters are unusual for Reynolds. Commissioned by Horace Walpole as a record of three close friends who often spent Christmas and Easter with him at his villa, Strawberry Hill in Twickenham, it shows an informal *salon* or 'Conversation Piece' in which the three friends examine the books in their host's antiquarian library. Walpole was a member of parliament, collector and man of letters and his friends, from left to right, are George Selwyn, 'Gilly' Williams and Lord Edgcumbe.

Sir Thomas Lawrence (1769-1830)
William Henry Cavendish-Bentinck, 3rd Duke of Portland (1738-1809)
oil on canvas, 1792
238.8 x 139.8 cm
Transferred, Bristol City Council, 2008
K6221

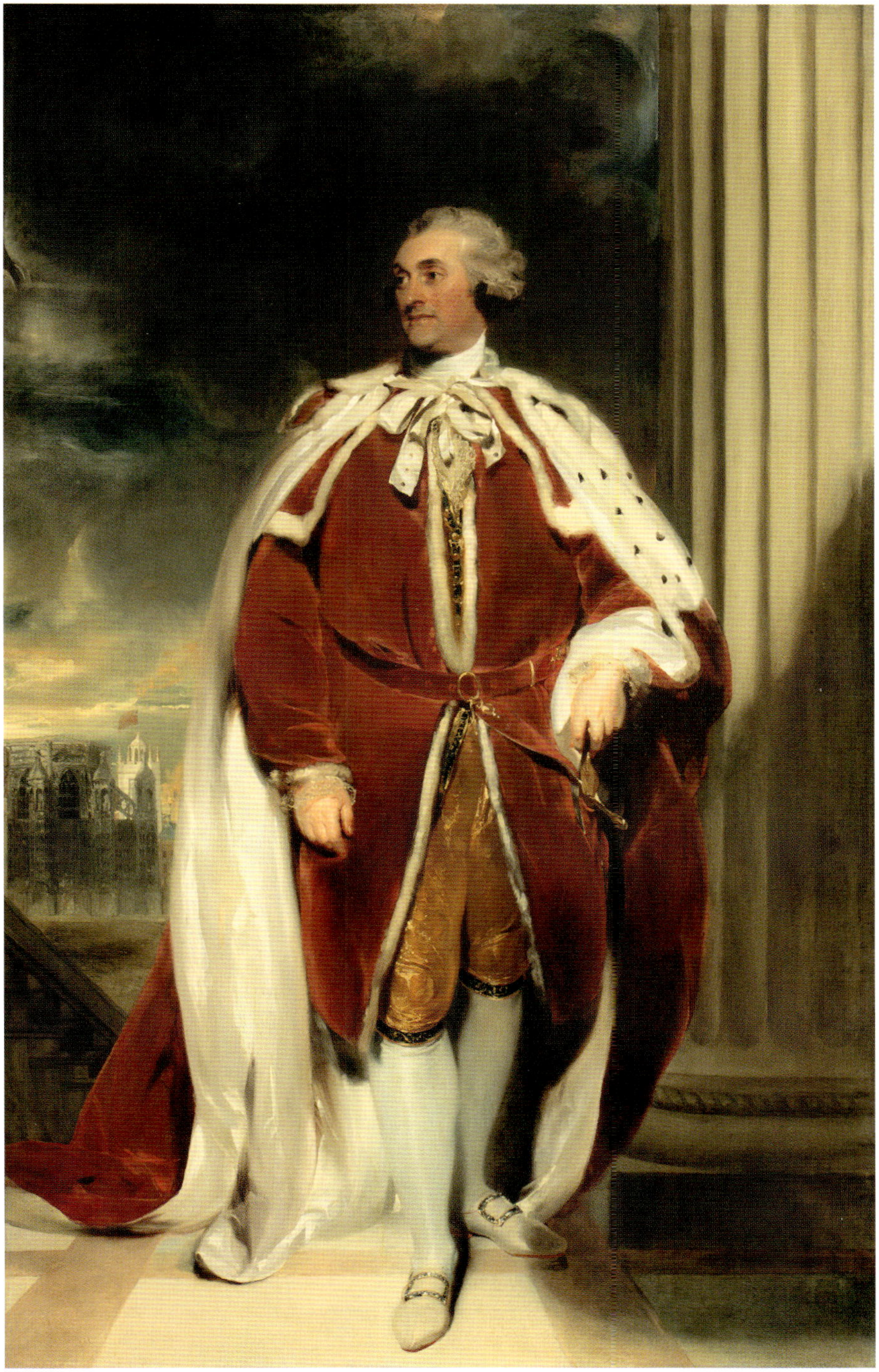

Thomas Lawrence painted this portrait aged just 23, two years after he painted Queen Charlotte. The Duke of Portland had been a Whig Prime Minister of a coalition government in 1783 and would return to that role as a Conservative in 1806. In 1786 he was High Steward of Bristol and this portrait was commissioned by the city to hang in the Mansion House in Queen Square. It cost 100 guineas. The painting narrowly escaped destruction in the Bristol Reform Riots of 1831, when the Mansion House was set alight. The painting was saved but the building was destroyed.

Portland is shown in his ducal red velvet and ermine robes, leaning against a classical fluted column that serves to frame the tempestuous sky beyond. Note the way that the natural world is framed and contained by the manmade column frames (which represent culture). As portrayed by Lawrence, the duke is an exemplary Enlightenment man.

Thomas Lawrence was born in Bristol but spent his childhood in Devizes. By his early teens, Lawrence supported the family by drawing pastel portraits of society visitors to Bath. He settled in London in 1787, where he was encouraged by Sir Joshua Reynolds, the President of the Royal Academy, and swiftly established his career. Although this portrait was painted early on, it already displays the bravura and sheer technical skill which would make Lawrence the greatest of Regency portrait painters.

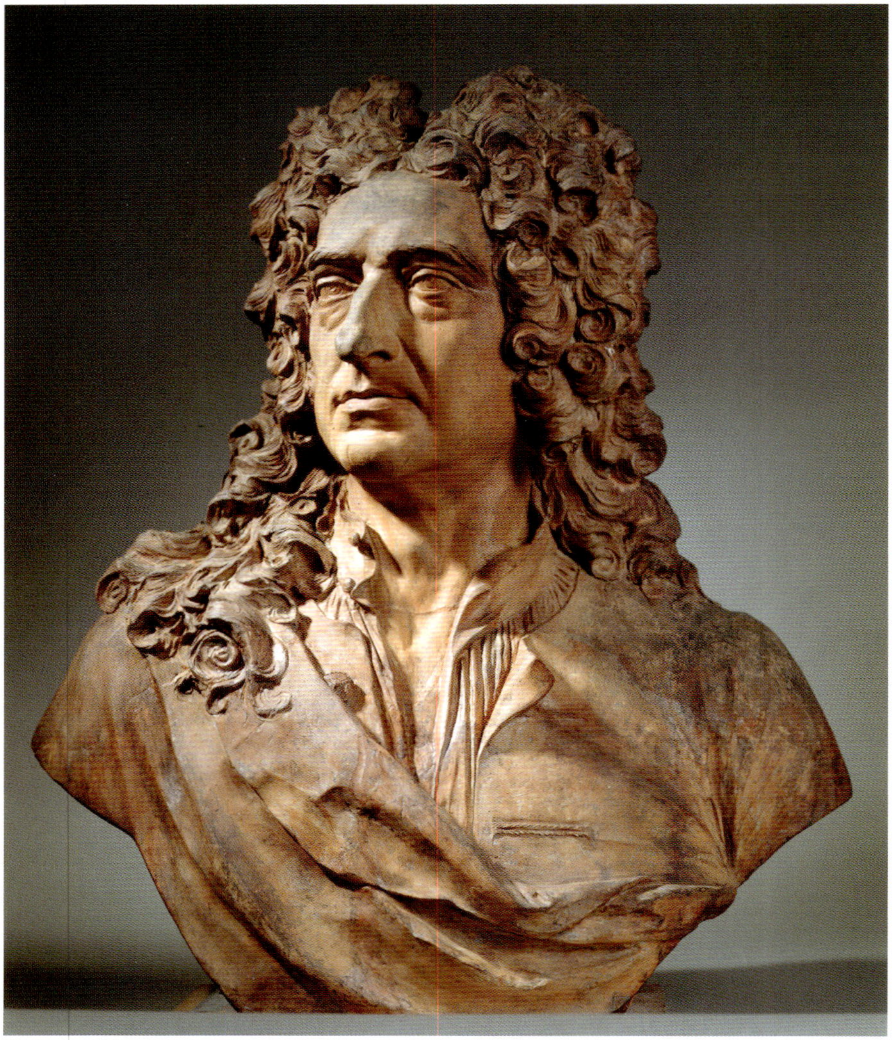

John Michael Rysbrack (1694-1770)
Edward Colston (1636-1721)
terracotta, about 1726
56 x 46 x 28 cm
Transferred, Bristol City Council, 1976
K4753

Many port cities in Britain, including Bristol, profited from the transatlantic slave trade. Edward Colston is probably the best known of the Bristol merchants who benefited. His wide-ranging business interests included trading in wine and cloth from Europe and sugar from St Kitt's, but it was as an official of the London-based Royal African Company (which from 1672 until 1698 held the British monopoly on the slave trade under Royal licence) that he was directly involved in the trade, organising the sale and transport of enslaved Africans to the Caribbean.

Colston was a shrewd merchant, but also a generous philanthropist, which is why his name is well-known in the city. He gave money to churches and built almshouses and schools. These gifts were hedged with restrictions, however: the recipients were to be Anglicans, and he laid down rules and regulations that matched his own High Anglican, High Tory beliefs. He donated about £140,000 to charitable causes, in Bristol and elsewhere. Today this would be worth more than £27,000,000.

John Michael Rysbrack came to London from Antwerp in 1720 and changed the nature of portrait sculpture in England, creating dynamic sculptures of Alexander Pope and George II. This terracotta bust was almost certainly made in preparation for Colston's monument in Bristol's All Saints' Church on Corn Street. The vivid posthumous portrayal is an image of Colston as a young man, based on a portrait by Jonathan Richardson.

Antoine-Jean, Baron Gros (1771-1835)
Madame Catherine Bruguière, née Sardon
oil on canvas, 1796
79.1 x 65.4 cm
Purchased, with the assistance of the Victoria & Albert Museum Purchase Grant Fund and the Penraven Bequest, 1967
K2992

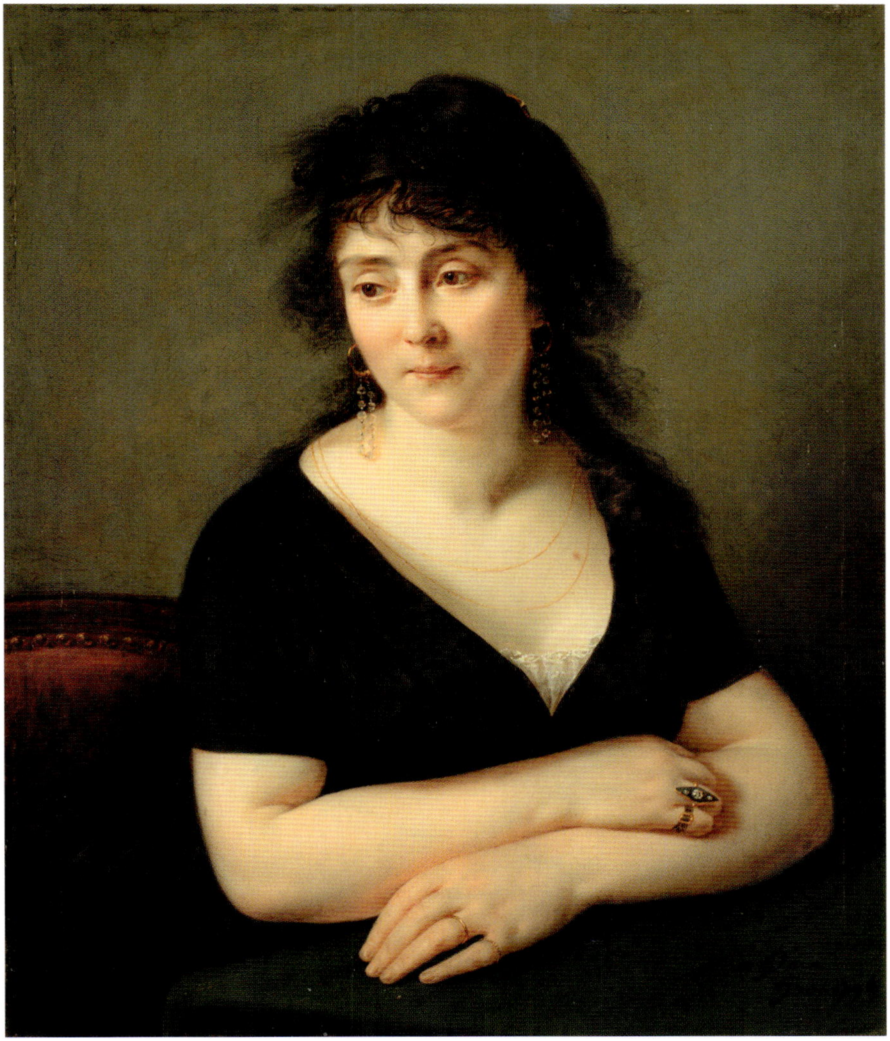

Trained by his father, a painter of miniatures, Antoine-Jean Gros then entered the studio of the Neo-Classicist Jacques-Louis David. The younger artist admired David, although he had a greater affinity with the colour and dynamism of Rubens. After the French Revolution, David helped Gros move to Italy in 1793, where he spent the next eight years. In Genoa, Gros met Josephine Bonaparte, the wife of the Emperor Napoleon, who took him under her protection and introduced him to her husband, whose portrait he painted. Gros went on to become the Emperor's propagandist and created stirring images idealising his military campaigns, such as the *Battle of Eylau* (now in the Louvre), which would influence Romantic artists such as Delacroix and Géricault.

It was in Genoa that Gros painted the Romantic portraits of the ship-owner François Bruguière and his wife Catherine, née Sardon. The portrait of François, which belongs to the Louvre, shows him as a Revolutionary with papers for a Radical Jacobin meeting and a passport to London. The muted background colours of *Madame Bruguière* concentrate our attention on the beauty of the sitter, with her black dress, white skin and distant gaze. Her face, which has been skilfully modelled by Gros, is framed by tendrils of black hair. The dark dress and hair accentuate her ivory skin, which is subtly modulated with a soft pink glow in her cheeks, as is the flesh of her smooth bosom and rounded arms, a technique reminiscent of Gros's idol, Rubens.

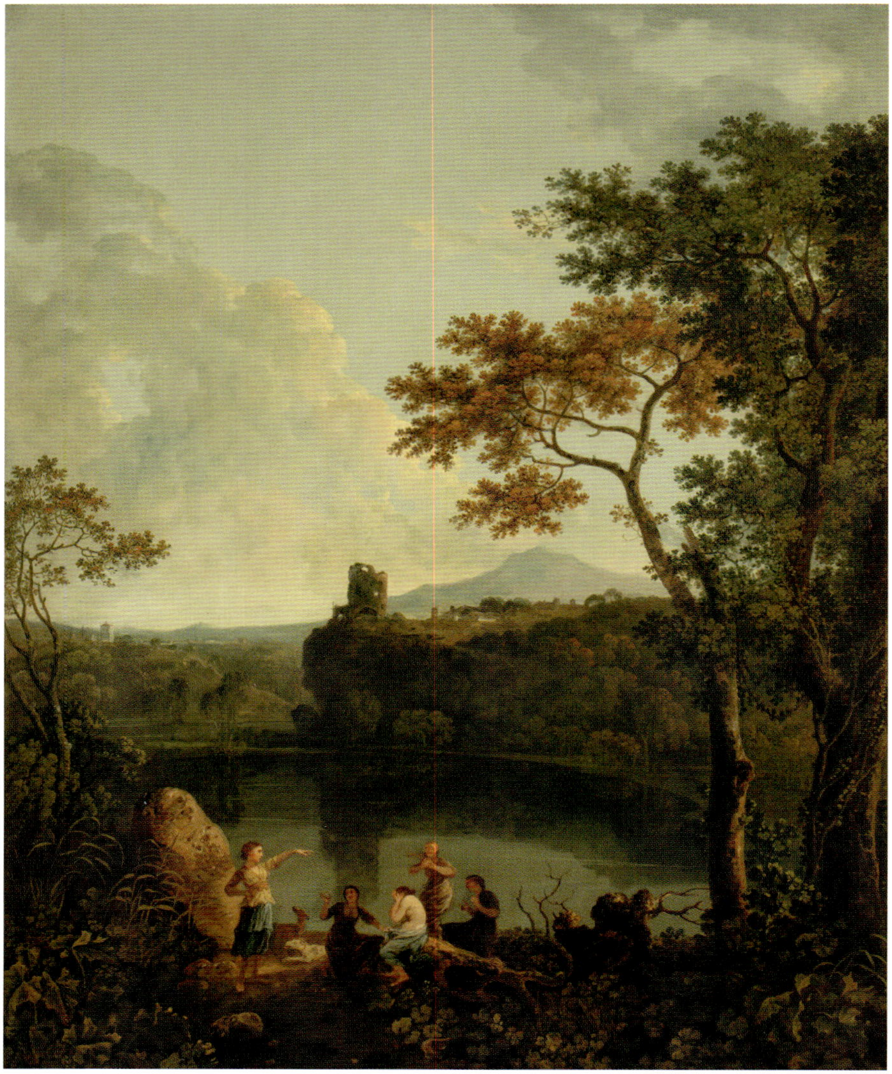

Richard Wilson (1714-1782)
Diana and Callisto
oil on canvas, 1764-65
229.2 x 183.4 cm
Purchased, 1955
K2413

In Ovid's 'Metamorphoses', Callisto, one of the goddess Diana's nymphs, was seduced by Jupiter. Wilson's painting shows the moment of confrontation when Diana admonishes the pregnant nymph in front of the other nymphs.

Richard Wilson pioneered landscape painting in Britain and was an important influence on Turner. He travelled to Venice in 1750 and settled in Rome for five years, returning to England as a landscape painter in the tradition of the great 17th-century masters, Claude Lorrain and Gaspard Dughet. His landscapes are characterised by the elegant arrangement of foliage to frame scenery bathed in soft golden light. Despite being born in Wales, Wilson was known as the 'English Claude'. He often introduced castles and mountains from his native Wales into his Italian scenes. He was a founder member of the Royal Academy in 1768.

Diana and Callisto is one of a set of four classical landscapes painted for Henry Blundell of Ince Hall, Lancashire (the other three remain at the Hall). Much of the preliminary work on these large canvases was painted by Wilson's apprentices. All depict scenery based on the countryside around Rome. The distant stone ruin, although so familiar in Italian landscapes, is actually the round tower of Dolbadarn Castle, seen standing at the foot of Snowdon in North Wales.

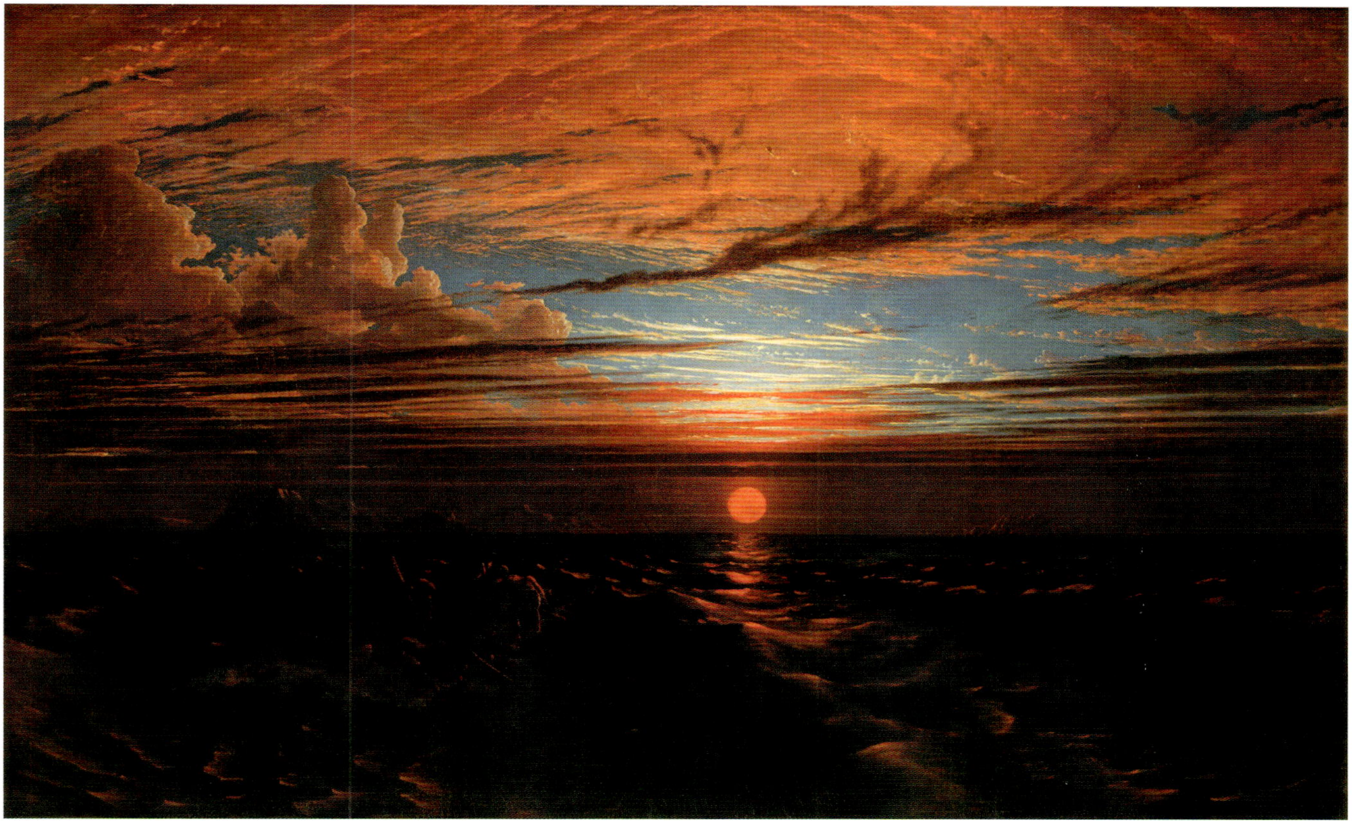

Francis Danby (1793-1861)
Sunset at sea, after a storm
oil on canvas, 1824
89.6 x 142.9 cm
Purchased with the assistance of the Victoria & Albert Museum Purchase Grant Fund, National Heritage Fund, Art Fund, Penraven Fund and the Friends of Bristol Art Gallery, 1981
K5008

'Forty years have passed since we saw this picture yet we could almost describe from memory the lurid red of the setting sun, the broken waves of the subsiding storm, the few survivors of the wreck, alone on the raft on the limitless ocean.' **Richard Redgrave** (A century of painters of the English School, 1890)

Francis Danby had been in Bristol some ten years when he painted this oil, having settled in the city after an ill-matched marriage in 1813. His personal life was in turmoil and he had many debts. The painting was first exhibited with the work of other Bristol School artists at the Bristol Institution before being sent to the Royal Academy, where it made Danby's reputation. It attracted the attention of Royal Academy President, Sir Thomas Lawrence, who purchased it for £100. Perhaps encouraged by this, Danby left Bristol for London.

In the painting a red sun descends into the horizon and casts its crimson glow across a darkening sky and sea. In the shadowy foreground a raft carrying the survivors of a shipwreck is just visible. The vivid contrasts of the red light and black sea are said to have inspired John Martin, and Danby commissioned mezzotint prints to be made of the image, exploiting the tonalities of the painting in the velvet texture of the prints.

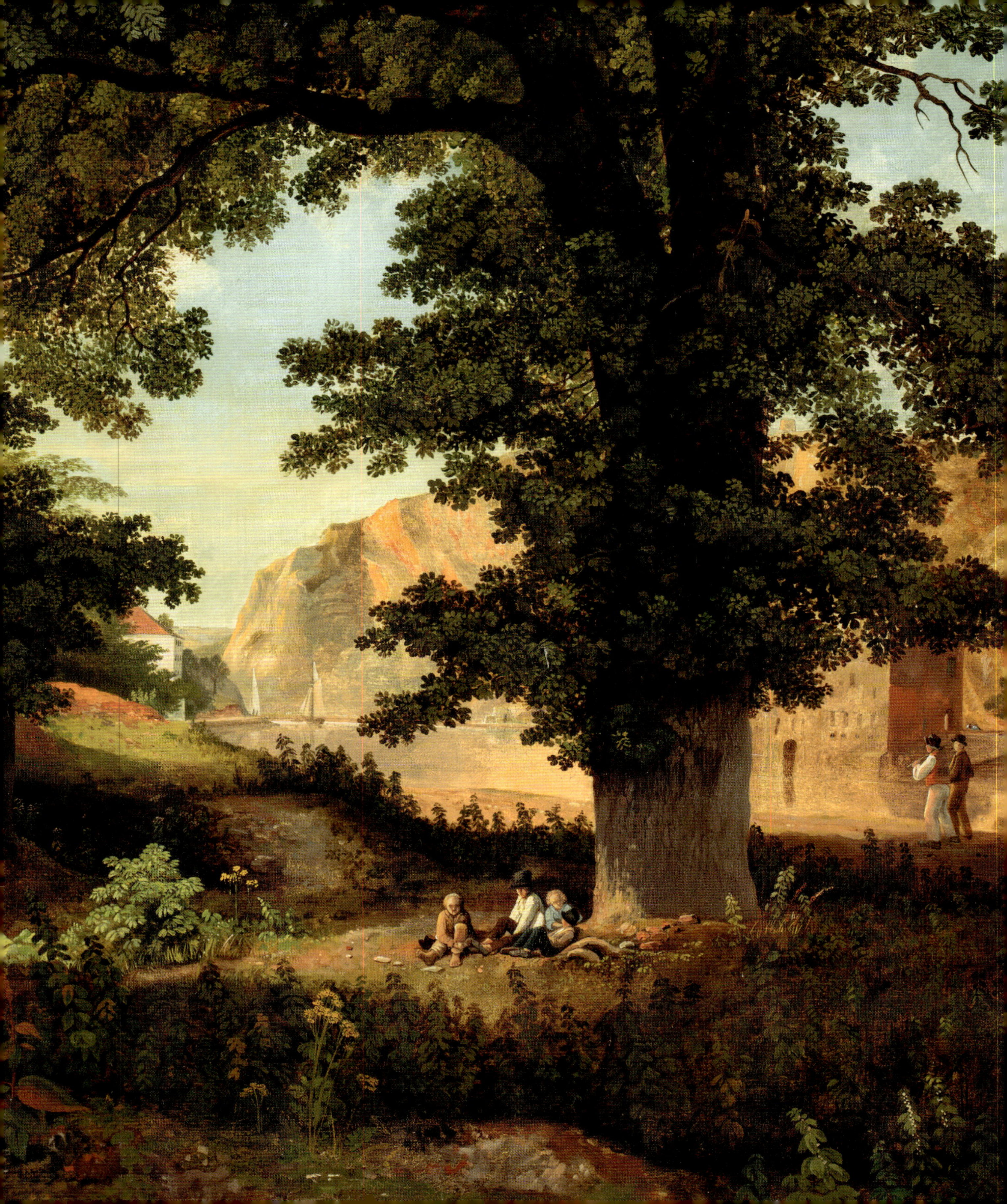

The Bristol School

'There existed in Bristol a society for the express association of the patron, the amateur and the artist. The party met ostensibly to sketch, and many pictures, which afterwards made some noise in the world, originated there. It was composed of men of high standing, and of the highest qualifications of the intellect, science and acquirement; it is unquestionable that Bird and others I could name profited by this.' **EV Rippingille**

In Britain in the early 19th century there was little in the way of formal art training outside the Royal Academy Schools. Young artists would be apprenticed to craftsmen or taught by drawing masters. Then, as now, they also worked as assistants to established artists or formed their own groups to pool and foster knowledge. In 1794 Edward Bird established a Gentleman's Drawing School in Bristol, which became the centre of an informal sketching society that included patrons and amateur artists as well as professionals. Although they did not consciously set out to develop a shared style or manifesto in the way that later groups of artists would do, the term 'Bristol School' was used as early as 1826 by the Reverend John Eagles, one of the amateur painters.

The Bristol School has come to refer to a circle of artists that included Bird, Edward Villiers Rippingille, Francis Danby, Samuel Jackson and William West, as well as a younger generation including James Baker Pyne and William James Müller. Bird's circle introduced the Bristol landscape to the world with their views of the Avon Gorge and Leigh Woods taken directly from nature. They held convivial sketching evenings too, exploring imaginative Romantic and exotic subjects. The social aspect of the group was vital, engendering friendships the artists would remember for the rest of their lives.

Bird was elected a Royal Academician in 1813 – the first Bristol artist to be honoured in this way. His genre painting, *The reading of the will concluded,* transposed the high morals and earthy bawdiness of Dutch genre painting to a domestic English setting. The painting was a success at the Royal Academy as well as a vital influence on the younger artist Rippingille, whose *Recruiting party* highlighted the dubious enlisting methods of the British Army.

The young Francis Danby learnt about landscape painting in Bristol, where he created intimate and atmospheric portrayals of Stapleton, Leigh Woods and the Avon Gorge in watercolour and oils. Danby was close to Samuel Jackson, who illustrated Brunel's designs for the Suspension Bridge and painted it in oils prior to its completion. Jackson was the only artist to enjoy a life-long career in the city. Danby left for London in 1824. Rippingille was involved in the early days of the Bristol Institution for the Advancement of Science and Art, organising the early art exhibitions which featured Danby's first Romantic masterpiece, *Sunset at sea after a storm*, but he too left in 1832. William West, who converted the windmill by the gorge into an observatory, left in 1857. Bird was well-regarded in the city but died in poverty in 1819 aged just 47.

The younger generation of sketchers was led by the artists Jackson, West, James Baker Pyne and William James Müller. The son of the geologist John Samuel Müller (who was also the first curator at the Bristol Institution), Müller was a prolific artist who painted the Bristol Reform Riots on October 31st, 1831, along with Pyne.

The influence of the Bristol School spread to other artists in the city such as Samuel Colman, the Yeovil-born Nonconformist artist, whose extraordinary *St James's Fair* owes some of its characters (if not its attitude) to Rippingille. And Rolinda Sharples was acutely aware of their work, as can be seen in her genre painting, *The cloak room at Bristol Assembly Rooms*.

The Bristol School artists reflected the manifold interests of their time, interests that would shape the 19th century, such as Romanticism, the study of nature, landscape, geology, archaeology, Egyptology, and even, in the case of Rippingille, radical politics. With their delighted wonder in the world around them the artists of the Bristol School anticipated the Victorian polymaths who followed.

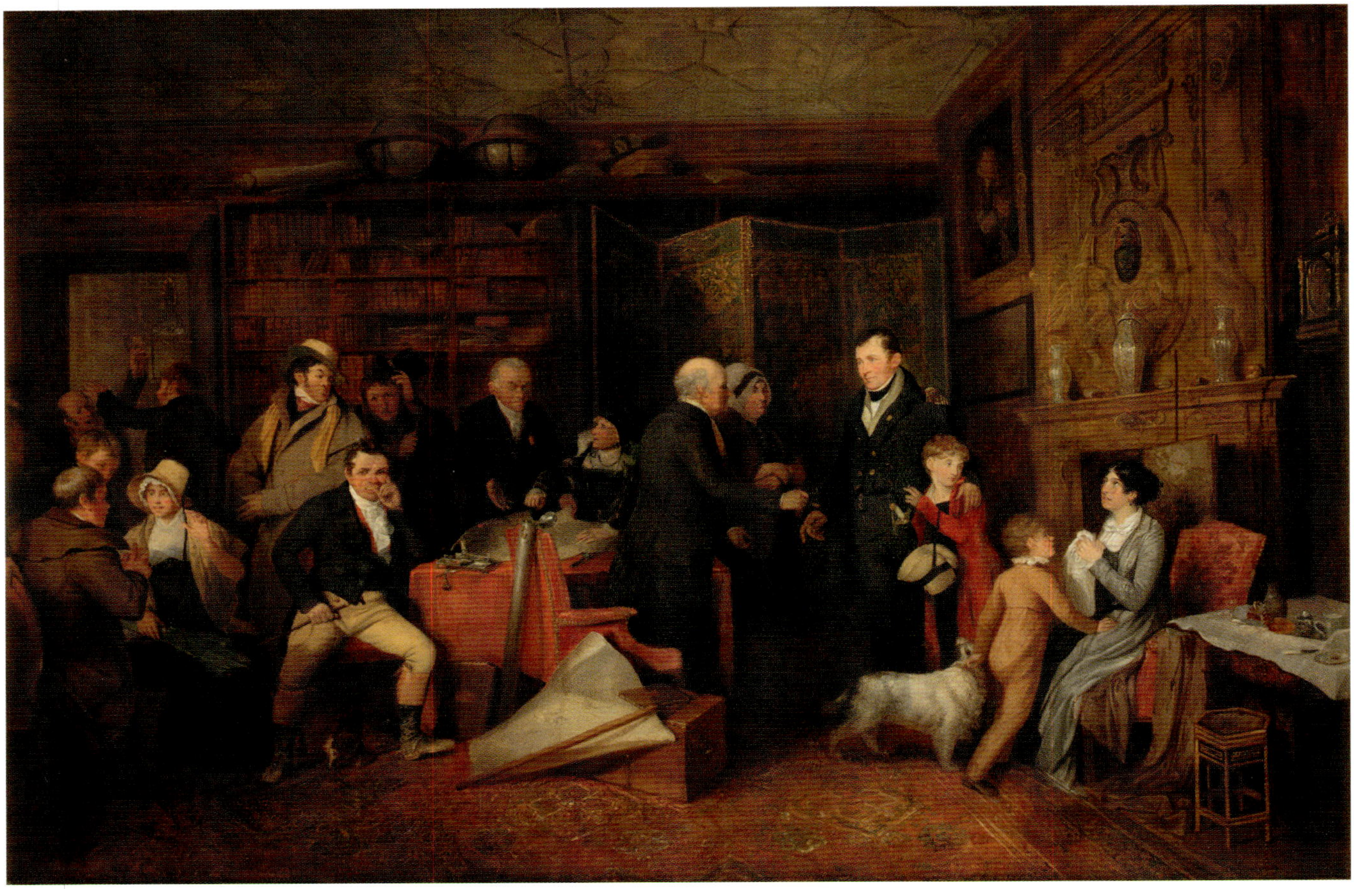

Edward Bird (1772-1819)
The reading of the will concluded
oil on canvas, 1811
97.7 x 62.2 cm
Purchased, 1917
K498

'[Bird's] society soon became the centre of attraction to all those who had enough of good taste... Thus was spontaneously [formed] a small society of art-loving friends, from which all that Bristol now can boast of artists and amateurs has descended.'
Dr John King

An old bachelor has died and named as his heir the modest naval officer, shown on the right with his family. The portrait of the younger man with the bachelor hanging above the family group is a clue to the affectionate relation between them. The bitter frustration of the relatives left out of the will is contrasted with the humble gratitude of those who have benefited. When the painting was shown at the Royal Academy in London, it had to be roped off to protect it from crowds, intent on reading every detail. Bird's achievement was to transpose the narrative quality of Dutch genre painting to 19th-century England.

Having trained as a japanning artist in Wolverhampton, decorating laquered tin-plate items, Edward Bird moved to Bristol in around 1794. He made a living japanning while he established himself as a 'Portrait, Landscape and Historical Painter' and opened an 'evening Drawing Academy' for young gentlemen. He befriended George Cumberland, Dr John King and Edward Villiers Rippingille, and began the sketching meetings at which the Bristol School artists met and worked together. Bird often included portraits of his friends in his genre paintings.

Bird advanced Bristol genre painting and influenced the work of Rippingille, Samuel Colman and Rolinda Sharples. He was the first Bristol artist to become a Royal Academician.

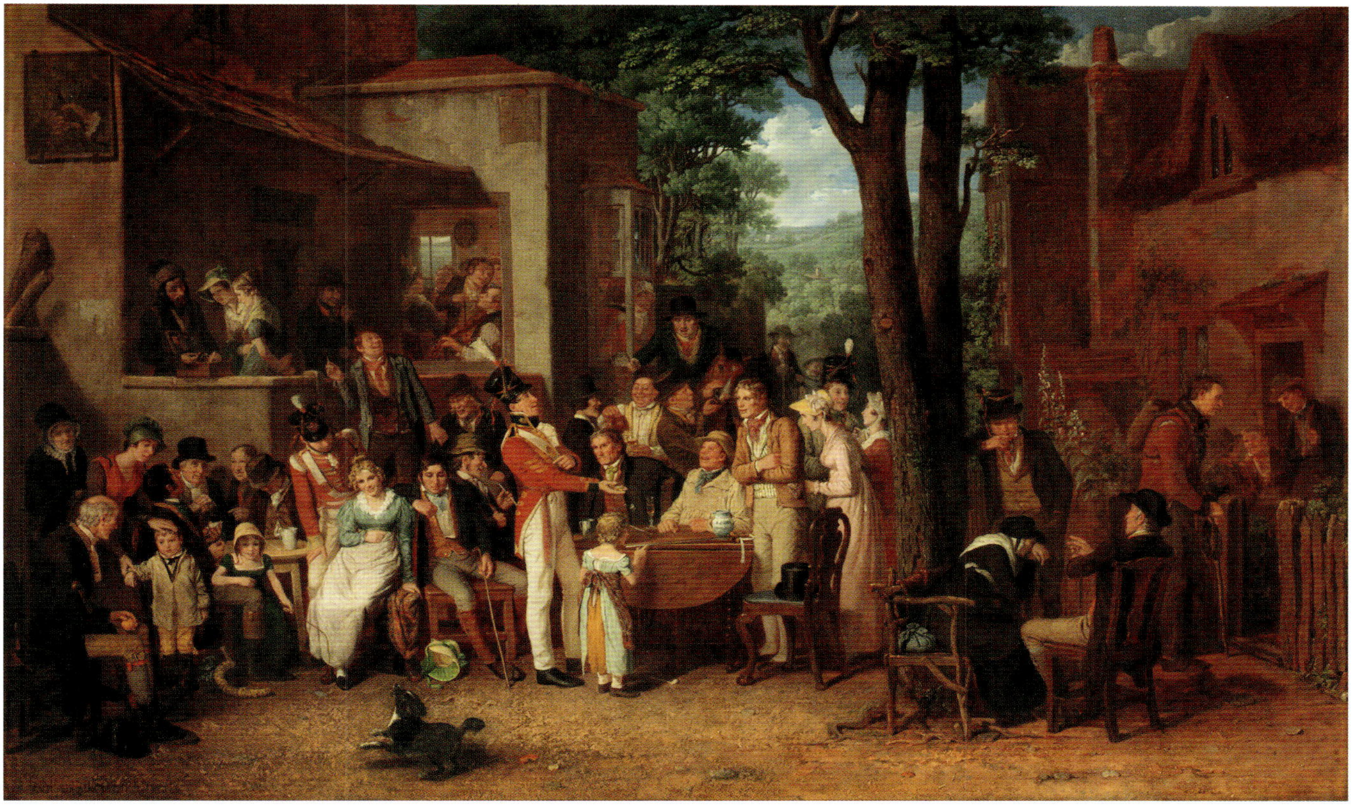

Edward Villiers Rippingille
(1788/89-1859)
The recruiting party
oil on canvas, 1822
83.4 x 135.9 cm
Purchased, 1917
K497

'[Rippingille] is a sour-tempered and unpolished being with little religion and little regard for anyone. He keeps no friends and his politics are radical in the extreme, but he don't want for talent in painting.' **George Cumberland**

Outside a village pub on a sunny day we see a recruiting sergeant trying to induce a callow young man to enlist in the Army. His sweetheart attempts to draw the young man away while a father figure looks on in impotent fury. A girl is seduced by a soldier and another young man declares his news to his distraught parents. The disorder set in motion by the arrival of the Army is highlighted by Rippingille in a critical twist on the genre painting practised by Edward Bird. Enlisting for life paid £23, 17 shillings and sixpence, a tempting amount of money when unskilled labourers were earning just a few shillings a week. 'Taking the King's shilling', which Rippingille illustrates at the centre of the painting, was the notorious enlistment contract, with a promise of glory and wealth. The reality is symbolised by the figure of the mature soldier in shabby clothes who enters to seek alms at the gate of the cottage on the right, unheeded by the crowd.

Having arrived in Bristol from Norfolk in 1817, Rippingille led a chaotic life but seems to have avoided some of the difficulties that beset his friend Danby. Largely self-taught, Rippingille learnt much from Bird and was at the hub of the Bristol art scene as a member of the sketching club. A dynamic force at the Bristol Institution, where he organised exhibitions and lectures, Rippingille was one of the only living artists in Bristol to receive its patronage (along with the sculptor EH Baily). His interests were various and distracting: he was an enthusiastic guitarist, and a writer who, in 1843, published *The Artist and Amateur's Journal*, as well as contributing to the *Art Journal* and *Bentley's Magazine*. As Cumberland asserted, Rippingille was a Radical.

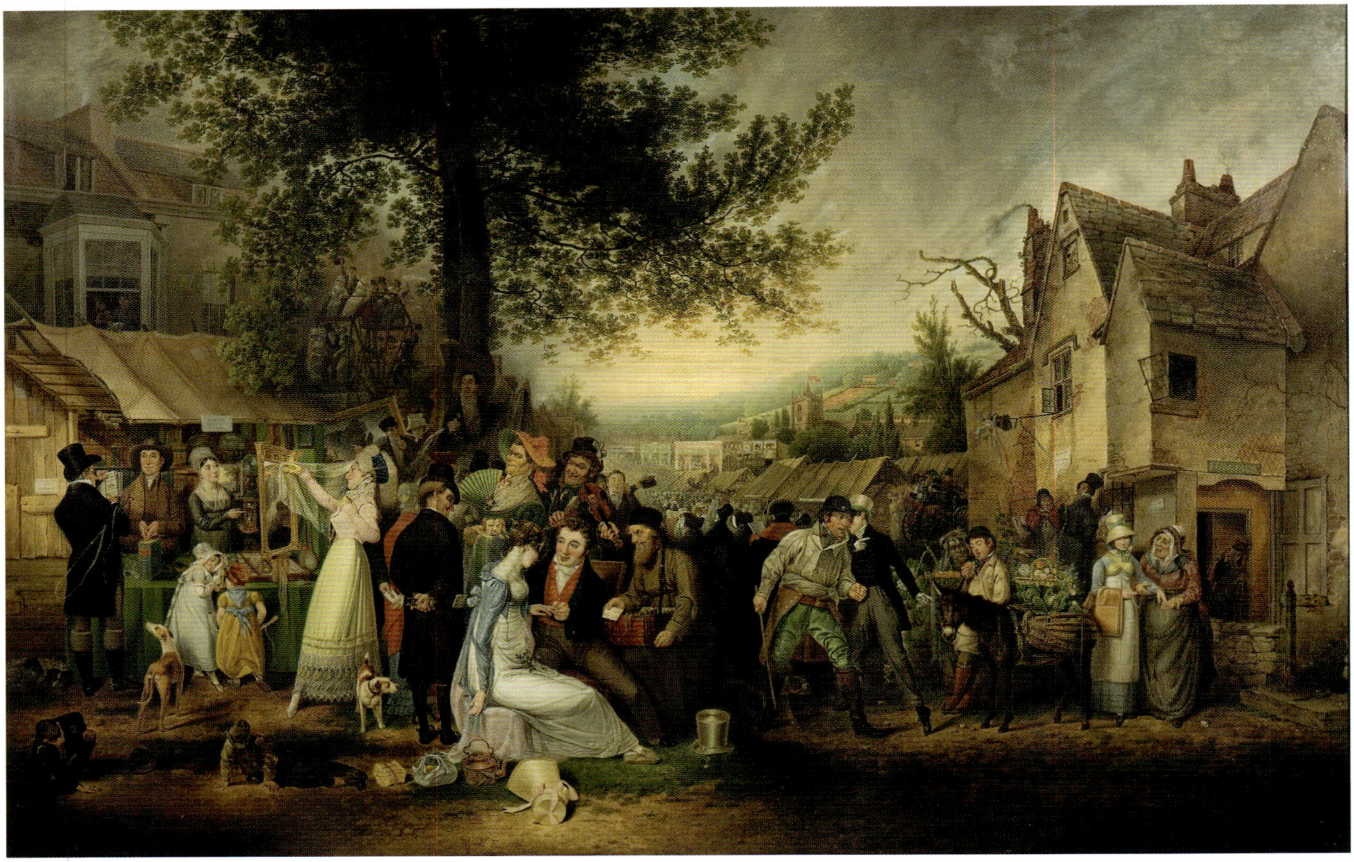

Samuel Colman (1780-1845)
St James's Fair
oil on canvas, 1824
87.6 x 133.9 cm
Bequest of J Anthony Bird, 1915
K353

This intriguing painting was intended as a nonconformist sermon targeting St James's Fair, which had taken place in Bristol since the 13th century. At the centre of the picture is a seduction scene, watched over by a group including a church warden, a violinist who serenades the couple, and a larger-than-life lady dressed in green. All around is wrong-doing.

Samuel Colman worked in Bristol between 1816-1838 as a portrait painter and drawing master, and in 1824 exhibited at the Bristol Institution's first exhibition of the work of the Bristol Artists. The apocalyptic themes of his religious epics such as *The coming of the Messiah* and his genre painting, *St James's Fair*, combined with his own history as a nonconformist, indicate that he may have had a religious patron.

As a nonconformist, Colman was not part of the salubrious social circle of the Bristol School artists, but this painting shows how much he learnt from the genre scenes of Rippingille and Bird. While Rippingille injected political commentary into his *Recruiting party*, Colman used the storytelling potential of genre painting to illustrate a religious tract, *Bristol fair but no preaching!*, written by the Reverend GC Smith who preached at the Zion chapel attended by the artist. Colman also used the painting to convey messages about other causes, such as the abolition of the slave trade, with a reference to the Bristol poet and anti-slavery campaigner Hannah More in the bookstall on the left. The peculiar group watching the young pair illustrates Colman's concern about the New Marriage Act of 1823, which made it easier for young couples to marry without the permission of their parents. Colman even makes reference to his own art, illustrating, on the left, his own painting, *St John preaching in the wilderness*, a hint perhaps of how he saw his role.

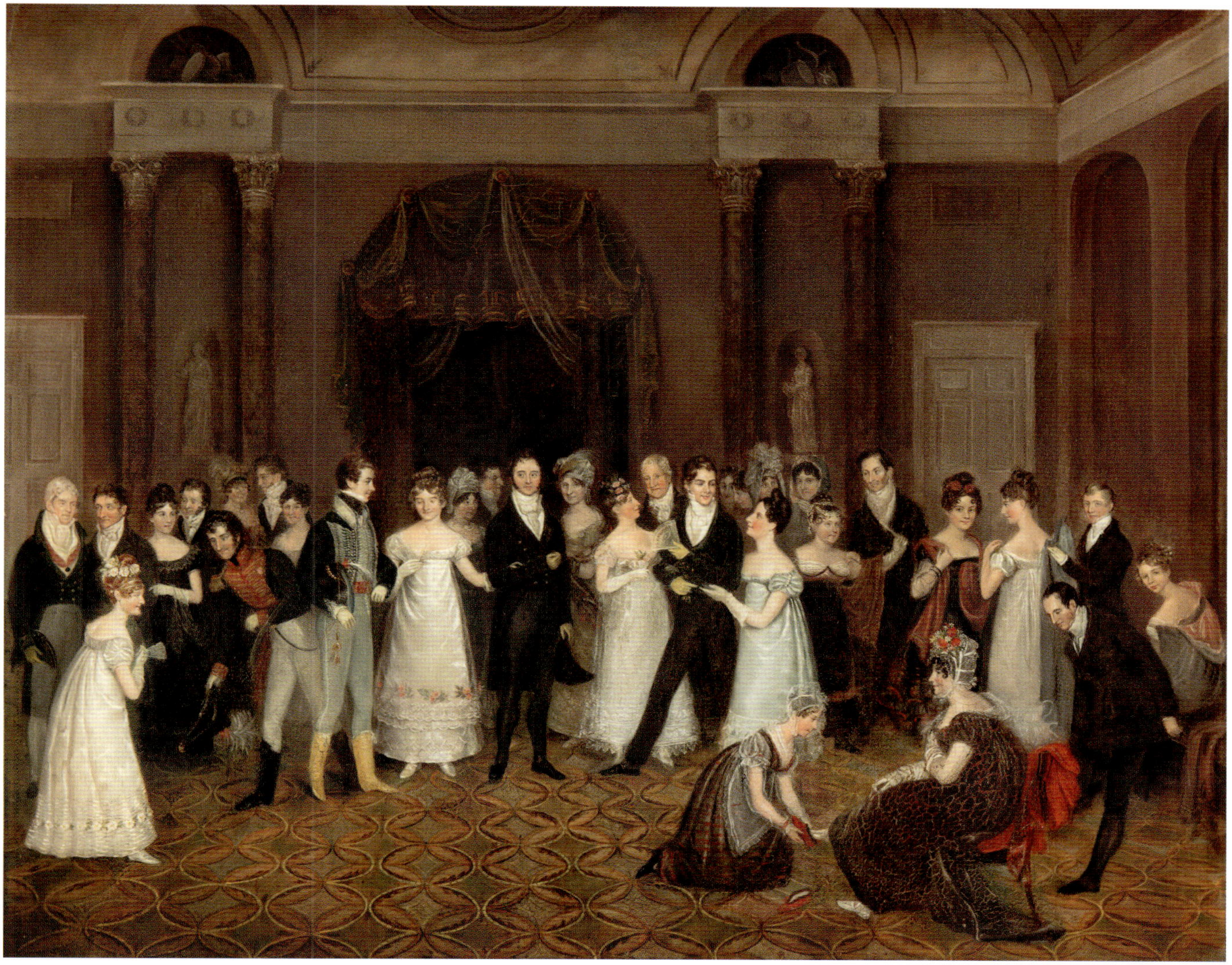

Rolinda Sharples (1793-1838)
The cloak-room, Clifton Assembly Rooms
oil on canvas, 1818
77 x 88.2 cm
Purchased, 1931
K275

Guests are arriving for a ball and a maid helps a lady with her overshoes. Two women greet a man at the centre while a couple flirt on the left. The Clifton Assembly Rooms had opened in 1811 and Rolinda Sharples chose a society gathering there for her first group painting. It bustles with the anticipation of the evening's festivities, like a scene from a Jane Austen novel. Sharples was at her best as a chronicler of middle-class life. She was born to a family of artists and spent her childhood in America where her father James was a portraitist. On his death the family returned to Britain, settling in Bristol.

As a woman it would not have been respectable for Sharples to join Rippingille, Bird and the others at their sketching parties. George Cumberland disdainfully wrote: 'Miss Sharples's pictures – 2 of them sold at an auction to Mr. Dance who knows nothing of painting for £50 – she had previously sold them to another simpleton for £150 or thereabouts'. Nevertheless Sharples was ambitious and responded in her art to contemporary events, as in her *Trial of Colonel Brereton* which depicts the scapegoating of Brereton after the Bristol Reform Riots in 1831.

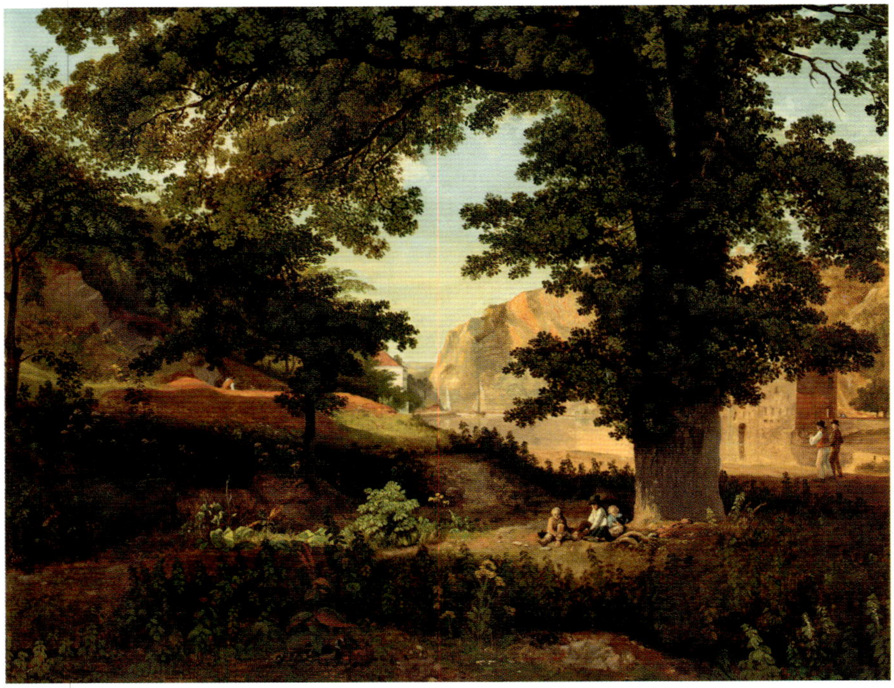

Francis Danby (1793-1861)
Clifton Rocks from Rownham Fields
oil on panel, about 1821
40 x 50.8 cm
Purchased, 1927
K850

Francis Danby left Dublin for London at the age of nineteen and when he ran out of money he walked the 120 miles to Bristol. He settled in the city, marrying Hannah Hardedge and meeting the Bristol School artists and his sympathetic patron, John Gibbons.

This is one of Danby's finest paintings from his years in Bristol. He focused on the contrast between the cool shade and the sunlit patch where young boys loll in the heat. The Avon Gorge is relegated to the background, but Danby included specific details - the Old Hotwell House on the right, the windmill on the summit of St Vincent's Rocks seen through the foliage of the oak tree, and the old lime-kiln on the left - which makes the scene unmistakable.

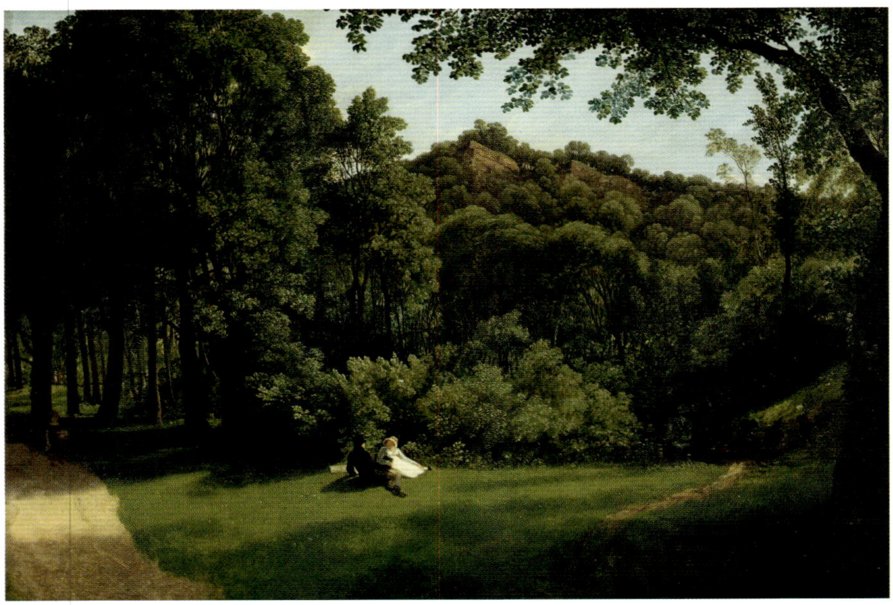

Leigh Woods
oil on panel, 1822
35.2 x 50.4
Purchased, 1956
K2654

Leigh Woods was a favourite haunt of the Bristol School. In this painting we see two sketchers relaxing in a glade. The woods are on the south side of Avon Gorge and were very secluded at that time. To reach them, visitors crossed the river at Rownham Ferry, then walked along the tow path and ascended Nightingale Valley. The Clifton Suspension Bridge did not yet exist. Danby boldly painted this work almost exclusively in green, in all its rich variety, with few other colours.

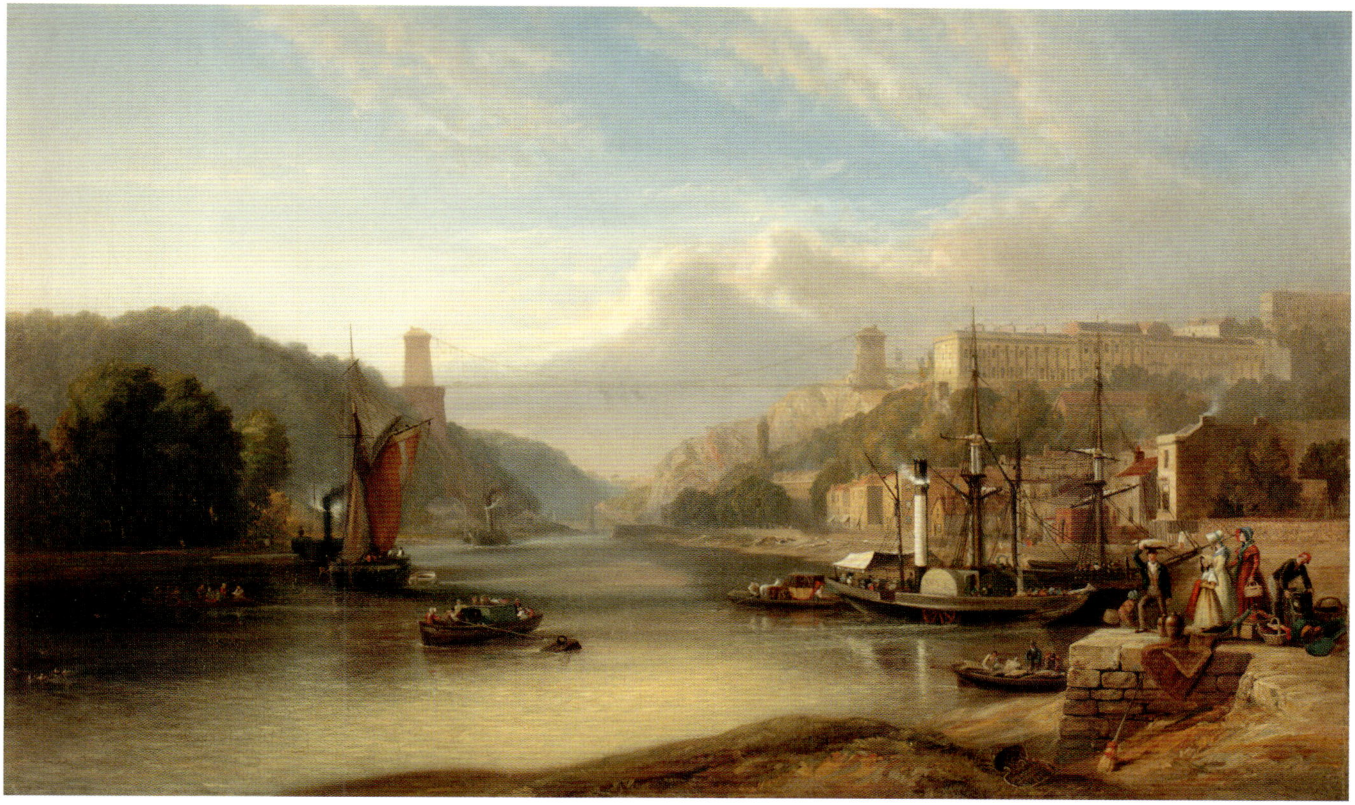

Samuel Jackson (1794-1869)
View of the Avon at Hotwells
oil on canvas, about 1840
62.9 x 101.6 cm
Purchased, 1903
K4

Brunel's Clifton Suspension Bridge had not been completed when this view was painted. Building work took place between 1836-43, and then the money ran out. For nearly twenty years Brunel's two towers faced each other across the empty gorge before the bridge was finally finished in 1864.

Samuel Jackson's reputation is as one of the quieter, more diligent artists of the Bristol School. Francis Danby wrote of him '...he has a genius which he has not shown'. Jackson remained in Bristol his whole life (although he travelled on excursions to the West Indies for his health, and later, in 1855 and 1858, to Switzerland) and supplemented his earnings as a drawing master and as an artist with commissions for the antiquarian, George Weare Braikenridge. His best work is close in mood to Danby, his fellow sketcher.

Jackson painted few oils but depicted the Suspension Bridge in watercolour several times, including landscape scenery commissioned by Brunel for his original four designs for the competition in 1830. Here the open space of the gorge is skillfully rendered. In the foreground there is much activity with the ferry and the steamboat, and the bustle as people await the boat-load of turtles by the pier, including a man carrying one on his head. Jackson would have known this scene well, as it includes the street where he lived, Freeland Place.

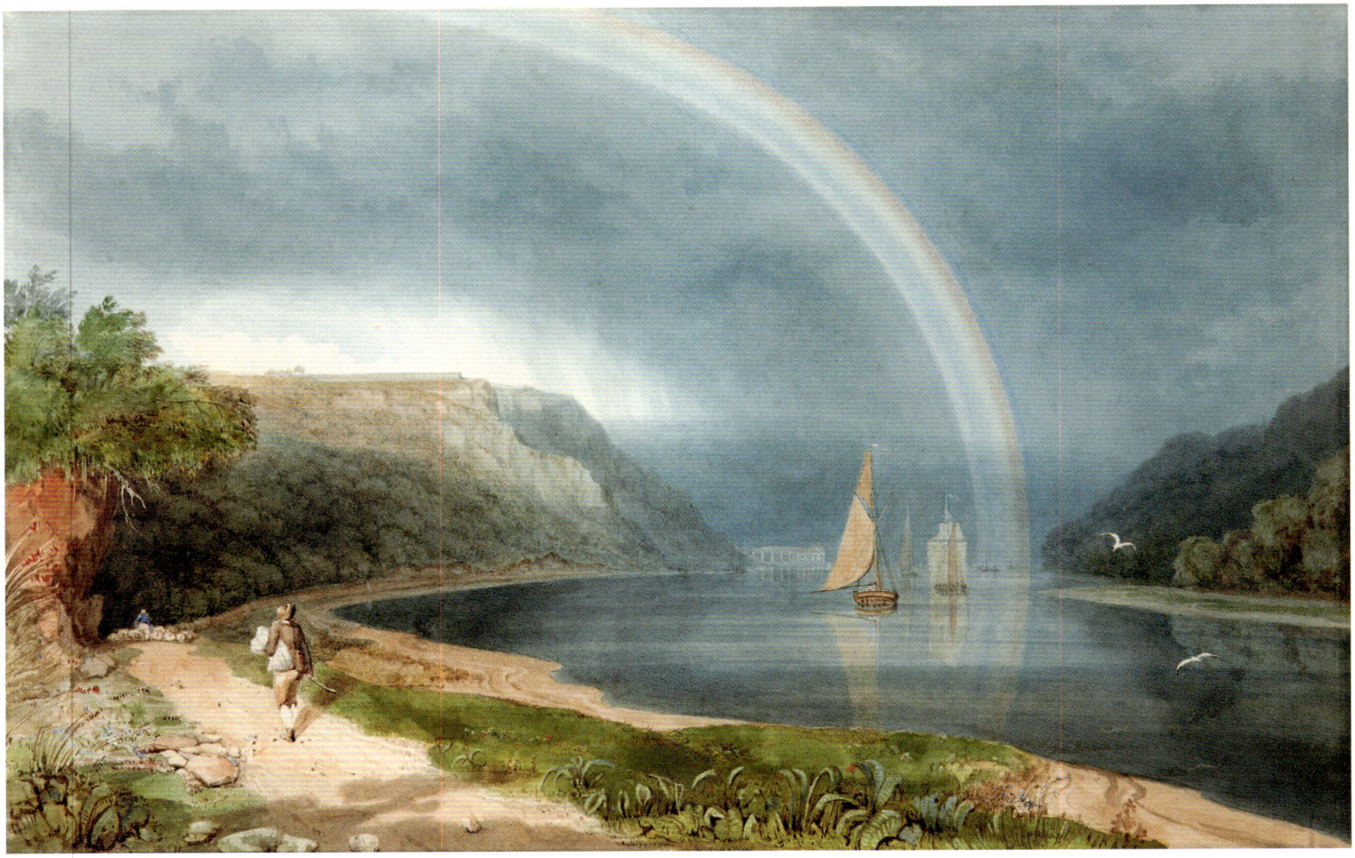

Samuel Jackson (1794-1869)
Rainbow on the River Avon
watercolour on paper, about 1825
29 x 44.7 cm
Gift, William Jerdone Braikenridge
K180

Jackson was made an associate member of the Old Watercolour Society in 1823 and went on to show 46 drawings there. The society was founded in 1804 to promote the use of watercolour painting as a medium to equal oil. This was so successful that by the 1820s artists such as Jackson were able to produce large finished watercolours such as The *Rainbow* for exhibition and sale at a more modest price for a new generation of patrons.

This is one of a series of four large watercolours of the Avon showing the different effects of a storm, moonlight and sunset. Under a glorious rainbow we see sheep being driven up the Avon along the tow-path. Sea Walls is on the left and the group of buildings beyond is the 'New Hotwell'. This thermal spring was leased out for development as a spa in 1730 but it was a lonely place and access was difficult. The spa enjoyed a brief revival after John Wesley visited in 1754, but the pump room ultimately fell into ruin and was used by quarrymen for shelter.

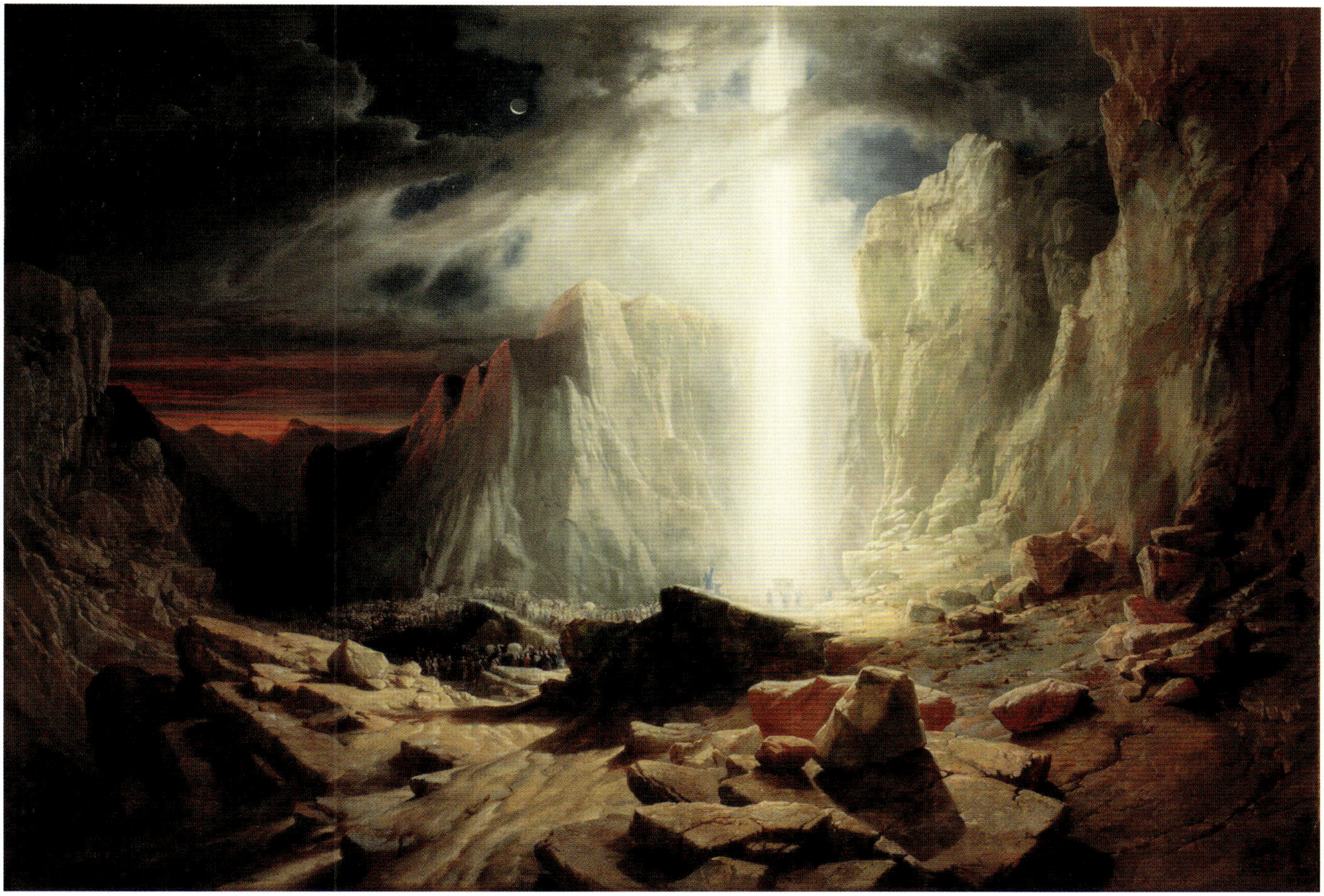

William West (1793-1861)
The Israelites passing through the wilderness preceded by the pillar of light
oil on canvas, 1845
111.7 x 167.6 cm
Purchased, 1974, with the assistance of the Victoria & Albert Museum Purchase Grant Fund
K4234

'[West] makes sketches at the drawing parties which delight all who see them, they are chiefly Eastern scenes, buildings, gardens, baths, fountains, subterranean scenes, dark interiors tastefully and ingeniously composed, illuminated by hot sun, cold moons, torchlight and all kinds of natural and preternatural light.' **Dr John King**

The Bristol School artists set themselves imaginary scenes which they sketched in monochrome washes. The discovery of the pyramids and tombs of ancient Egypt led to great excitement among artists who used them for Romantic paintings. William West drew with the sketching club, but ceased painting between 1826 and 1832 to pursue other interests. He rented out the derelict windmill on Clifton Down and installed a telescope, then a *camera obscura*. A keen geologist, he excavated a tunnel to Giants Cave nearby, and opened it to the public in 1837. He also involved himself in the plans for Clifton Suspension Bridge. West returned to painting and showed his *Israelites passing though the wilderness...* at the Royal Academy in 1845.

The flight of the Israelites is told in the Old Testament book of Exodus. God guided the Israelites at night with the light from a pillar of fire. This dramatic night scene, with the light streaming down on the minute figures of Moses and the Israelites is a Romantic history painting in the Sublime manner. West emphasises the powerlessness of humanity in the imposing landscape.

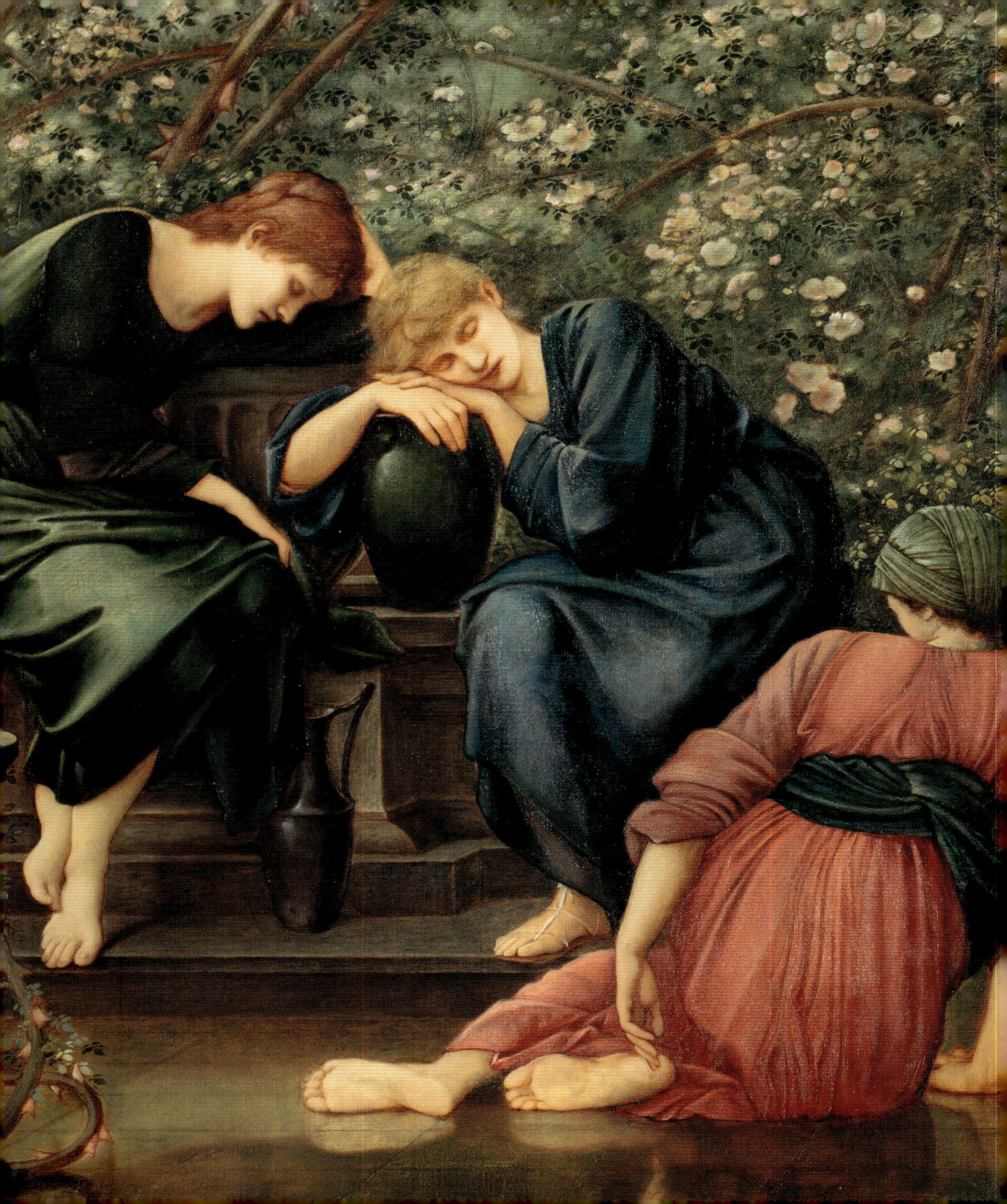

Art, landscape, travel and romance: British art 1790-1920

Landscape painting became a popular and established genre in Britain in the 19th century after the pioneering work of artists such as Gainsborough and Richard Wilson in the previous century. The so-called Golden Age of Watercolour began in the 1770s, when the newly produced watercolour boxes designed for Captain Cook's South Sea voyages made it easier to paint whilst travelling.

The Grand Tour had inspired artists to paint dramatic scenery abroad, but the Napoleonic Wars prevented travel and so artists had to look closer to home, and in doing so discovered the British scenery that inspired the Romantic Sublime and the quirky, irregular Picturesque. It is probably no coincidence that the rise of landscape painting in Britain occurred at the time of the Industrial Revolution when the expansion of cities began to change the fabric of Britain. Turner began his career exploring the more rugged and little-known corners of Britain such as North Wales and Yorkshire, as well as the South West. As a teenager in the 1790s he visited Bristol, where he painted an early finished watercolour of the Avon Gorge as seen through the mouth of a cave.

In 1838-39 WJ Müller was one of the first British artists to travel to the Near East (as Turkey, Greece and Egypt were then described), where he is said to have sailed along the Nile at the same time as the Scottish artist David Roberts. Following Napoleon's invasion of Egypt in 1798 an explosion of 'Egyptomania' occurred as archaeologists discovered the pyramids, tombs and hieroglyphs of ancient Egypt. The excitement generated by these discoveries can be seen in Müller's richly-coloured Egyptian scenes.

Roberts's *Temple of Dendera* records in vibrant colour the since-faded painted exterior of the temple and populates it with a party of Ottomans seated amongst the ruins. It is as if the artist is contrasting the grandeur of the ancient temple with the informality of the picnickers. The tendency to portray the East as exotic and mysterious and therefore less than rational is relatively muted in the work of Müller and Roberts, who both sought to create a reliable record of what they saw. What is notable about Roberts's scene is the absence of any Western figures. It is as if the Egyptian past and present were equally distant from any Western experience, although this was a time when Western powers were competing for influence in the Ottoman Empire.

Artists also looked back to early Renaissance art and to the aesthetics of the Middle Ages. The Pre-Raphaelite Brotherhood rebelled against the idealised portraiture and history painting of the Royal Academy. Instead, they turned to legend and literature or reinterpreted biblical subjects, often using contemporary sitters with strikingly modern features. The young Edward Burne-Jones was an admirer of the Pre-Raphaelites, and he and the socialist artist William Morris befriended their founder, the poet and painter Dante Gabriel Rossetti.

'Beautiful romance dreams' was Burne-Jones's term for the courtly mediaeval painting he wanted to make. *The garden court* is from a series of four images illustrating Charles Perrault's 17th-century tale, 'The sleeping beauty', or 'Little Briar Rose' as it was named by the Brothers Grimm. The draped sleeping women form a frieze of mannered, rhythmic postures that owes more to a classical relief carving than the receding perspective pioneered during the High Renaissance. By the time he completed the series, Burne-Jones had experienced success at the 1889 Paris International Exhibition, where his work was seen by the Symbolists Odilon Redon and Gustave Moreau. He had also been invited to become an Academician by the progressive President of the Royal Academy, Lord Leighton. He accepted but then later resigned.

The Victorian admiration for classical antiquity is evident in Sir Lawrence Alma-Tadema's *Unconscious rivals*, which depicts two distracted female companions sitting on a balcony decorated with a sculpture of Cupid. The Aesthetic artists downplayed narrative and sought to evoke mood, describing their paintings as arrangements or compositions, like pieces of music. Alma-Tadema's classicism hovers between narrative art and the subtle tonal arrangements of 'Art for art's sake'.

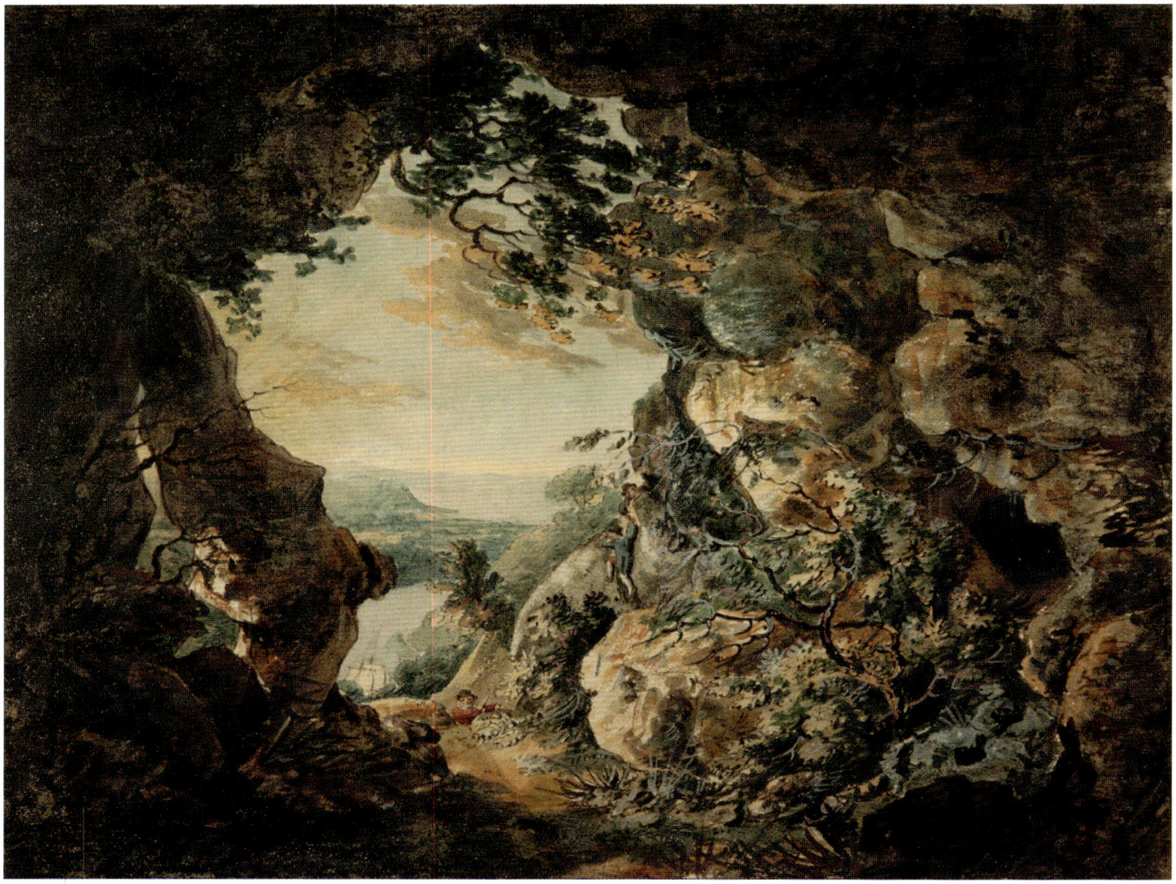

Joseph Mallord William Turner (1775-1851)
The mouth of the Avon near Bristol, seen from the cliffs below Sea Walls
watercolour and bodycolour over pencil, 1791/1792
22 x 28.3 cm
Purchased with the assistance of the Art Fund, the Friends of Bristol Art Gallery and the Peter John Blyth Art Fund, 2013
K6431

This watercolour beautifully illustrates why his hosts, the Narraways, nicknamed Joseph Mallord William Turner the 'Prince of rocks', gently teasing the teenager for the time he spent climbing, exploring and sketching in and around the Avon Gorge.

The view of the mouth of the River Avon towards the Severn and South Wales appears to be captured from inside a cave in the rock face of the Gorge. It is actually an amalgamation of two views: the slightly enlarged image of the cavern interior located below Sea Walls, which still exists, and the west-facing view taken from outside the cave. Turner had already exhibited at the Royal Academy in 1791 aged just sixteen, having entered the RA Schools in 1789. He was familiar with the compositional manipulations of topographical artists whose work he studied and emulated in order to pay for his tuition. His visit to Bristol and the South West established what would become his lifelong practice of gathering material for landscapes on the spot.

Turner has shown warm sunlight spilling into the cave and illuminating the three figures clambering up the rock. A narrative element which reappears in other images made on this visit in the Bristol and Malmesbury Sketchbook, is the passing vessel at the bottom of the composition, just visible from this high vantage point. Yet this is Turner's invention, as the cave is located much too high in the rock face for any passing masts to be seen.

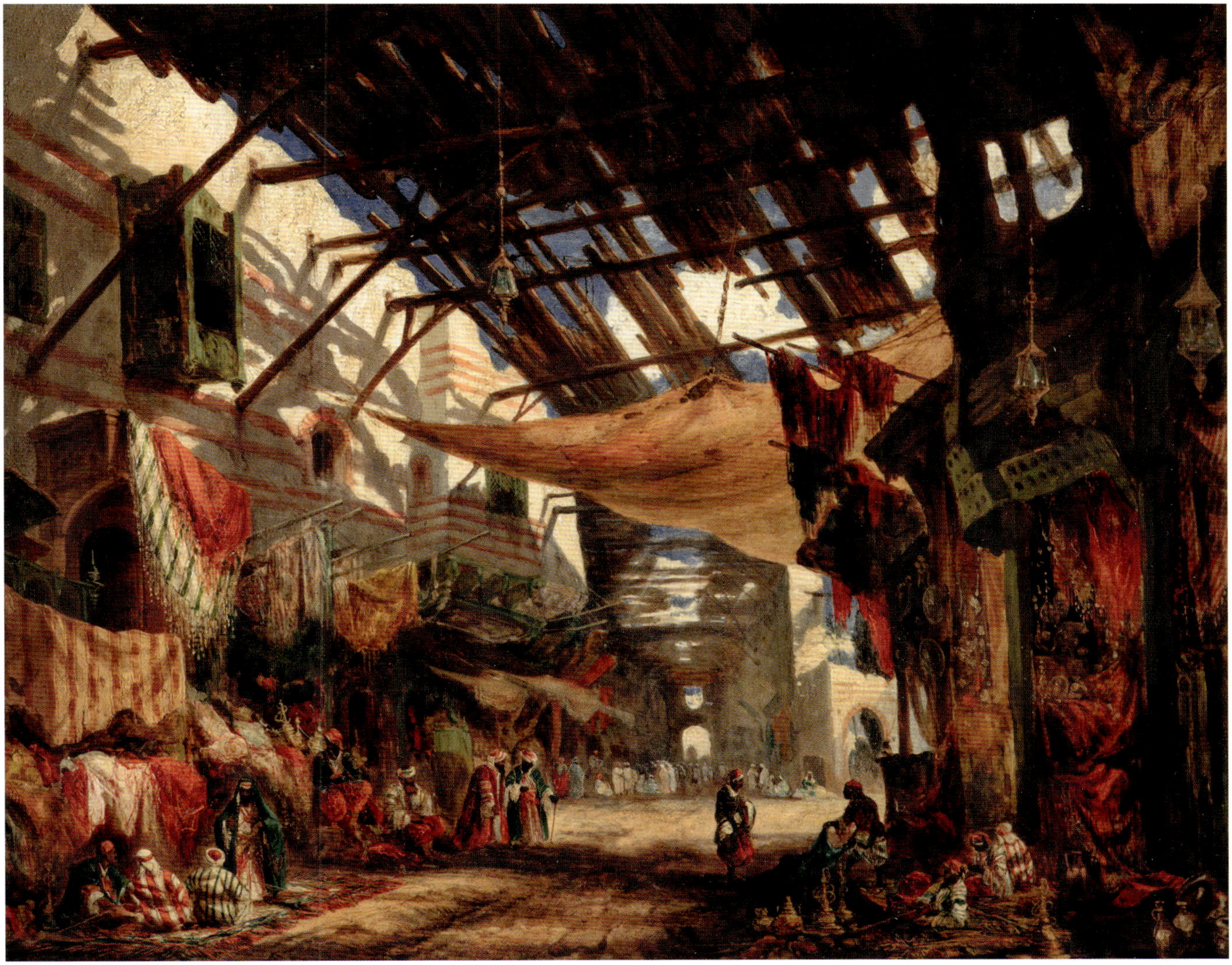

William James Müller (1812-1845)
The carpet bazaar, Cairo
oil on panel, 1843
62.2 x 74.9 cm
Gift, Mrs Samuel Lloyd, 1918
K509

Under a shabby wooden awning a street lined with white-washed buildings and tall market stalls leads into the distance. Sunlight strays into the half-darkness, lighting the silverware on the stalls and heightening the jewel-like quality of the colourful fabrics on display. Brightly clothed figures are shown resting and in conversation throughout the composition.

William James Müller, born in Bristol and for many years the city's best-known artist, visited Egypt in 1838-9. This was at the same time as David Roberts and both artists were in search of subject matter. Müller described Alexandria as 'like humanity put into a kaleidoscope' but soon admitted that Cairo was better still. The streets and bazaars excited him most, and the rich shadows and shafts of light he found there reminded him of the art of Rembrandt. This picture is the recollection of a bazaar painted several years after his return to Bristol.

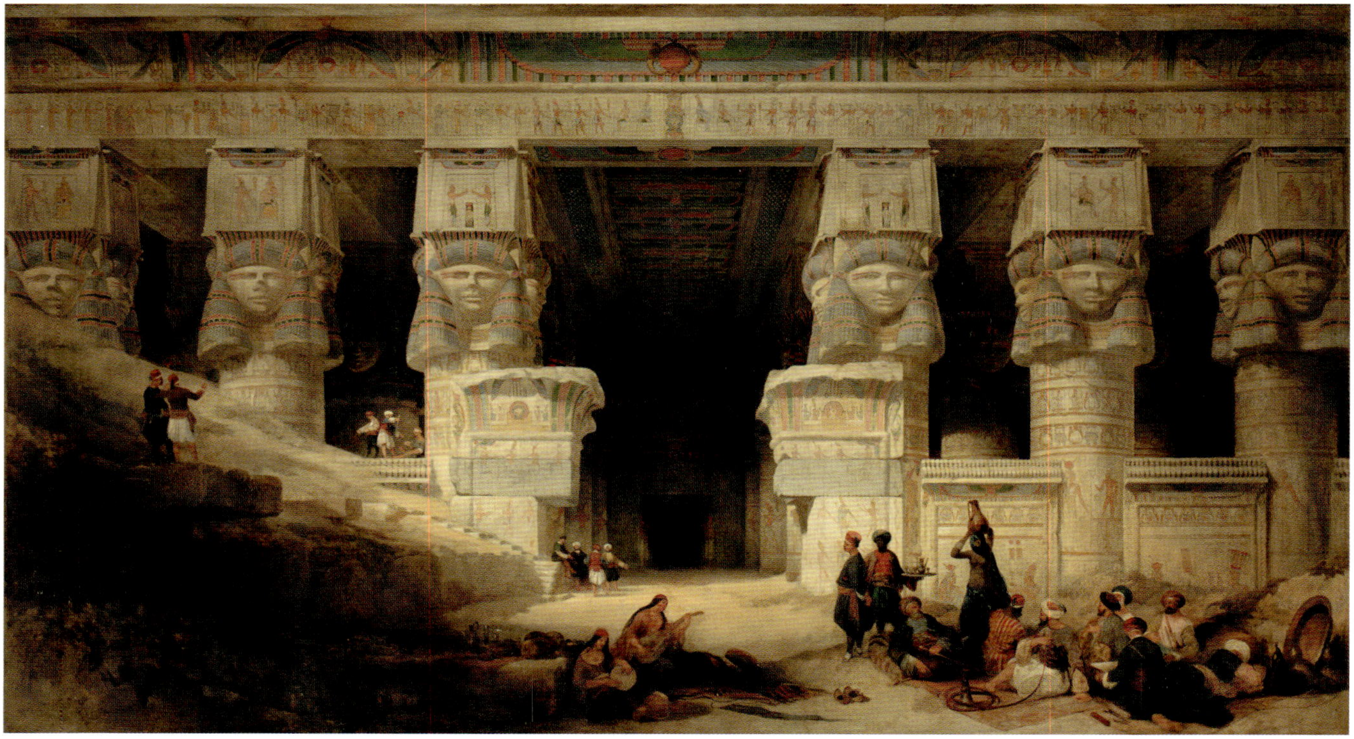

David Roberts (1796-1864)
The Temple of Dendera, Upper Egypt
oil on canvas, 1841
119.3 x 212 cm
Gift, Lord Winterstoke, 1910
K203

The dark interior of the Temple of Hathor at Dendera seems to recede endlessly beyond the elaborately decorated façade of the colossal building. The figures in the foreground heighten the scale of the ancient Egyptian architecture and dramatic lighting enhances the effects of sublime grandeur. David Roberts began his career as a set painter, and settled in London to make designs for the Drury Lane Theatre. His skill at rendering monumental forms was used to great effect in his Romantic masterpieces. Notice how the the leisurely picnicking Ottoman figures contrast with the grandeur of the ancient temple.

Roberts had been encouraged by Turner to paint. His visit to the Near East in 1838-9 was of crucial importance to his career. He was already acclaimed as a painter of European topographical and architectural views but he needed new subject matter and was one of the first British artists to visit Egypt. The sketches he made there and in the Holy Land gave him a supply of subjects that lasted the rest of his life. At Dendera he noted the temple's good state of preservation in his diary. However, the faces on the columns of the portico had eroded and he embellished them in this painting for greater dramatic impact.

Frederic, Lord Leighton (1830-1896)
The fisherman and the syren
oil on canvas, 1856-58
66.4 x 48.9 cm
Gift, The Honourable Mrs Lyell, 1938
K1401

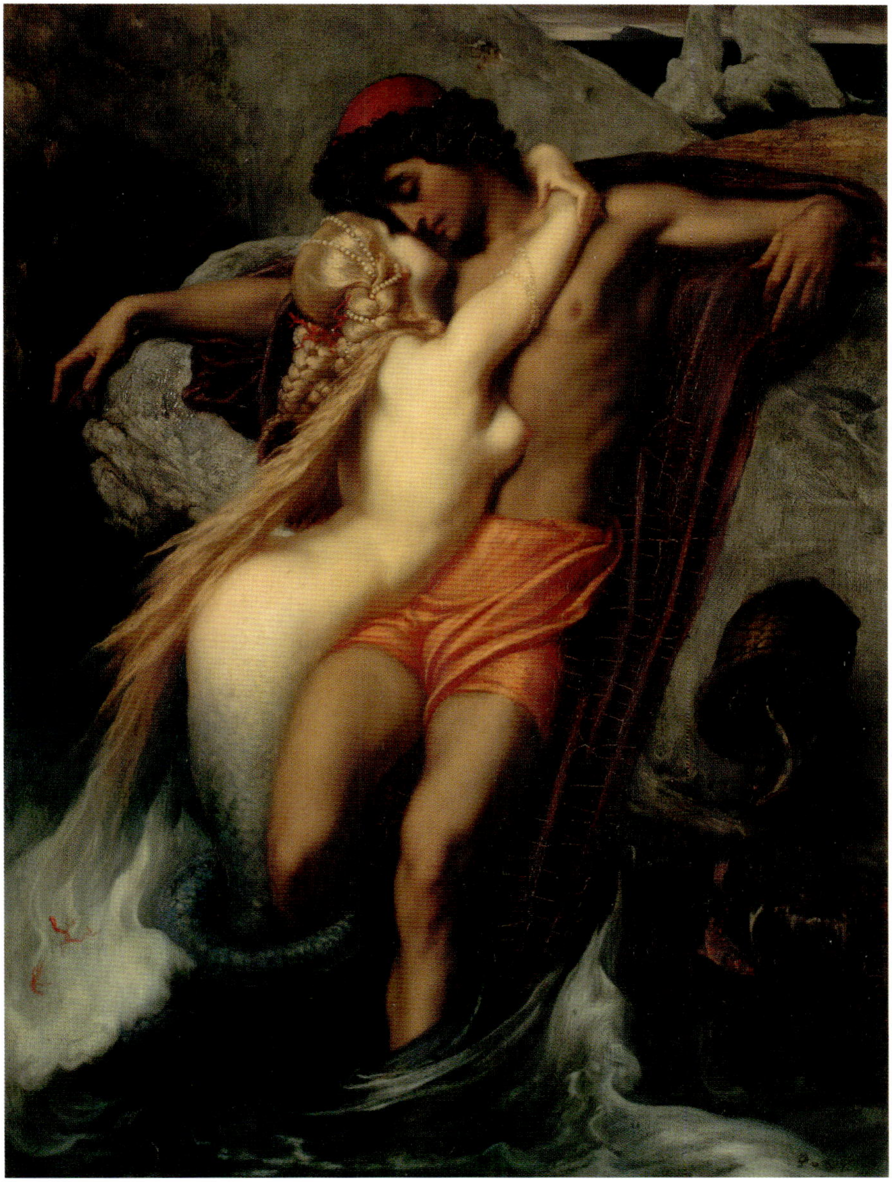

This early work by Frederic Leighton illustrates the poem by the German Romantic writer Goethe in which a mermaid lures a fisherman to his death in retribution for killing her children:

> *'Half drew she him*
> *Half sunk he in*
> *And never more was seen.'*

His arms outstretched, the fisherman resembles Christ on the cross as he surrenders to the fair-haired siren who presses her body to his: it is a highly eroticised image. A contemporary critic noted the 'irresistible seductiveness' of the mermaid but also observed that this 'young artist has plainly drunk long and eagerly at the fount of beauty that assuaged the thirst of Leonardo, Michelangelo and Raphael'.

Leighton travelled extensively through Europe in his youth, studying in Frankfurt under the Nazarene artist Edward von Steinle. His work was self-consciously academic, often looking back to the Renaissance artists. The year before *The fisherman and the syren* he painted *Cimabue's celebrated Madonna is carried in procession through the streets of Florence* which was purchased by Queen Victoria, and is now in the National Gallery.

Leighton was elected President of the Royal Academy in 1878 where he was a progressive influence, encouraging the membership of Burne-Jones.

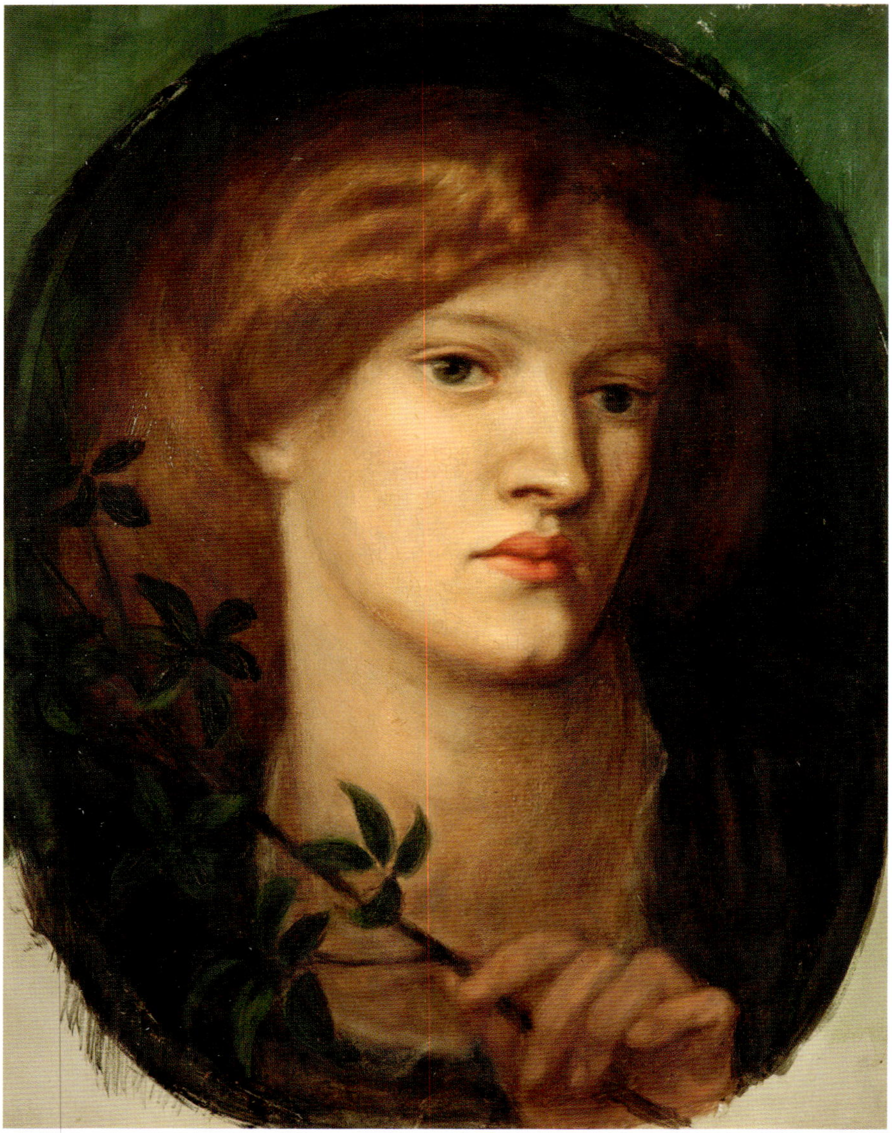

Dante Gabriel Rossetti (1828-1882)
Portrait of Louisa Ruth Herbert
oil on panel, 1858-59
45.1 x 35.6 cm
Gift, Ms Virginia Surtees, 2014
K6465

In this portrait of the Victorian actress Louisa Ruth Herbert, Dante Gabriel Rossetti has painted the features according to Pre-Raphaelite ideals of female beauty. The young woman's pouting lips, voluminous red hair and strong neck have been particularly emphasised. The oval format of the composition focuses the viewer's gaze onto the face. Louisa Ruth Herbert was born in Bristol in 1831 and had a successful stage career, even managing the St James's Theatre in London from 1864 to 1868. She modelled for Rossetti between 1858 and 1860.

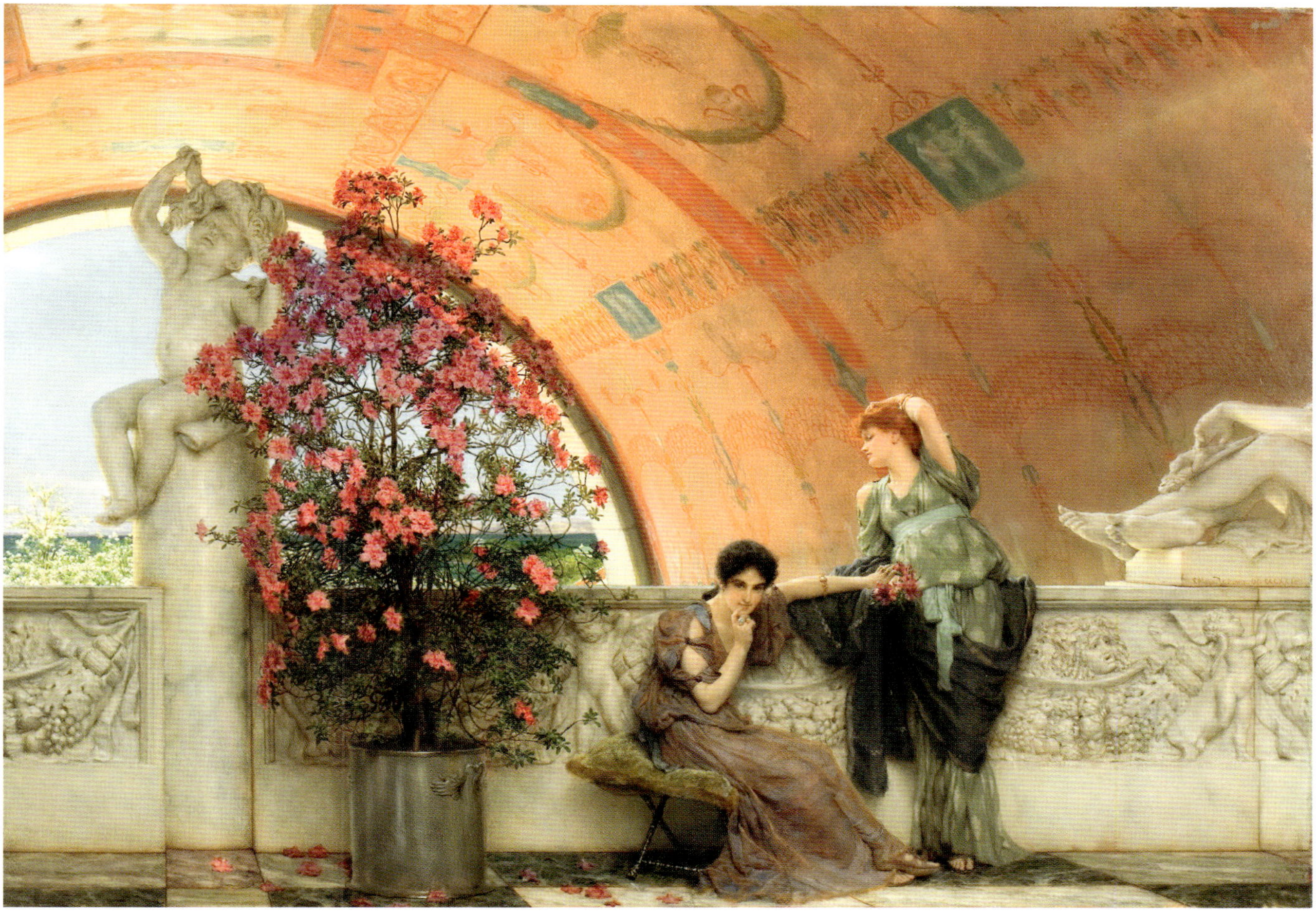

Sir Lawrence Alma-Tadema
(1836-1912)
Unconscious rivals
oil on panel, 1893
45.1 x 62.9 cm
Bequest of Jessie and Robert Bromhead, 1935
K1248

This meticulous depiction of two glamorous women lounging in an ancient Roman villa exemplifies the work of Lawrence Alma-Tadema, who became interested in daily life in ancient Greece and Rome after visiting Pompeii in 1893. From the marble-clad wall in the foreground the eye is drawn along a decorated ceiling towards a view of the Mediterranean coast beyond. The warm colouring of the coral ceiling and the dark pink hibiscus blossoms heightens the sensuality of the scene with the languorous women.

Critics have interpreted the young women as rivals in love waiting for the same man. The large marble statue to the left shows Cupid, the god of love, taking off the mask of a Silenus, companion to the god of wine Bacchus, which suggests that the women's love rivalry is about to be unmasked. The artist based the sculpture on artefacts found in Roman museums, photographs of which he owned.

Alma-Tadema was Dutch-born but settled permanently in London in 1870, where he enjoyed a highly successful career.

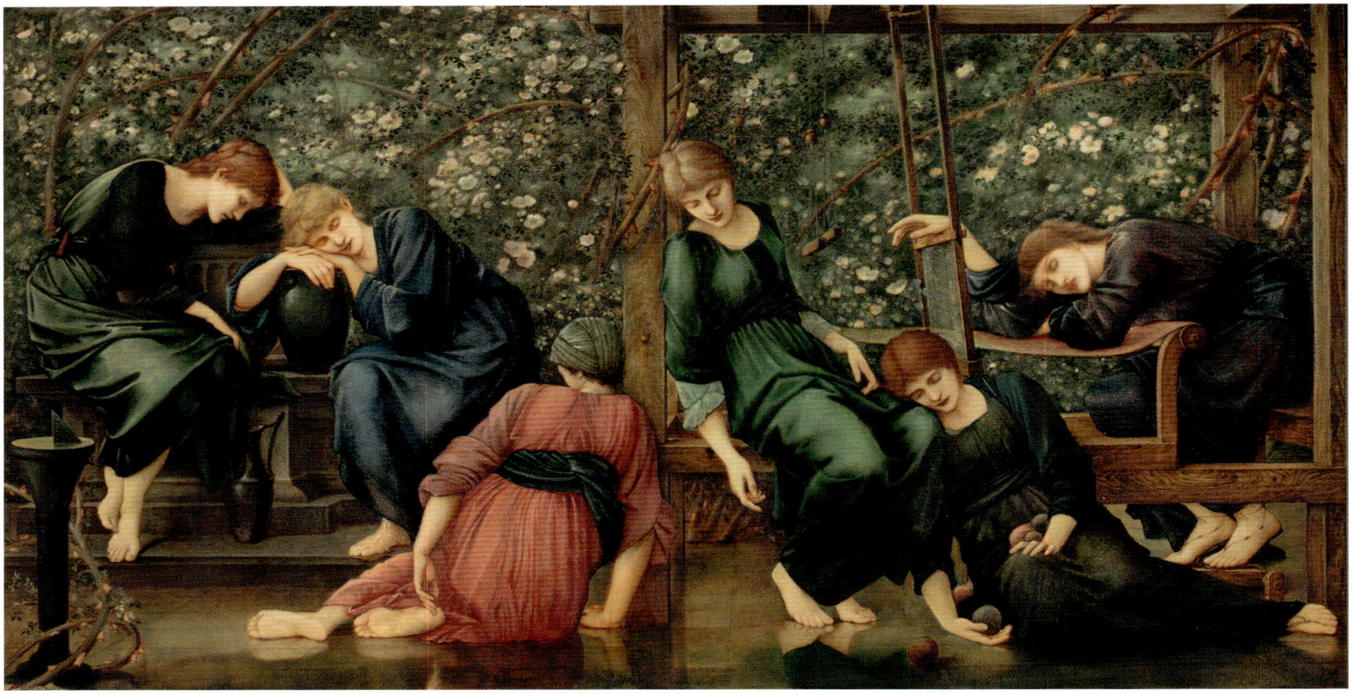

Sir Edward Coley Burne-Jones (1833-1898)
The garden court, from the 'Briar Rose' series
oil on canvas, 1894
126.3 x 237.4 cm
Gift, Conrad P Fry, Mrs Cooke-Hurle and Sir Geoffrey Storrs Fry, in memory of their parents, Francis James Fry and Elizabeth Fry, 1930
K928

Throughout his career Edward Burne-Jones was captivated by the fairy tale of 'The sleeping beauty'. For some twenty years he worked on a cycle of paintings illustrating the story which were finally presented at Agnew's Bond Street gallery in London in 1890. The four large paintings were purchased by Alexander Henderson, Lord Farrington for his home Buscot Park in Oxfordshire. Burne-Jones returned to the story several times and *The garden court* is from the third series.

This dreamlike scene takes the viewer inside the enchanted palace where sleep reigns supreme. Before a thicket of sweet briar roses (*Rosa rubiginosa*) six young women appear to have fallen asleep while weaving and fetching water. The stylised bodies of the women form a decoratively flowing frieze across the picture's narrow foreground.

Burne-Jones met Rossetti in 1856 and worked with him and William Morris on the *Morte d'Arthur* wall paintings in the Oxford Union Debating Society Room in 1857. Burne-Jones's early work was influenced by mediaevalism, but on his travels to Italy he developed an admiration for Botticelli which can be seen in the composition and the draperies of *The garden court*. As an artist Burne-Jones was a nonconformist, resigning from the Old Watercolour Society and the Royal Academy and showing instead at the independent Grosvenor Gallery. He was knighted in 1889 and awarded a baronetcy in 1894.

The inertia of the willowy forms of *The garden court* contrasts with the active figure of the New Woman in the 1890s, written about by novelists including Henry James. A generation of women was beginning to campaign for equal education and the right to vote. This included the women of the Pre-Raphaelite circle, but it is hard not to see a tension in the Pre-Raphaelite portrayals of women.

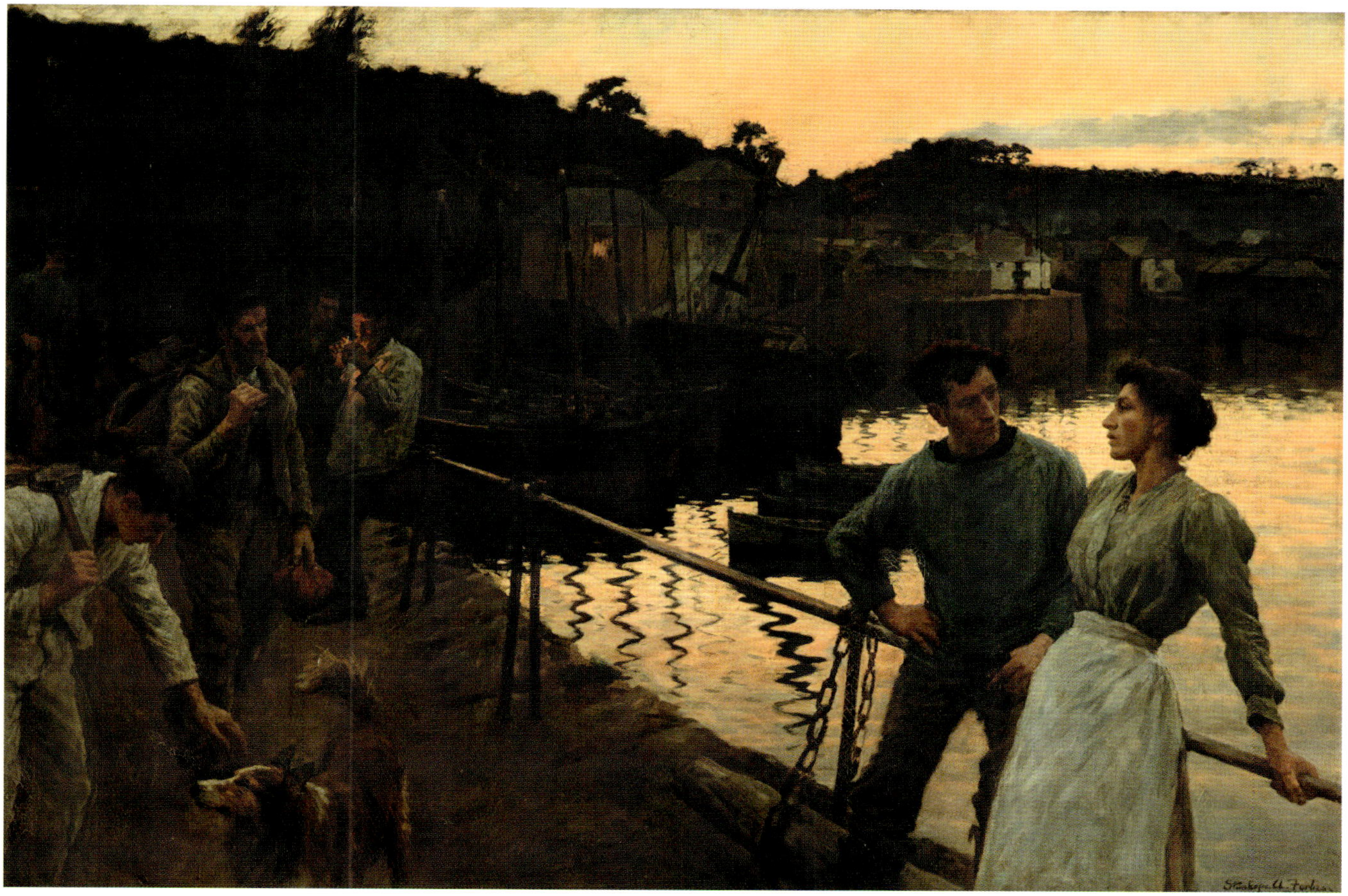

Stanhope Alexander Forbes
(1857-1947)
Home-along: evening
oil on canvas, 1905
120.6 x 180.9 cm
Purchased, 1910
K204

'Home-along' is dialect in Cornwall and here suggests the return home in the evening. In 1884 Stanhope Forbes settled in the small fishing village of Newlyn. He was the centre of a 'colony' of like-minded *plein-air* (open air) painters who followed the 19th century French Impressionists and Realists in depicting contemporary life lived by ordinary people. Forbes's models were the villagers who wandered the quay and he could often be seen at work with his easel on the cobbled streets. He was interested in using photography to achieve dynamic composition effects, following pioneers such as Edgar Degas. The cropped figure bending to greet the collie anchors the panoramic sweep of the view. The atmosphere of the darkening evening is conveyed by the red glow on the face of the man lighting a pipe seen against the flattened black silhouette of the coastal background. In contrast, the couple in the foreground are still lit by the last rays of the setting sun.

Purchased in 1910, this was the first work by a living artist that the museum had acquired since *Eve at the fountain* by EH Baily in 1825. As a young artist Forbes had been a founder member of the New English Art Club which was established to challenge the supremacy of the Royal Academy over the art scene in England. By 1910 however, Forbes was happy for *Home-along: evening* to be exhibited at the RA.

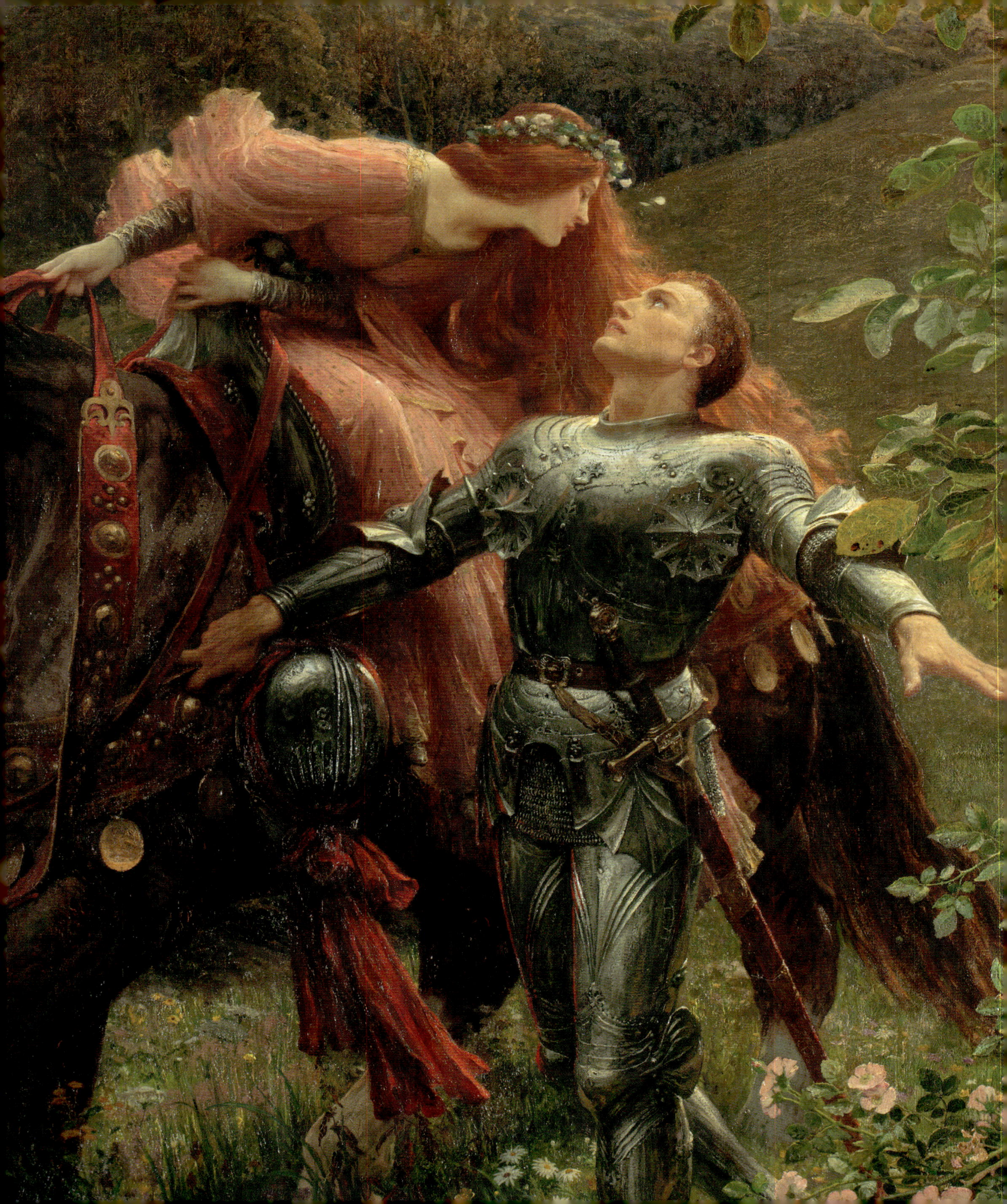

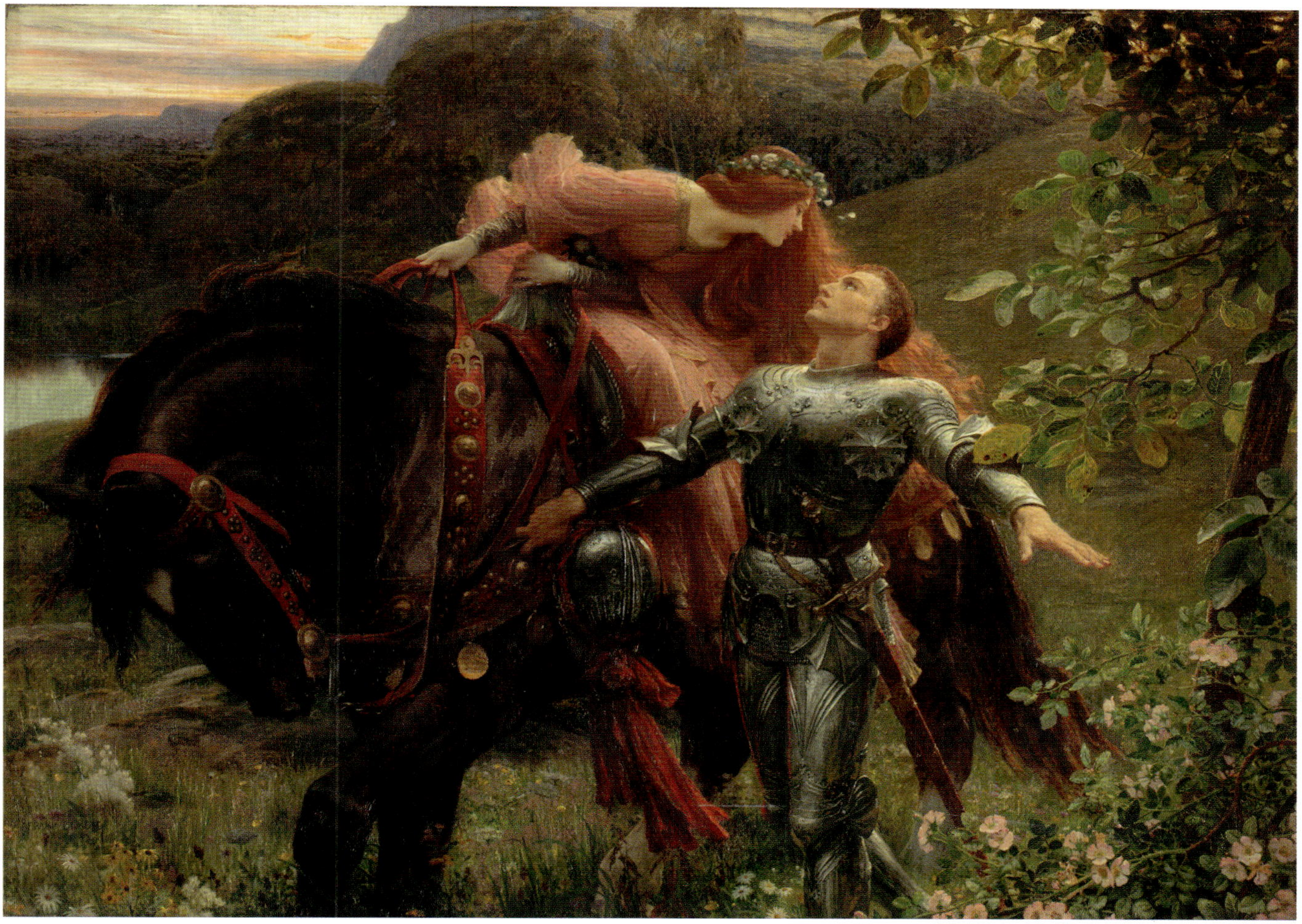

Sir Frank Dicksee (1853-1928)
La belle dame sans merci
oil on canvas, 1901-1903
137.2 x 188 cm
Gift, Mrs Yda Richardson, 1913
K328

Blind to the beauties of the surrounding meadows and wooded hillsides, a young knight in polished armour dramatically throws back his arms and appears to surrender himself to the lady on horseback who leans down – as if to kiss him. The encounter is inspired by Keats's poem of 1819:

'I met a lady in the meads,
Full beautiful – a faery's child,
Her hair was long, her foot was light,
And her eyes were wild.
...
I set her on my pacing steed,
And nothing else saw all day long;
For side long would she bend, and sing
A faery's song.'

Frank Dicksee did not depict the dark outcome of the story, which leaves the knight devastated, but focuses the composition on the seductive power of the *femme fatale*. A fascination with chivalry had existed throughout the Victorian era, but this painting reflects a rising anxiety over gender roles at the turn of the 20th century.

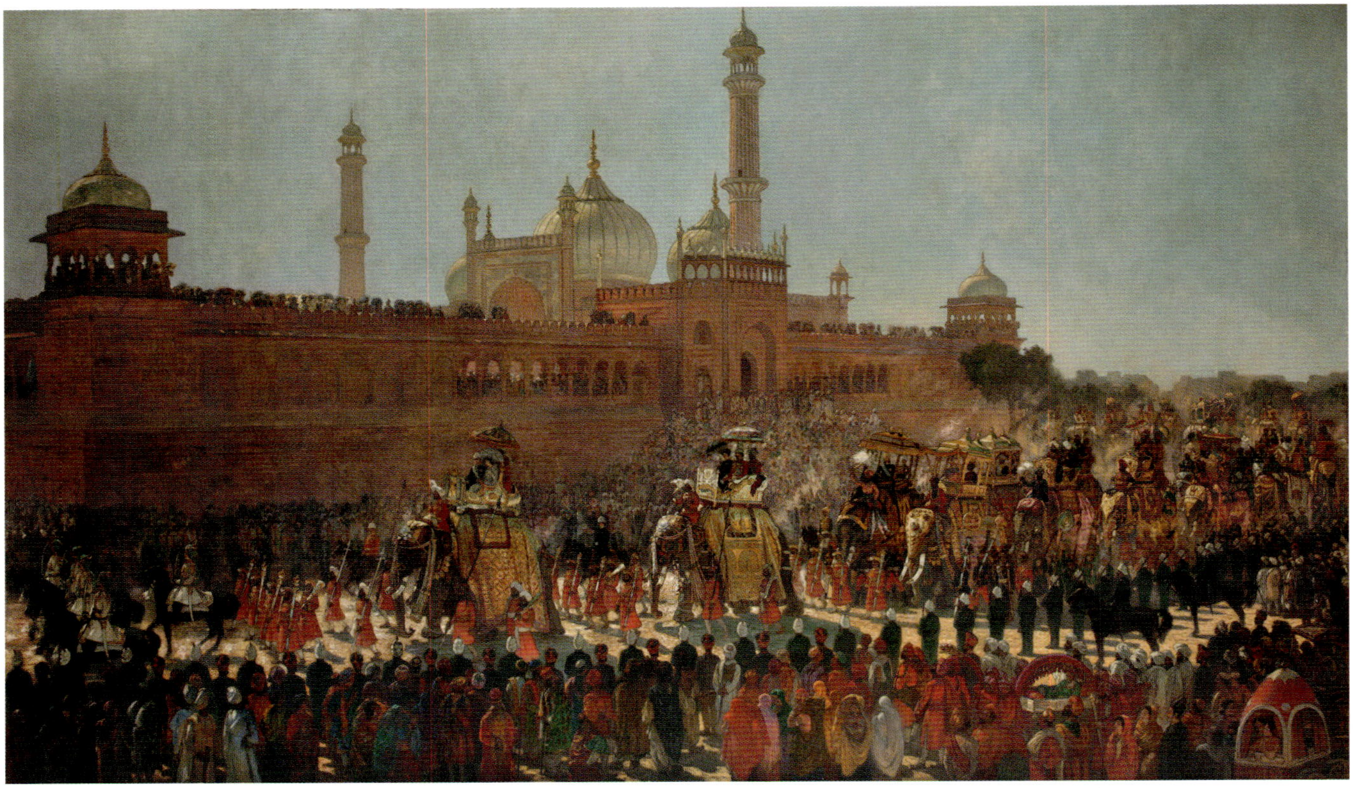

Roderick McKenzie (1865-1941)
The state entry, 1903
oil on canvas, 1907
3660 x 5790 cm
Transferred, British Empire and Commonwealth Museum, 2012
2002/156/001

The three Delhi Durbars, or ceremonial gatherings, held in 1877, 1903 and 1911, were spectacular state occasions to mark the declaration of a British monarch as Empress or Emperor of India. In 1901, Edward VII became King, and a durbar was organised to declare him Emperor of India on 1 January 1903. Edward VII did not attend in person, but sent his brother, the Duke of Connaught. The event was organised by Lord Curzon, Viceroy of India, with two weeks of processions, sports, balls and dinners.

Curzon commissioned Roderick McKenzie, a British artist living in India, to paint the ceremonial procession of British officials and Indian Maharajas as they entered the Durbar grounds on elephants, passing the Jami Masjid or Friday Mosque.

The procession was led by the Viceroy, then the Duke and Duchess of Connaught, representing the British royal family, and then by Indian rulers, headed by the Nizam of Hyderabad and the Maharaja of Mysore. The first version of the painting is in the Victoria Memorial Hall in Kolkata, India.

After he left India, McKenzie made this second version for Lord Roberts, who served in India from 1851-1877. The image offers an insight into the historical mechanisms of the British Empire. The local detail, vast scale and composition create the impression of an exotic and at the same time orderly and harmonious event. Like the durbar spectacle, the painting's original aim was to celebrate British rule in India – from a British perspective.

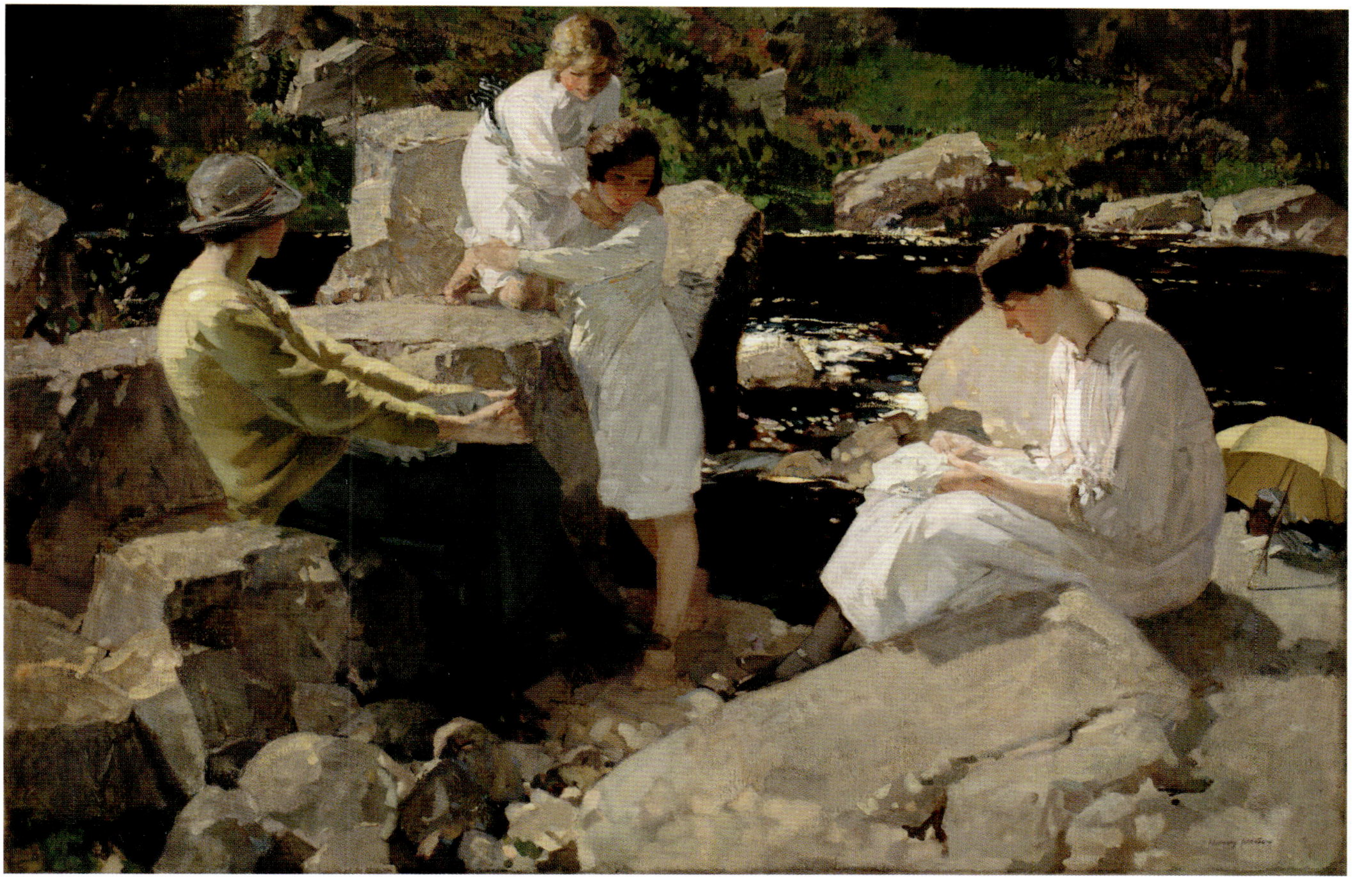

Harry Watson (1871-1936)
Holidays
oil on canvas, about 1920
102.8 x 154.9 cm
Purchased, 1922
K720

Harry Watson was born in Scarborough and trained at the Royal College of Art in London where he was a gold medallist and won a scholarship to travel to Italy. Watson generally painted outdoors (*en plein air*) capturing weather effects, especially the play of sunlight, in breezy portrayals of people at play.

In *Holidays* Watson shows a carefree day by a river running through a mountain landscape. Two girls play in the sunshine, while the young women in the foreground perch elegantly on large boulders, all in light summer clothes and sporting fashionable 1920s bob hairstyles.

Beyond the rushing stream in the middle-ground, the far bank of the river is visible, rather like a painting by Watson of North Wales on the River Lledr which is in the collection at Leighton House in London. Watson has painted the scene in fresh, confident brushstrokes, omitting the sky and concentrating on the play of light over the rocks, the water and the relaxed holiday atmosphere. In the 19th century the Impressionists had begun to paint people at leisure. Such scenes became more widespread in Britain as changing work patterns in the 20th century gave more workers greater leisure time.

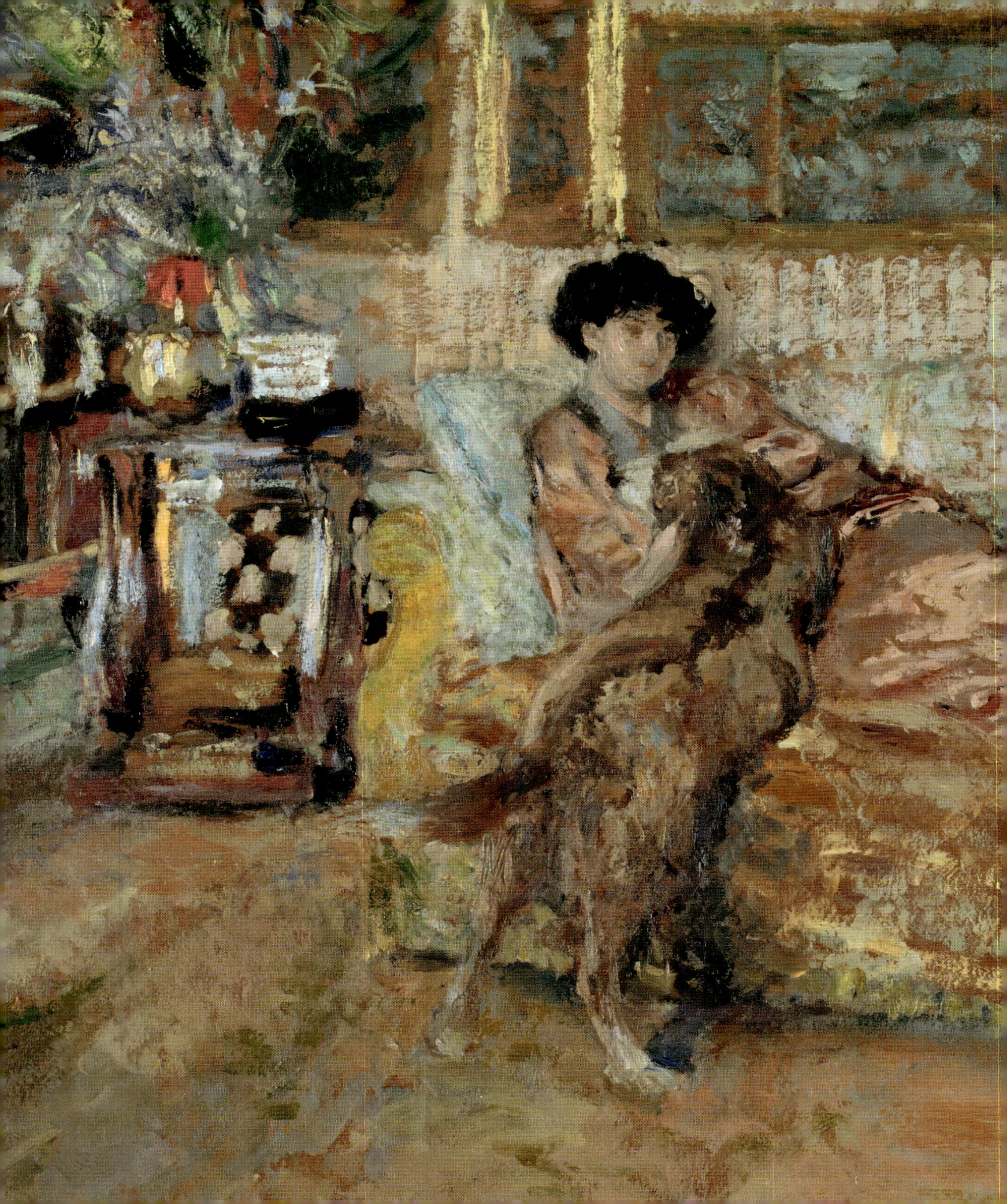

Radical changes: French art 1831-1910

The 19th century in France was a period of tumultuous change which saw the Napoleonic Wars (1803-1815) along with the Franco-Prussian War and the Paris Commune in the 1870s, and this stormy history is reflected in its art.

French art in the 19th century was even more dominated by its Academy than British art. Artists often faced rejection from the annual *Salon* exhibition in the Louvre, then the only public exhibition of art. At the same time as the Pre-Raphaelites were forming in England, their French contemporary Gustave Courbet was writing a Realist manifesto. Just as the young English artists used unconventional models in their paintings of religious subjects, Courbet was applying the grand scale of history painting to working-class subjects. Courbet's career marked the start of a process of increasing self-reflection that characterises modern art. The seascape *Eternity* was painted in the 1860s when he visited Trouville on the north coast of France. In a departure from Realist subjects, the mystical title lends the painting a Romantic sensibility. It might well be interpreted as the calm before the storm of Courbet's involvement with the Commune in 1871.

Eva Gonzalès was taught by the notorious artist of the *Salon des Refusés*, Edouard Manet. In 1863, artists rejected by the *Salon* were offered the chance to show their work in the *Refusés.* Manet's art was mocked because he painted recognisably real people, and many viewers could only see ordinary undistinguished men and women. The subject of Gonzalès's painting, *The donkey ride*, is similarly informal. The composition, in which the artist's sister Jeanne is seated on a donkey, appears natural and unposed. The painting is unfinished and its liquid handling has the loose quality associated with Impressionism.

The *Refusés* opened a path for artists to organise exhibitions outside the mainstream. The first show by the Impressionists was held in 1874 and displayed their concentration on modern subjects similar to those of Courbet, as can be seen in Auguste Renoir's interior with its portrayal of two young girls.

It wasn't just everyday subjects and sitters that made these artists radical. The Impressionists painted light and shadow in colour, a method that looked unfinished to contemporary viewers. The name Impressionist actually came from a critic's scornful summation of Claude Monet's *Impression, sunrise* of 1872. Its atomised dabs of complementary colour – purple with yellow, green with red, orange with blue - incorporated modern optical theory and anticipated the fragmented visual language of Cubism. Such methods marked a shift from representing a supposedly objective reality to expressing the artist's perception of a changing world. This was mirrored in the shift from a type of art made for patrons to one created to solve aesthetic problems the artists set for themselves. It was an art that existed outside the official *Salon,* promoted by a new generation of art dealers and patrons who were sympathetic to the work of the artists.

Symbolism is perhaps the opposite of Realism but can be seen as an extension of the subjectivity of Impressionism. Gustave Moreau and Odilon Redon both turned away from contemporary life for their subjects. In 1870, after Moreau shunned public life following harsh criticism of his work, he painted the mythological figure of Andromeda awaiting her rescue from the sea monster by Perseus. Burne-Jones had also painted the story of Perseus, and the Symbolists were close to the Pre-Raphaelites, both in subject matter and their desire to find a new way to express spirituality. Redon's *Rider on the beach* occupies the same imaginary sphere as Burne-Jones's 'beautiful romance dreams', but its execution is fragmentary and intimate.

Edouard Vuillard took what he had learnt from Symbolism and the methods of the *Nabis* (prophets) group and applied it to the realm of ordinary domesticity, like the Impressionists. Over and over he portrayed Lucie Hessel, the wife of his dealer, in her home. The writer André Gide said of Vuillard that it was as if he was whispering and beckoning the viewer to come closer. This 1910 portrait brings us back to the subjective artist's eye of Impressionism and reminds the viewer that photography has been invented. Lucie Hessel is blurred, a frozen moment in a stolen snapshot. *Madame Hessel* looks ahead to the Modernism of the 20th century.

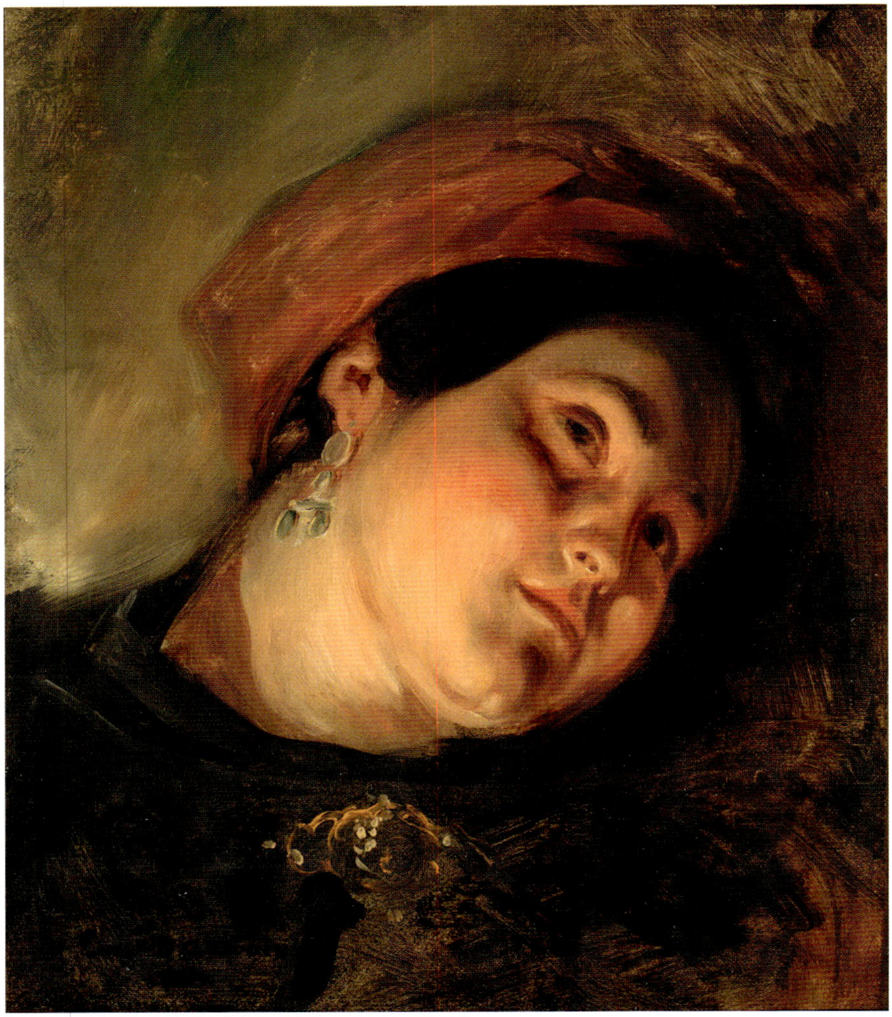

Eugène Delacroix (1798-1863)
Head of a woman in a red turban
oil on canvas, 1831
45.3 x 41.3 cm
Purchased with the assistance of the Victoria & Albert Museum Purchase Grant Fund and the Art Fund, 1962
K2873

According to Frédéric Villot, a close friend of the artist and the original owner of the painting, this vibrantly coloured study of a woman's head was painted by lamplight. The vigorous treatment shows the influence of Rubens on the work of the Romantic painter, whose work would become so influential to French art in the 19th century.

Eugène Delacroix travelled to Morocco and Algeria in 1832 with the entourage of the Comte de Mornay, King Louis-Philippe's diplomatic representative to the sultan. He used the trip to gather imagery that would inform his painting for the rest of his life. *Woman in a red turban* was painted prior to that tour, but indicates Delacroix's long interest in the Middle East, which was partly inspired by Delacroix's admiration for Byron and his exoticised subjects. In Morocco the artist discovered how to paint light and shade in colour. The Neo-Impressionist Paul Signac suggested in 1899 that Delacroix's use of colour freed art from the shadowy *chiaroscuro* of Baroque painting and looked forward to the optical experiments of the Impressionists.

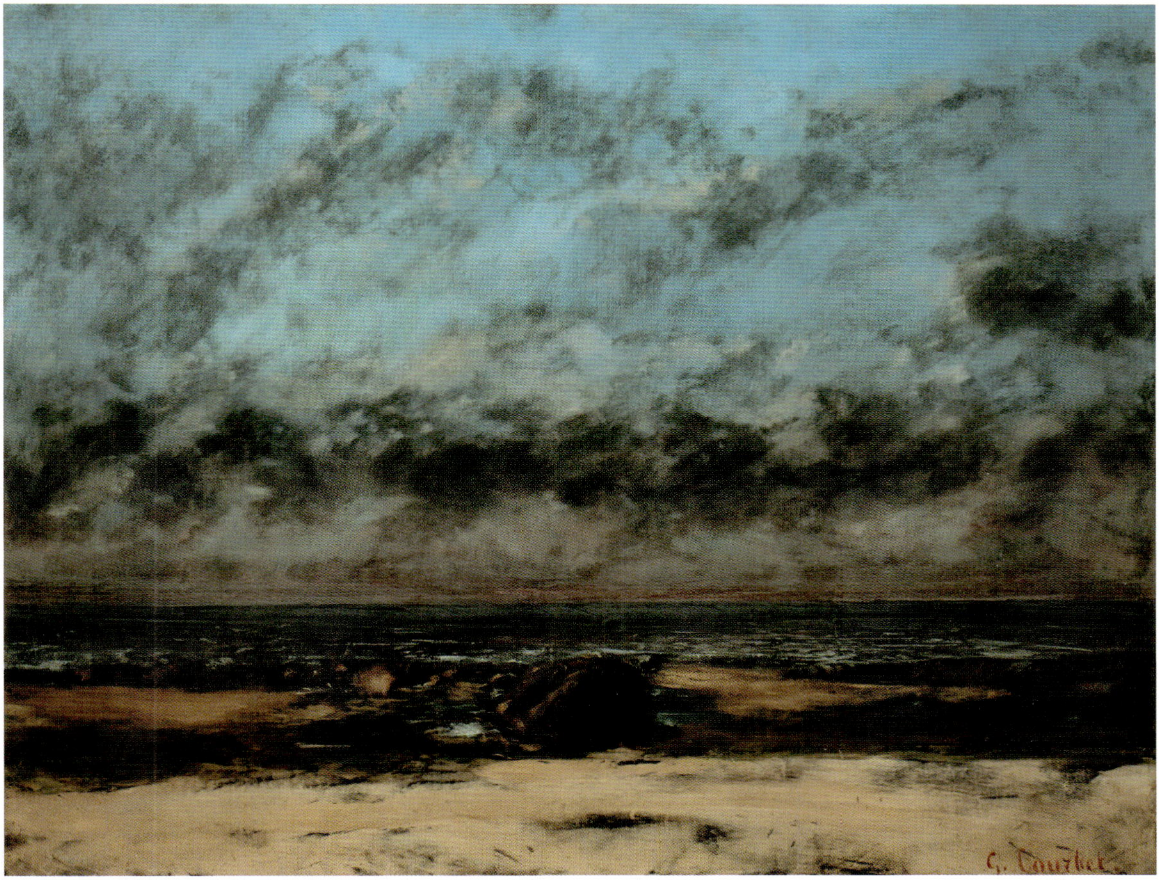

Jean-Désiré-Gustave Courbet
(1819-1877)
Eternity
oil on canvas, about 1865-69
64.7 x 79.3 cm
Purchased with the assistance of the Art Fund, 1952
K2239

Gustave Courbet, who did not see the sea until he was 22, declared 'how strange it is for a valley-dweller'. His first 'sea landscape', as he called them, was painted at Palavas near Montpelier in 1854. In 1865 he visited Trouville on the Normandy coast for the first time. The railway had opened there in 1863 and the seaside was becoming a place of leisure. This can be seen in 19th-century portrayals of the sea that emphasise its calmness and mystery especially when compared to the shipwrecks and thunderstorms of Romantic art. The artist Whistler was convalescing at Trouville when Courbet arrived and he painted Courbet's portrait on the beach. Courbet painted several views during the 1865 visit, including six pure 'sea landscapes'.

In *Eternity* the beach is depicted at low tide and the view stretches out across a calm sea to the low horizon. Because the scene doesn't attempt to depict a specific location or a particular point of interest, it could even be seen as semi-abstract. In contrast to the Impressionists, who used white canvases, Courbet worked in the traditional manner on a dark ground, a technique which intensifies the melancholy mood. He explained: '*nature, without the sun, is also dark and black. I do as the light does, I illuminate the parts that project, and the picture is done*'. He nevertheless rejected the high finish of French establishment painting, applying the paint with a palette knife.

Courbet was revolutionary in his life as well as his art. He later went to prison for his role in the revolutionary *Commune* that took control of Paris between March and May of 1871.

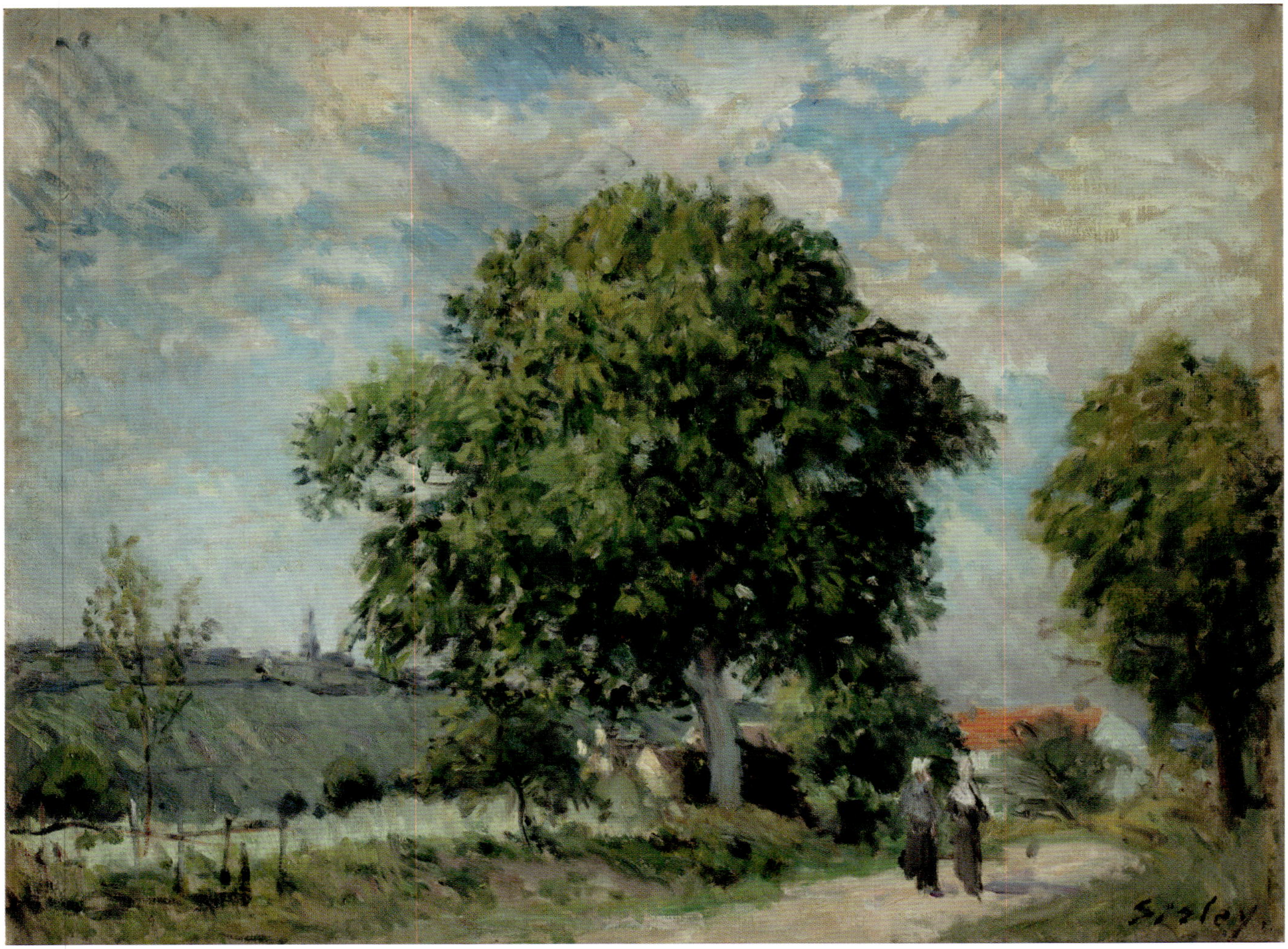

Alfred Sisley (1839-1899)
The entrance to the village
oil on canvas, 1876-1880
49.5 x 64.1 cm
Purchased with the assistance of the Victoria & Albert Museum Purchase Grant Fund and Estate Duty exemption, 1972
K4132

The English artist Alfred Sisley met Monet and Renoir in the Paris studio of Charles Gleyre in 1862, after abandoning his business career in London. Sisley painted with Monet and Renoir at Barbizon during the period when the ideas of Impressionism were crystallised. Like Monet, Sisley concentrated on landscape throughout his career.

Entrance to the village exhibits the spontaneous, 'unfinished', handling of paint for which the Impressionists were derided. A tree dominates the centre of this view near to where two women in bonnets walk along a country road. Sisley employs a range of brushstrokes: light dabs for the billowing clouds, feathery greens for the foliage, diagonal hatches for the grass, blocks of red and white for the distant buildings and a few shorthand strokes for the strolling figures.

The experimentation of Impressionism sustained Sisley's painting all his life. The failure of his father's business after the Franco-Prussian War meant that he had to make a living from his art. He did not achieve the success of his friends, although he was promoted by several important dealers, including Paul Durand-Ruel who handled this picture in 1892.

Lucien Pissarro
(1863-1944)
The turkeys (*les dindons*) or Esther in the garden, Eragny
oil on canvas, 1893
55.2 x 45.7 cm
Given by Mrs AMT Barrett
(neé Marjorie Sherlock), 1972
K4126

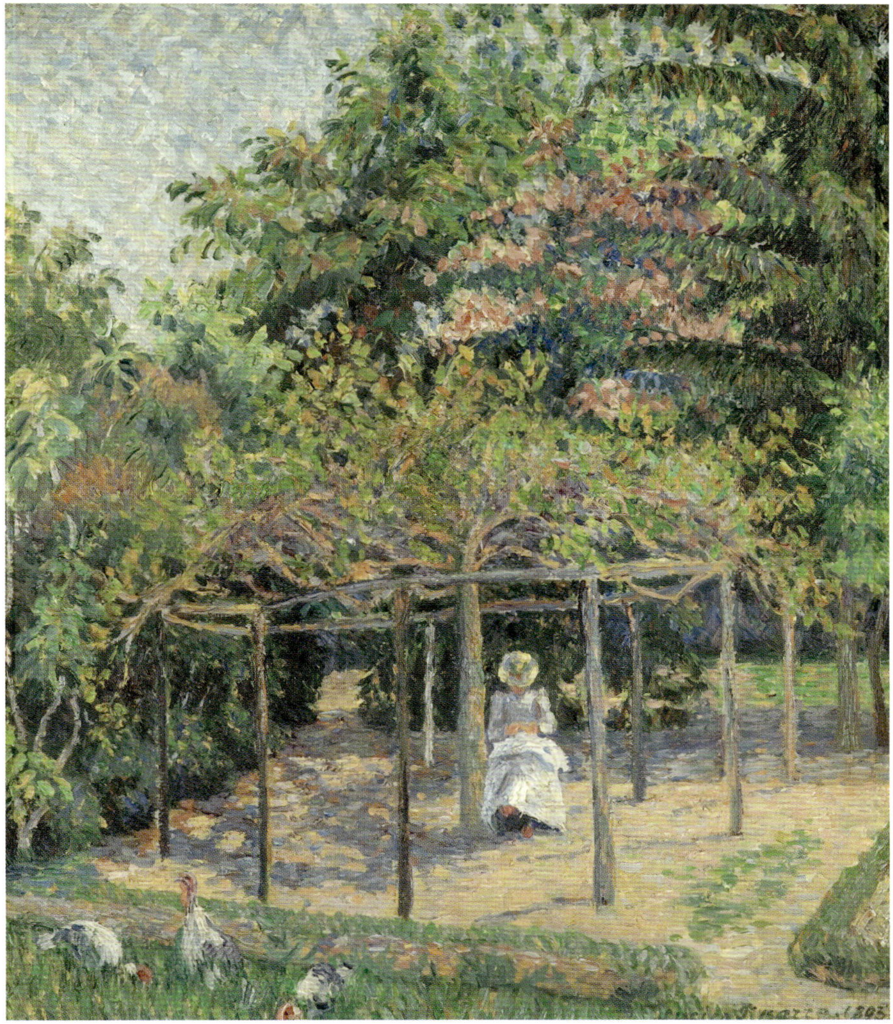

Lucien Pissarro has portrayed his wife Esther sitting in the shade of a tree in the garden of their home. The dappled light is evoked using Neo-Impressionist techniques. Lucien was taught by his father, Camille Pissarro, who exhibited in all eight Impressionist exhibitions. By the 1880s, Camille had become interested in the colour theory of Eugène Chevreul and he supported the inclusion of the proponent of 'scientific' Impressionism, Georges Seurat in the 1886 Impressionist show. The application of the paint in separate dabs shows Lucien's engagement with Seurat's divisionist optical theory: the distinct colours of each brush-stroke are 'mixed in the viewer's eye rather than on the palette' and colour appears to vibrate on the canvas.

Lucien Pissarro moved to England in 1890 and later adopted British nationality, becoming a member of the Camden Town Group along with Walter Sickert and Spencer Gore.

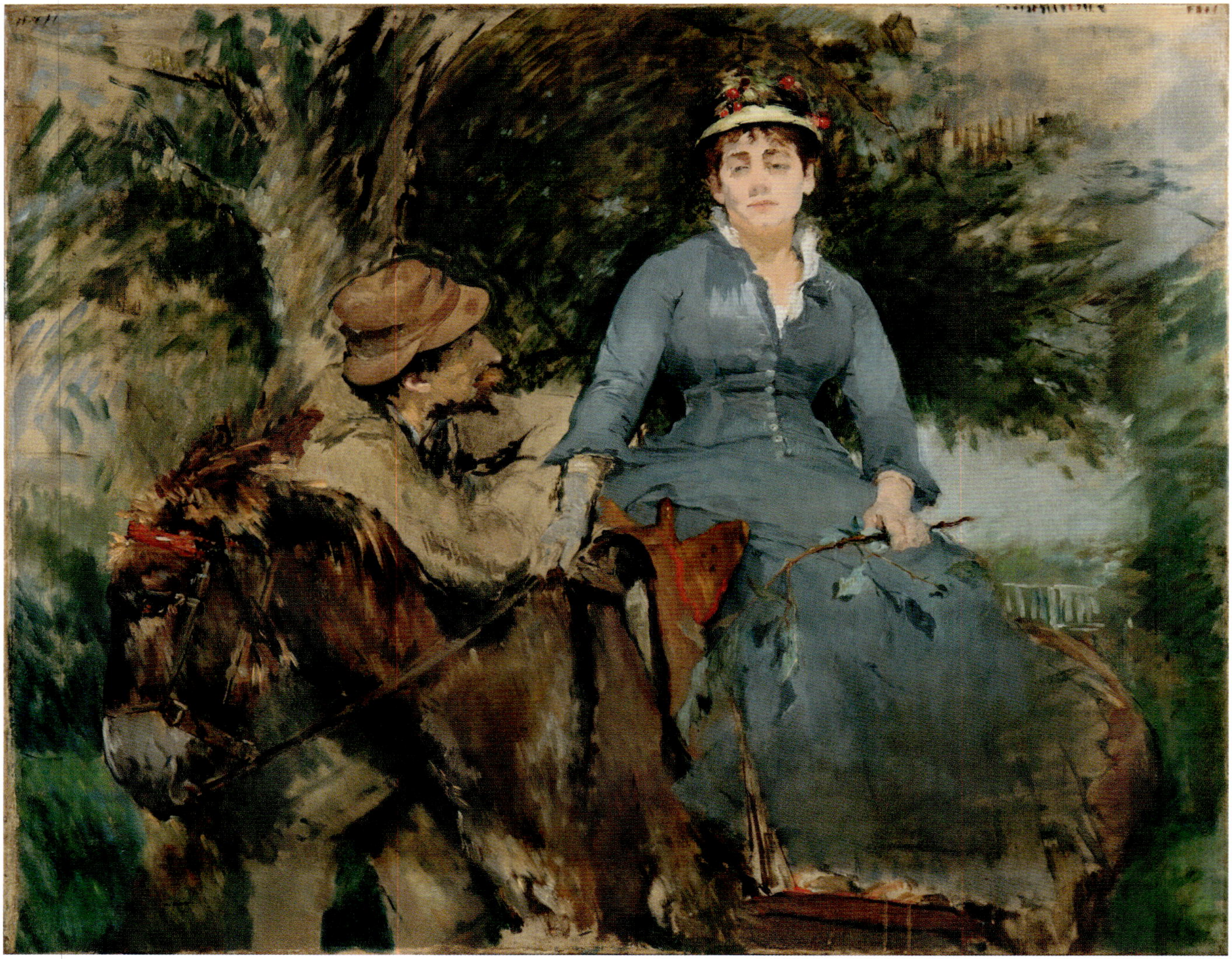

Eva Gonzalès (1849-1883)
The donkey ride
oil on canvas, about 1880
80 x 100 cm
Purchased with the assistance of Alfred Daber, 1966
K2988

Because of her fresh approach and modern subjects, Eva Gonzalès is often associated with the Impressionists, although she never exhibited with them. She was taught by Edouard Manet whose portrait of Gonzalès at work hangs in the National Gallery, London.

The donkey ride is the only painting by Gonzalès in a British collection. The artist's sister Jeanne sits on a donkey, attended by Eva's husband, the engraver Henri Guérard. The pair often modelled for Gonzalès, such as in her *Loge aux Italiens* in 1874. Gonzalès's loose handling of paint shows how this generation of artists took the vigorous Romanticism of Delacroix in a new direction. The rough diagonal hatches of paint suggest the movement of light. The painting was discovered in Gonzalès's studio after her death and would not have been exhibited unfinished. Nevertheless, we can see the radicalism of Cézanne in the energetic mark-making.

Pierre-Auguste Renoir (1841-1919)
The two sisters
pastel on paper, about 1889
79 x 63.5 cm
Accepted by Her Majesty's Government in lieu of tax and presented to Bristol City Art Gallery, 1976
K4349

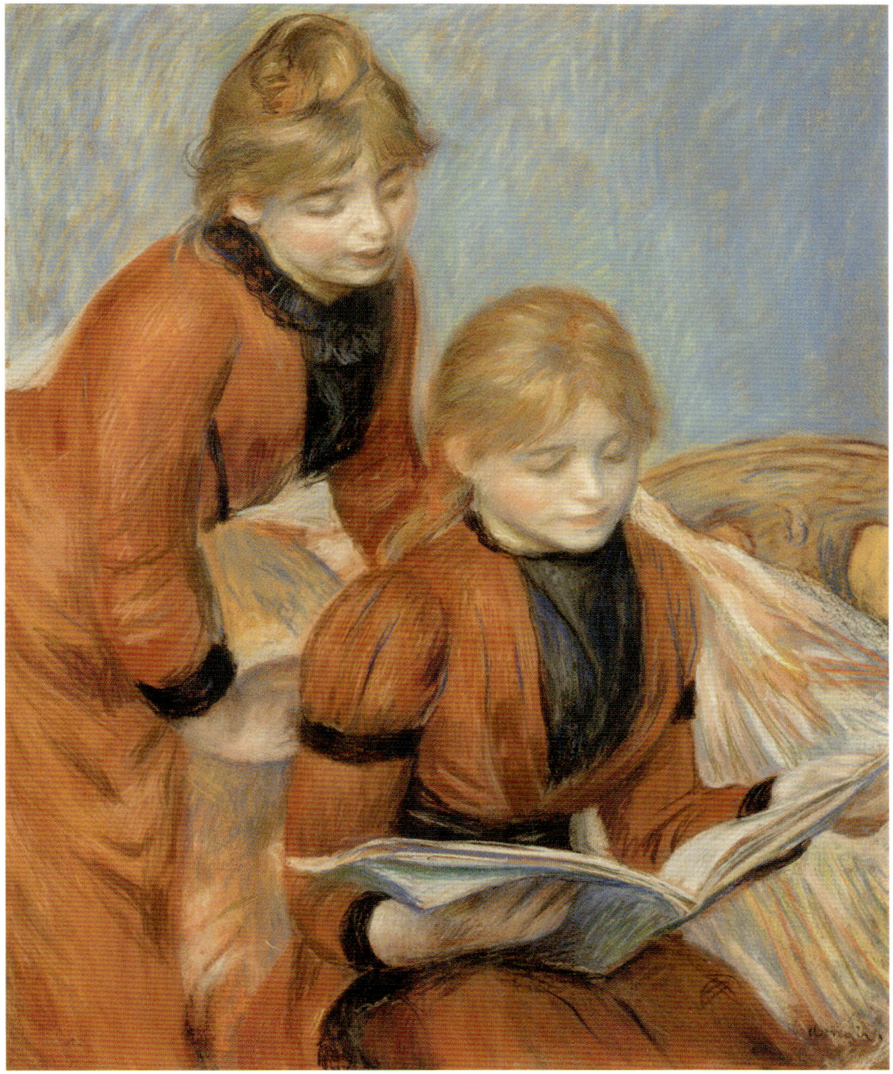

Pierre-Auguste Renoir portrayed these unknown girls several times including an oil painting (*The piano lesson*) now in Nebraska. They are portrayed with a natural and relaxed intimacy.

Compared to the scandal of Manet's nudes or the abstraction of Monet's landscapes, Renoir's art displayed an uncomplicated pleasure in showing attractive people at leisure. He is said to have shocked his studio master Charles Gleyre when he declared that he wouldn't paint if he didn't enjoy it. By 1881, Renoir said he had 'travelled as far as Impressionism could take me'. He returned wholeheartedly to the Rococo artists such as Fragonard and Watteau he had admired when he first befriended Monet in 1862.

Pastel became increasingly popular during the 1880s especially with the Impressionists: the sticks of pure colour were the perfect medium for artists to maximise the effects of colour and light. Pastels are quicker and cheaper to work with than oil paint and large-scale drawings such as this portrait could sell to a wider range of clients. The two young women were swiftly sketched with the light feathery strokes characteristic of Renoir. Note for example his tactile tracing of their soft cheeks, the orange fabric of their dresses and the purple hatches of the cover of the portfolio.

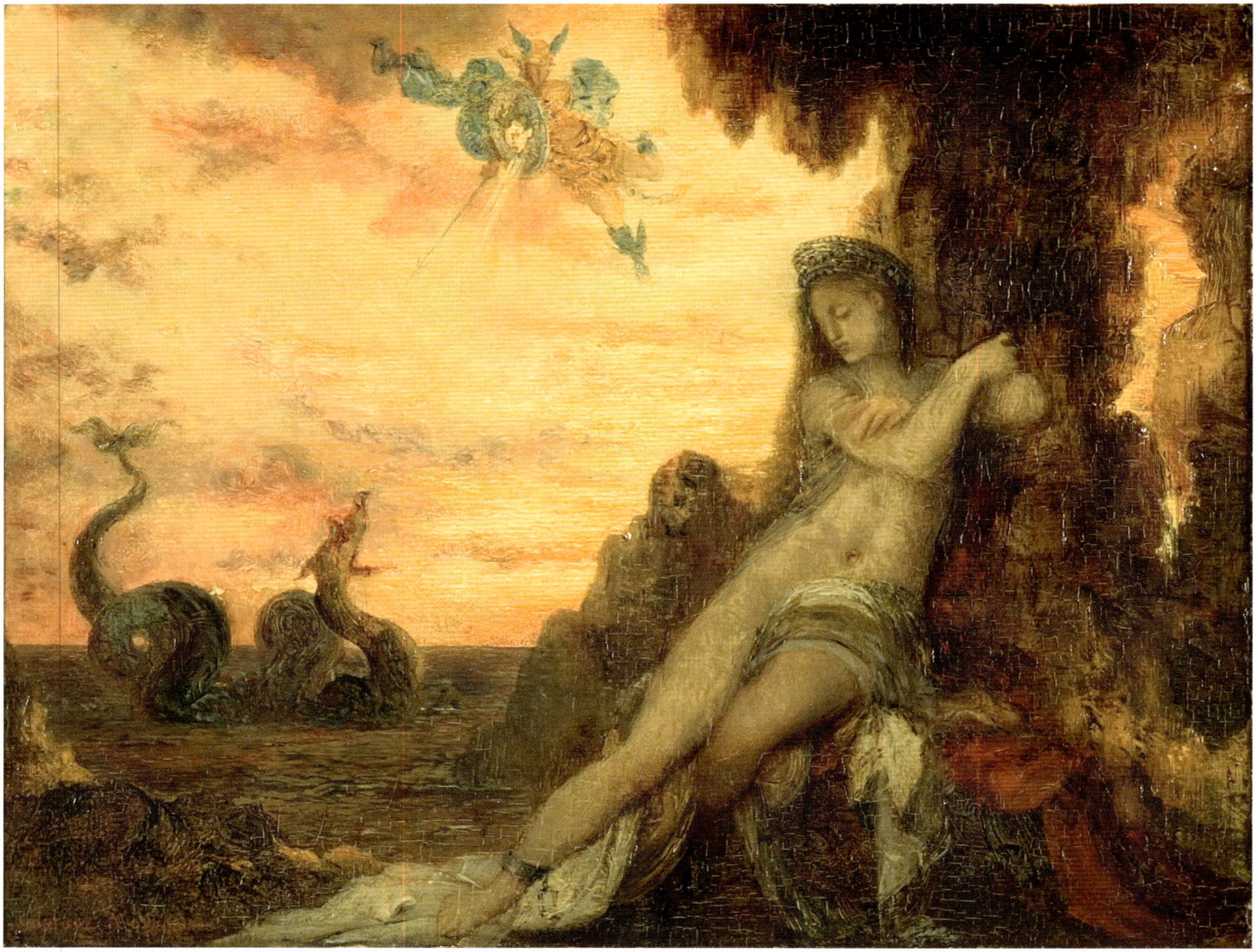

Gustave Moreau (1826-1898)
Perseus and Andromeda
oil on panel, about 1870
20 x 25.4 cm
Purchased, 1965
K2953

In Ovid's 'Metamorphoses', Andromeda, an Ethiopian princess, was chained to cliffs as a sacrifice to the sea monster sent by the vengeful god Poseidon to terrorise the land. The princess's captive body dominates the composition of this jewel-like painting, with her face turned away in desolation. Her liberator is Perseus, a golden figure in the sky who bears a shield with the Gorgon's head which will turn the monster into stone.

Like Odilon Redon, the Symbolist Gustave Moreau rejected the theories of Impressionism, preferring subjects taken from classical mythology or the Bible. He was far more influenced by the Romantic art of the 19th century and in the 1890s became a professor at the *Ecole des Beaux Arts*. Moreau's paintings depicted a decadent world of high drama in a richly coloured palette. In *Against nature* the novelist Joris-Karl Huysmans describes in detail Moreau's painting of Salome, the seducer of King Herod. Moreau left his paintings to the French nation and his pupil Georges Rouault became the first curator of the Gustave Moreau Museum in Paris. In the 20th century the museum was a haunt of the Surrealist André Breton and in Moreau's painted fantasies it is possible to see a clearly-delineated precursor of the Surrealists' tapping into the unconscious.

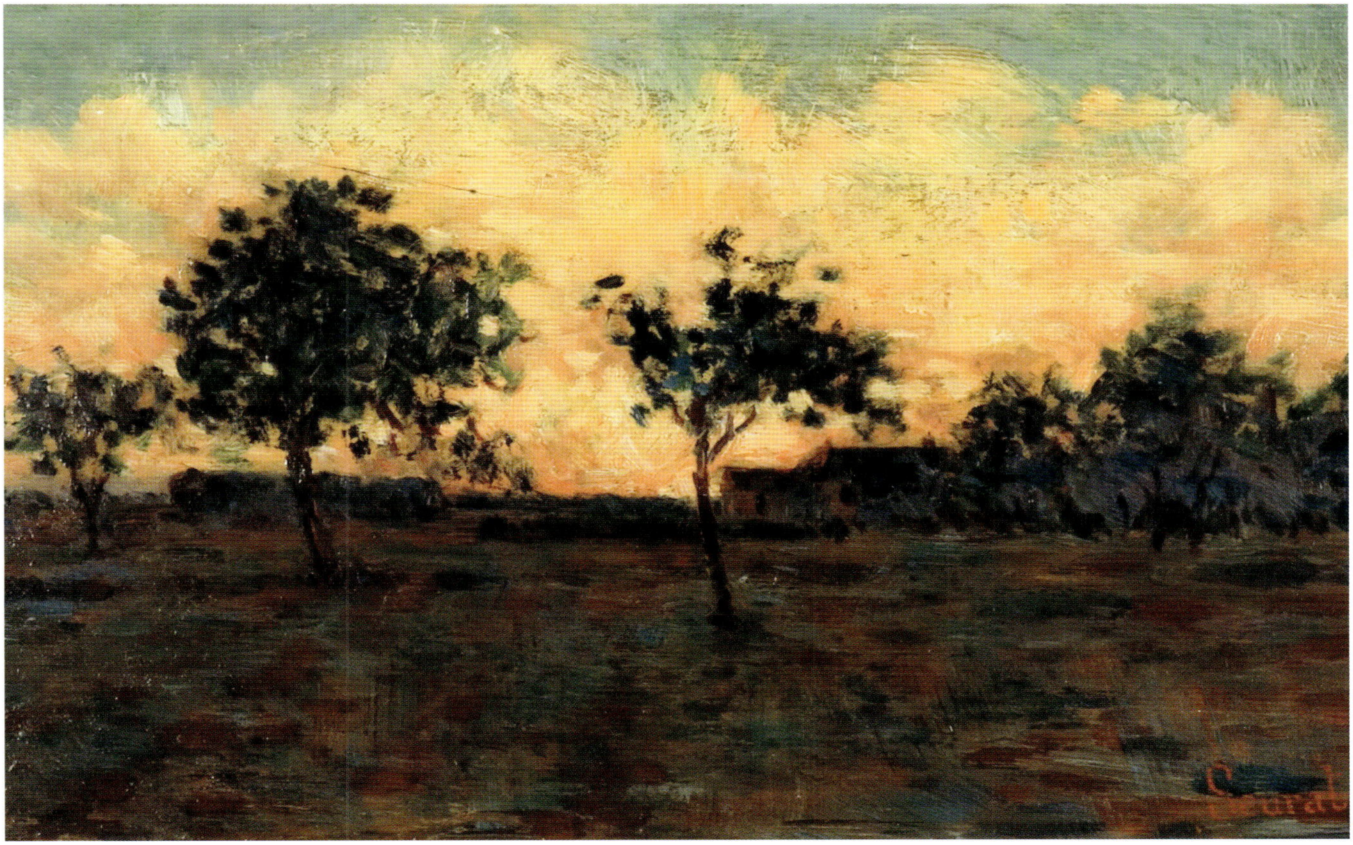

Georges-Pierre Seurat (1859-1891)
Sunset
oil on panel, about 1881
15.2 x 24.8 cm
Purchased with the assistance of the Victoria & Albert Museum Purchase Grant Fund and donations from Bristol citizens, 1963
K2892

Sunset is one of the many '*croquetons*' (little sketches) that Georges Seurat painted on cigar-box lids in the early 1880s, mostly showing landscapes from the region around Paris. The red-brown colour of the wooden lids provided a warm ground that suited Seurat's landscapes.

This tiny sketch predates the Neo-Impressionism that Seurat pioneered with Paul Signac, where the artists utilised the theory of Eugène Chevreul to bring scientific rigour to the optics of Impressionism. They were encouraged to experiment by the 'father figure' of Impressionism, Camille Pissarro. Seurat would go on to minimalise his brushstrokes to minute spots, creating the effect of veils of coloured light sometimes known as 'Pointillism'. It was a precision technique that can appear stilted in the artists that followed Seurat. In *Sunset* the ideas of Impressionism are tested with colours applied in rough strokes that appear more spontaneous than the control of Seurat's later experiments.

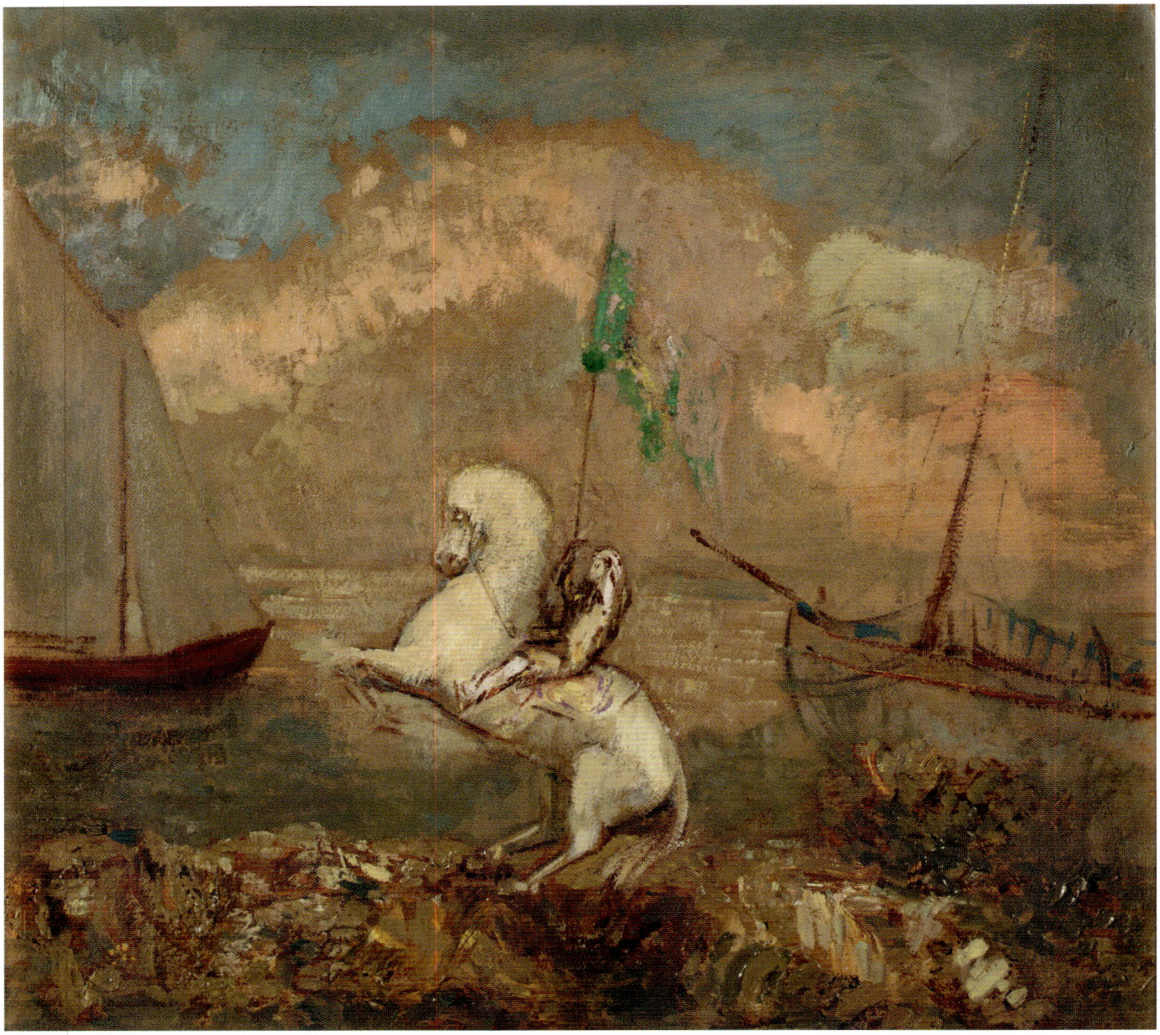

Odilon Redon (1840-1916)
Rider on the beach with two ships
oil on cardboard, 1905-08
61.1 x 64.5 cm
Purchased with the assistance of the Victoria & Albert Museum Purchase Grant Fund, 1964
K2911

This delicately painted scene shows a rearing white horse whose rider is holding a green standard like a mediaeval knight. The imagery is fragmented, with motifs such as the mast and prow of the ship on the right lightly outlined in blue and brown. The figure of the knight is an ambiguous form – is it St George or Don Quixote?

Odilon Redon regarded the Impressionists as slaves of the visual world and their interest in light effects as an extreme form of naturalism. His own Symbolist art rejected external realities instead turning inwards to a realm of dreams populated by mysterious creatures, a realm that the Surrealists would return to in the 20th century. For 50 years Redon worked in monochrome, creating unsettling images in charcoal and lithographs he called *'noirs'* (blacks). In *Against nature*, Joris-Karl Huysmans's Symbolist novel of decadence, the protagonist Des Esseintes collects prints by Redon. It was only in the 1890s that Redon began to work in colour.

For the Symbolist artists suggestion and mood were key. The elusive quality of light pursued by the Impressionists becomes the trace of a half-remembered dream.

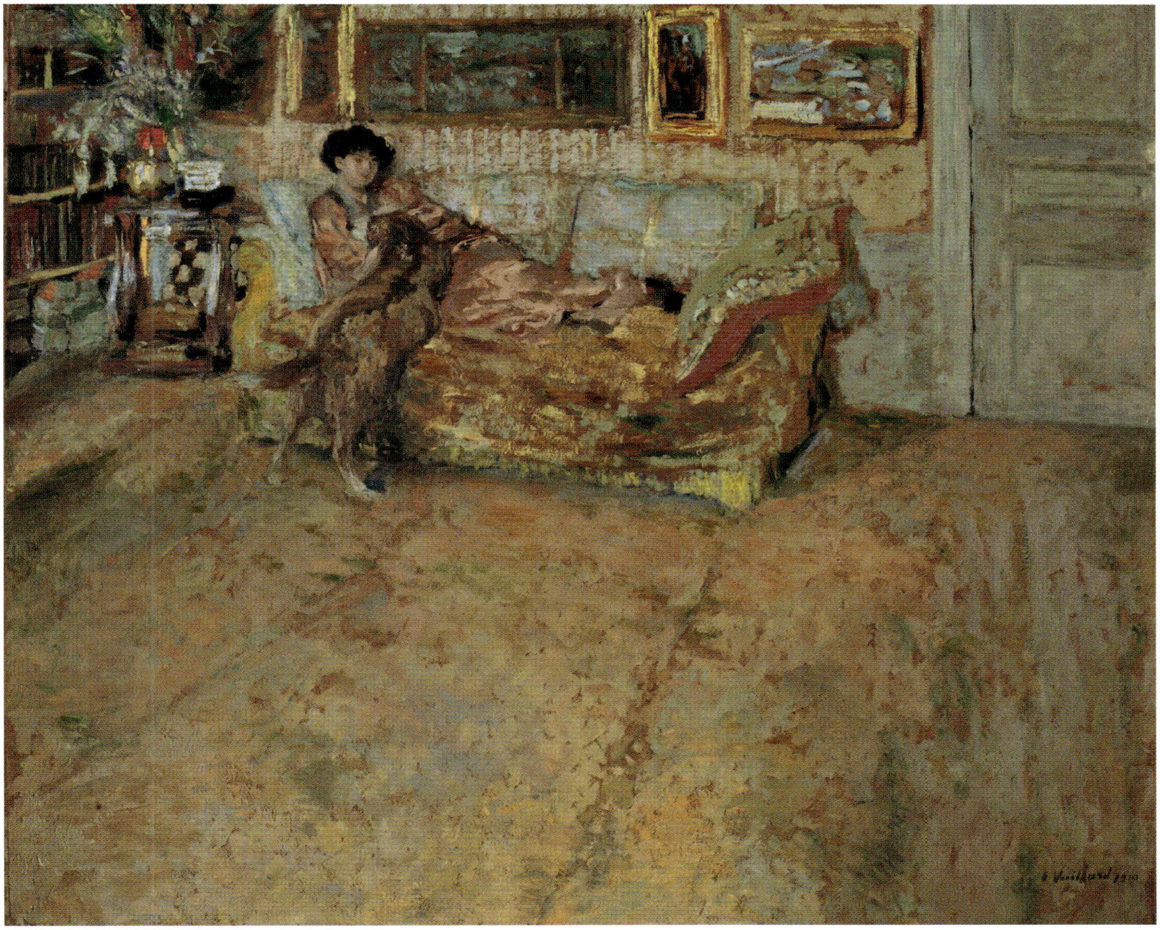

Edouard Vuillard (1868-1940)
Interior with Madame Hessel and her dog
oil on cardboard on panel, 1910
98 x 113 cm
Purchased with the assistance of the Art Fund and the Victoria & Albert Museum Purchase Grant Fund, 1961
K2832

'I've only ever lived with women in the places from which I drew my subjects.'

Edouard Vuillard's portraits of women in interior settings reveal a distinct intimacy and rapport with his subjects. The sense of quiet domestic privacy is close to Vermeer and these scenes are often described as *intimiste*. Vuillard's corset-maker mother Marie was his first female model but he was a *confidant* to many women throughout his life.

Vuillard became close to Lucie and Jos Hessel in 1900 when Jos's company, Bernheim-Jeune, began to sell his work in its gallery. The three dined and holidayed together and Vuillard painted Lucie frequently in her home – having manicures, in her dressing-room, or in animated conversation with the artist, wearing her fashionable kimonos and tea-dresses, attire for entertaining in the home. Here she is a hazy presence, affectionately patting her dog. A row of paintings behind her reveals the couple's taste for contemporary art – what looks like a Roussel landscape, perhaps a Moreau, and possibly even a seascape by Vuillard himself on the end.

Daringly Vuillard devotes much of his composition to the play of light on the floor, with areas left untouched by paint. The image has the feel of a cropped photograph, or a scene glimpsed through a window. Lucie seems blissfully unaware of being captured in this private moment.

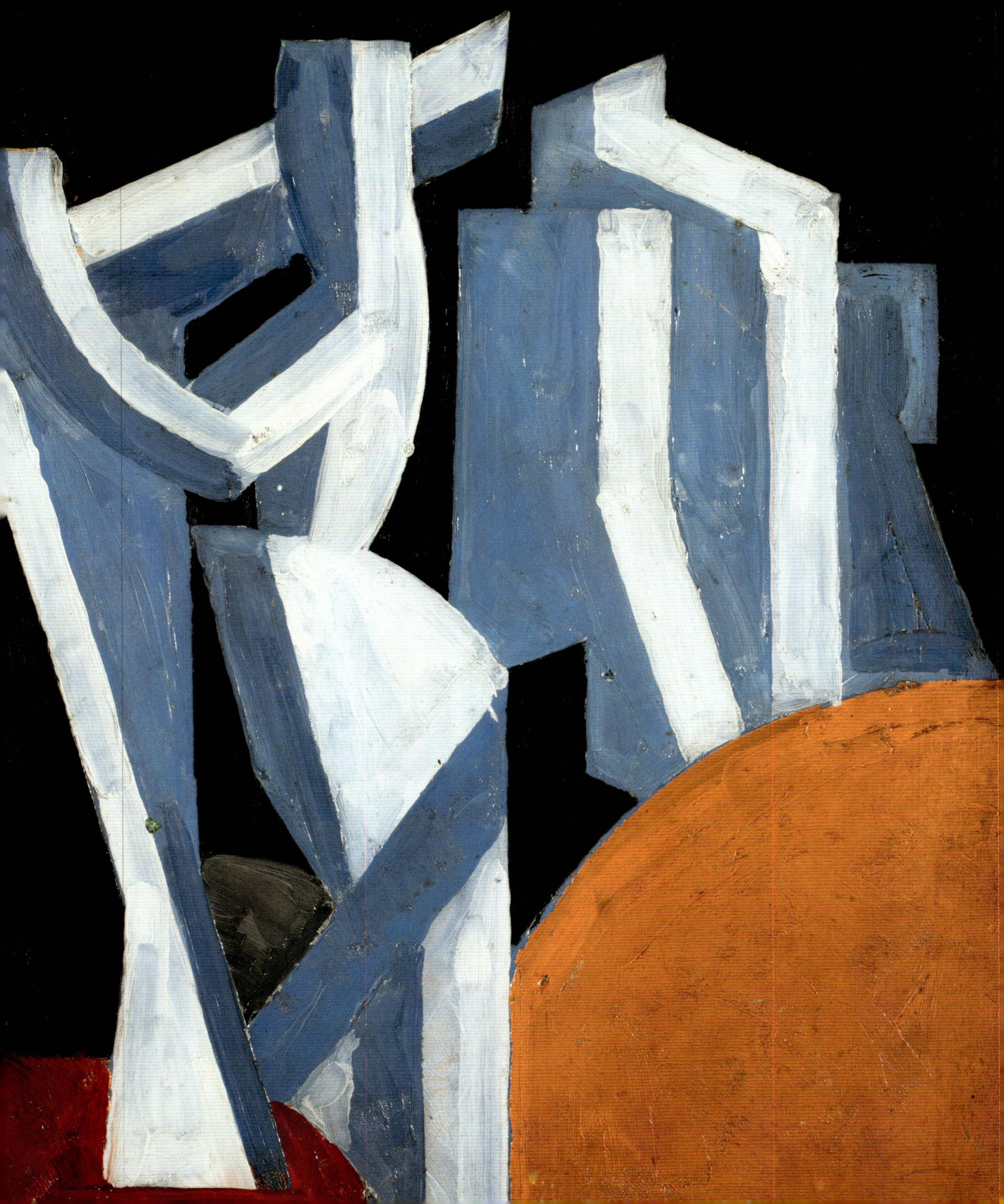

Modern art in Britain

The art revolution that began in 19th-century Europe had spread to Britain by the turn of the 20th century. David Bomberg was expelled from the Slade School of Art for his experiments paring down the human figure to basic shapes like parts in a machine. Bomberg and Christopher Nevinson were dazzled by the exhibition of Italian Futurism in the Sackville Gallery in 1912, particularly the way the Italian artists sliced up their subjects using a radical new visual language designed to convey speed.

Where Cubism illustrated multiple perspectives side-by-side, Futurism seemed to shake up this cracked imagery to release the disparate energies of the new century. Bomberg followed the sculptor Jacob Epstein to Paris where he met Picasso. The two wars bisected the first half of the 20th century. On the eve of World War I Nevinson found in Futurism a style powerfully suited to capturing the reality of mechanised warfare.

The French artist Henri Gaudier-Brzeska spent time in Cardiff and Bristol as a business student before becoming an artist. Along with peers from Picasso to Epstein, he found inspiration in the direct forms of African and Oceanic sculpture. Like the Futurists, Gaudier-Brzeska sought to convey movement in his work. *The wrestler* (1912) conveys both solidity and rhythm as the corpulent figure appears to weigh up his rival. Gaudier-Brzeska was killed in action in the war, aged only 24.

Between the wars, the English artist Eric Ravilious used the experimental techniques of European modernism to depict a quintessentially English domesticity. Looking back to mediaeval art, Ravilious worked with tempera, a method predating oil paint which combines pigment with a binder such as egg. The weightless tennis players of the decorative panels he made for Geoffrey Fry seem to float like angels in a 13th century fresco.

During World War II, Barbara Hepworth and her husband Ben Nicholson established a circle of artists at St Ives and invited their close friend, the Russian artist Naum Gabo, to join them. An influential artists' colony was formed, with Nicholson teaching members of the younger generation, such as Peter Lanyon. The crisis of the war affected artists in diverse ways: Hepworth and Nicholson relocated from London to the coast; Lanyon signed up and served as an engineer; and the German artist Karl Weschke came to Britain as a prisoner of war.

Not surprisingly, the war affected the art made in its aftermath. Mid-century abstraction has been seen as a refusal of artists to verbalise what they had seen in the war. At the same time a generation of artists in America were taking the abstract experiments of Europe to a dramatic new level of gestural mark-making. Peter Lanyon's painterly gestures share common ground with the Abstract Expressionism of his American peers but were designed to evoke his native Cornish coast. Lanyon and his St Ives circle felt strongly that they belonged to a specifically European tradition of art.

The aftermath of World War II saw major social initiatives in Britain, and through them a sense of hope for the future. Hepworth made her Hospital Drawings at the London Clinic and the Princess Elizabeth Hospital in Exeter in 1947-49 when the National Health Service was being established. A self-conscious connection is made in the drawings between the skill of the sculptor and the surgeon. Hepworth seems to be displaying a show of solidarity with this groundbreaking post-war scheme.

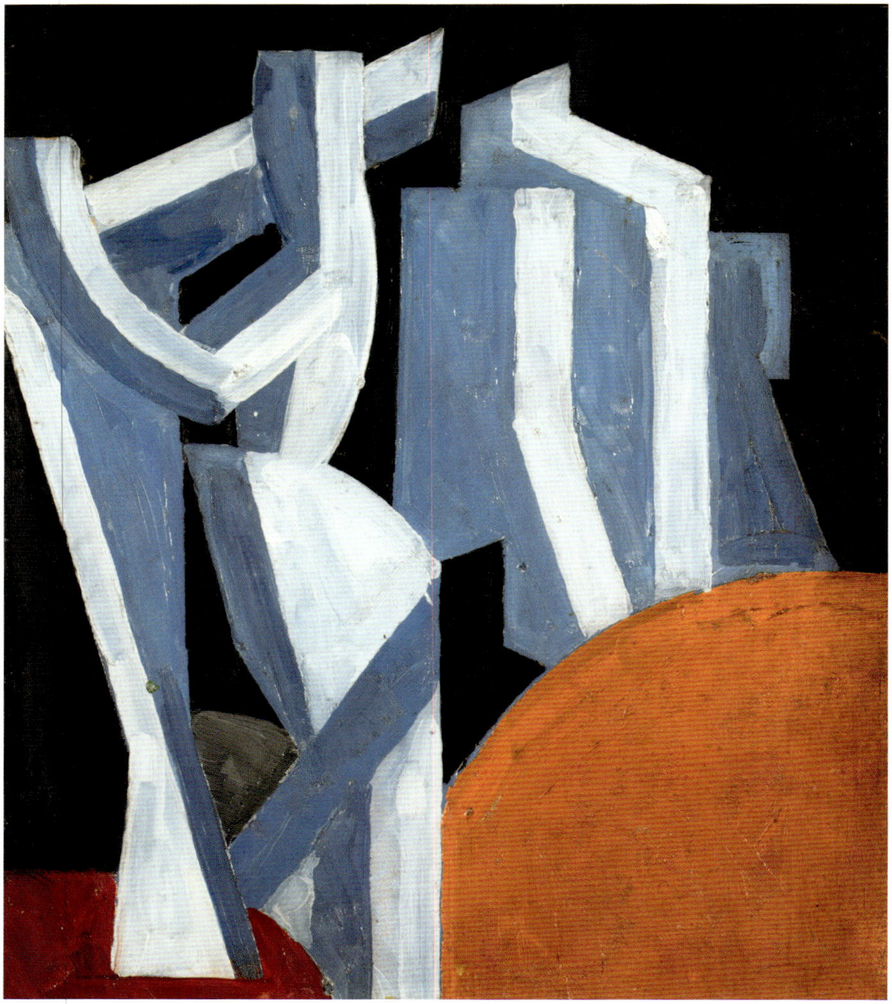

David Bomberg (1890-1957)
Figure composition
oil on panel, 1913
41 x 33 cm
Purchased, 1969
K3054

'I want to translate the life of a great city, its motion, its machinery, into an art that shall not be photographic, but expressive.'

Having been encouraged to study art by Walter Sickert, David Bomberg attended the Slade with Christopher Nevinson and Mark Gertler where he was taught by the English Impressionists Henry Tonks and Philip Wilson Steer. The 1910 *Manet and the Post-Impressionists* exhibition at the Grafton Galleries was a major inspiration. However Bomberg's experiments with form, especially Cubism, led to his expulsion from the Slade in 1913. He travelled with the sculptor Jacob Epstein to Paris, where he met Picasso. As with the Italian Futurists, machines symbolised the essence of modernity for Bomberg. *Figure composition,* made the year he was expelled from the Slade, reduces human figures to dynamic angular forms in blue and white planes against the orange wedge in the foreground.

Although Bomberg exhibited with the Vorticists, he was never a part of the English Cubist group. It has been suggested that his experience of the destructive power of machines during World War I (his brother was killed in the war) destroyed Bomberg's faith in the machine age. In the 1950s, he taught Frank Auerbach and Leon Kossoff at Borough Polytechnic in London where he promoted a more expressionist form of abstraction.

Christopher Richard Wynne Nevinson
(1889-1946)
Dog tired
oil on canvas, 1916
76.2 x 64.8 cm
Purchased, 1954
K2394

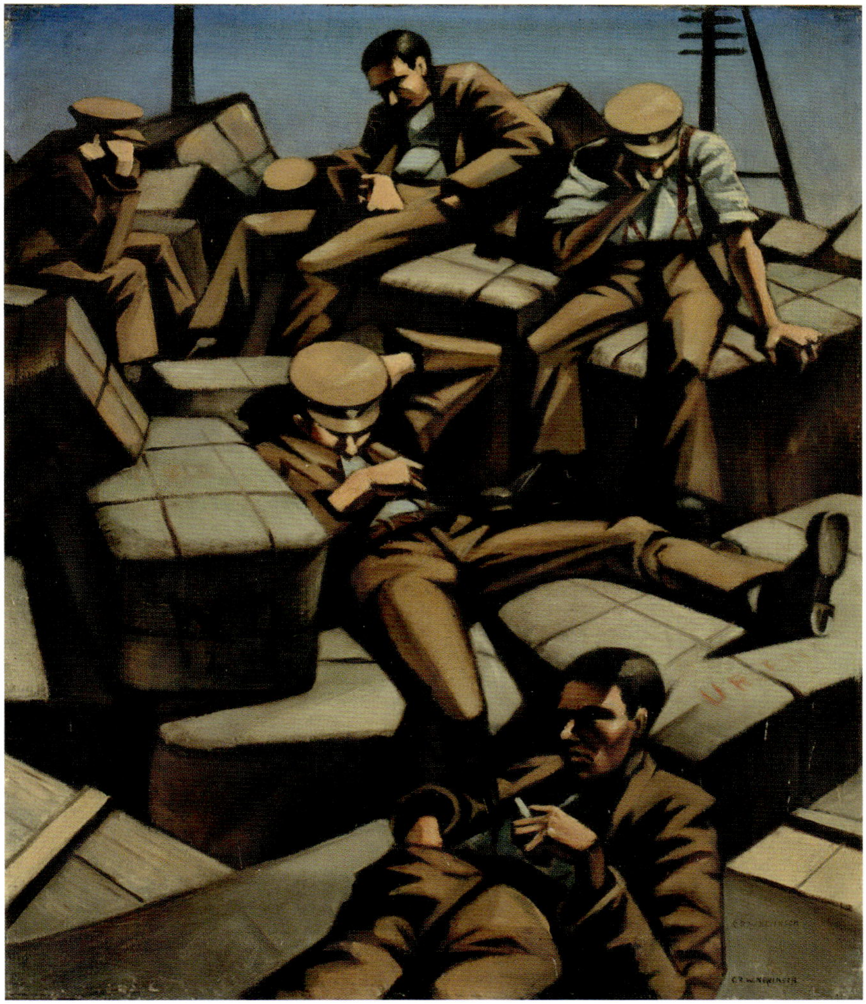

The Futurist exhibition at the Sackville Gallery in London 1912 was a key moment in Christopher Nevinson's career. The show's unprecedented celebration of the dynamism of the machine age prompted Nevinson to paint London's Tube and the Strand in the same angular kinetic style. While studying in Paris, Nevinson met Filippo Tommaso Marinetti and joined the Futurists, after which he published a satire on the English art scene *A vital English art*.

Nevinson was the son of the war correspondent Henry Nevinson and the women's suffrage campaigner Margaret Nevinson. He trained at the Slade between 1909-12 with David Bomberg, Stanley Spencer, Paul Nash and Leonora Carrington. His friendship with the Futurists caused him to fall out with another British artist, Wyndham Lewis, who founded the Vorticists in response to Futurism.

At the outbreak of World War I Nevinson went to France to volunteer with the Red Cross. With his father and other volunteers he treated the wounded French soldiers who had returned from the front. When he was invalided home Nevinson declared that he would use Futurism to depict the true horror of war. *Dog tired* uses the zigzagging angles of Futurism to convey the dragging fatigue of the sleeping soldiers, creating a pyramid of figures, who are seen catching a rare moment of rest. Nevinson was appointed an Official War Artist in 1917.

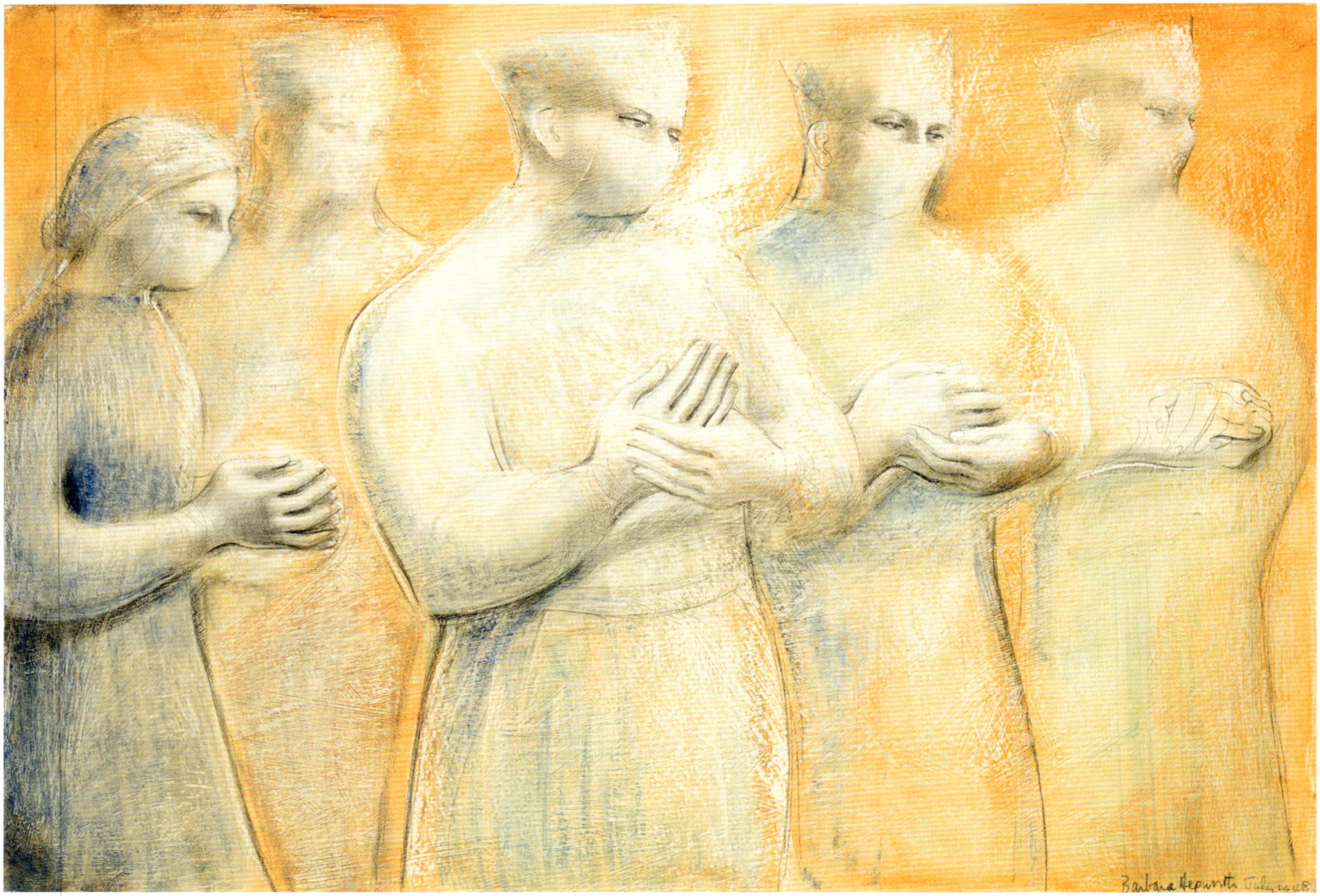

Dame Barbara Hepworth (1903-1975)
The hands
oil and pencil on panel, 1948
38 x 51.4 cm
Presented by Friends of Bristol Art Gallery, 1949
K1899

Barbara Hepworth made her 'Hospital Drawings' after befriending the surgeon Norman Capener who had operated on her daughter Sarah. Hepworth was a pioneer of abstract art in Britain and helped to reinvent stone-carving for the 20th century. She was co-founder, with Paul Nash and her husband Ben Nicholson, of the Unit One group which sought to promote Surrealism and abstraction in Britain. The Hospital Drawings were a return to the figurative human form, and to drawing.

Hepworth hesitated when Capener first invited her to draw in the operating theatre, but she quickly became inspired by the joint efforts of the surgeons and produced around 100 drawings using sterilised sketch books.

'[A] special grace of mind and body induced a spontaneous space composition, an articulated and animated kind of abstract sculpture very close to what I have been seeking in my own work...In a fearful emergency everybody goes into the right sort of place and the most extraordinary shapes are made.'

Hepworth shows the surgeons standing in a frieze-like composition that is reminiscent of the carved reliefs she saw in Italy as a student. The focus is on the ritual of scrubbing-up. Paint is scratched through to the white gesso ground, a technique used to inscribe sculpture known as *sgraffito*. The close connection Hepworth felt between her art as a sculptor and the skilled hands of the surgeon is expressed in *The hands* with an almost religious intensity.

Henri Gaudier-Brzeska (1891-1915)
The wrestler
bronze, 1912-13, cast, 1945
63.5 x 27 x 45 cm
Purchased, with the assistance of the Victoria & Albert Museum Purchase Grant Fund, the Friends of Bristol Art Gallery and the Wills Fund, 1984
K5164

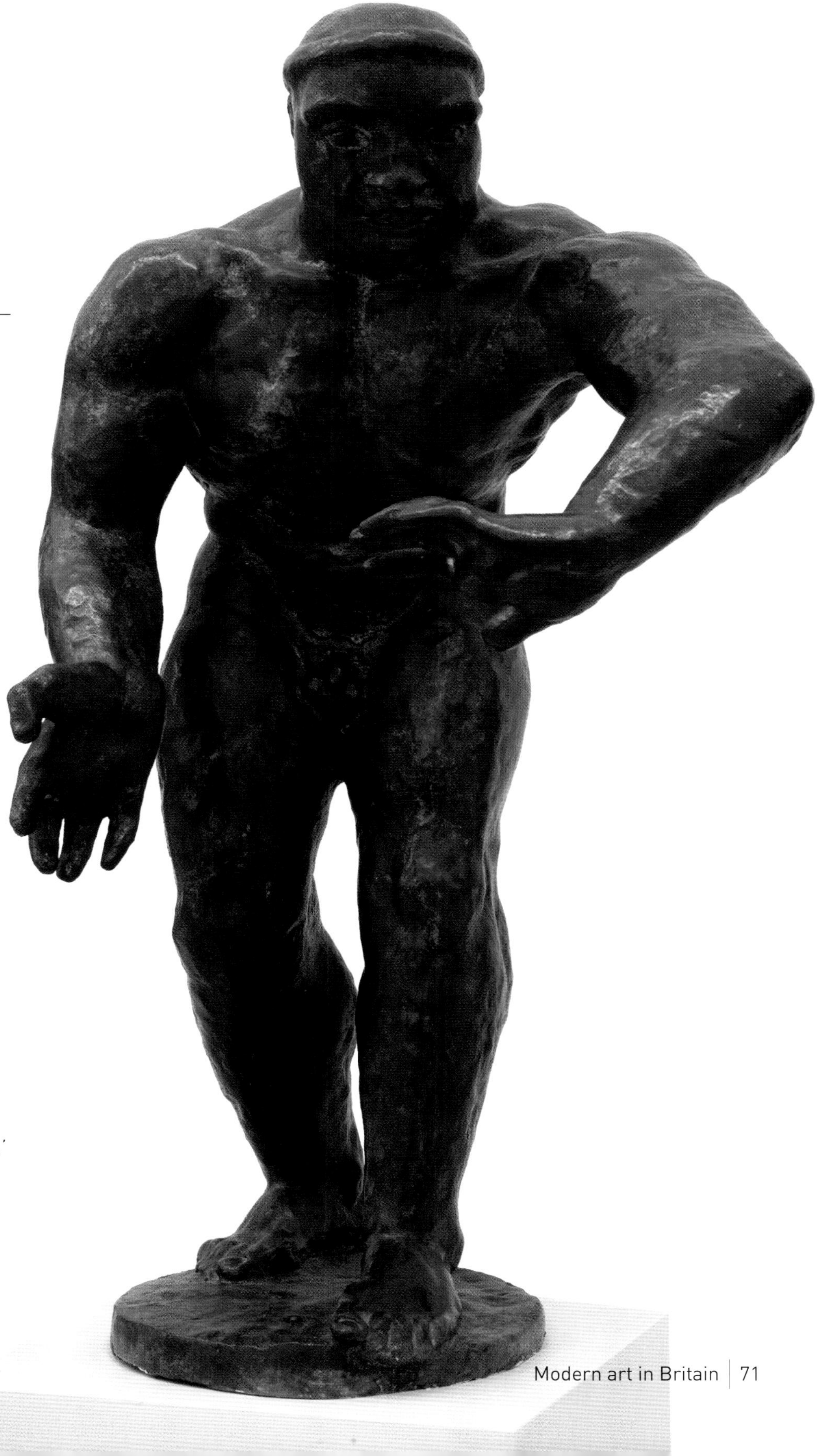

Henri Gaudier-Brzeska was born in France and settled in London in 1910. In just four years he created a vital body of work including drawing, painting and especially sculpture. In London he became close to the Imagist poet Ezra Pound and the Vorticist Wyndham Lewis, as well as contributing to the Vorticist journal BLAST. Initially a follower of Rodin, Gaudier-Brzeska was inspired by African and Pacific sculpture at the British Museum and also studied minute Japanese *netsuke* figures. Through Pound he became interested in ideograms, a method of concentrating a subject into the sparest of forms, the results of which can be seen in the direct expression of his sculpture.

Gaudier-Brzeska shared the Modernists' desire to convey rhythm in his work. He became fascinated by wrestling and visited the London Wrestling Club to make sketches:

'Last night I went to see the wrestlers - God! I have seldom seen anything so lovely - two athletic types, large shoulders, taut, big necks like bulls, small in the build with firm thighs and slender ankles, feet sensitive as hands.'

The dynamism of the sport is evident in the rhythmic gesture of the monumental figure as he contemplates his opponent.

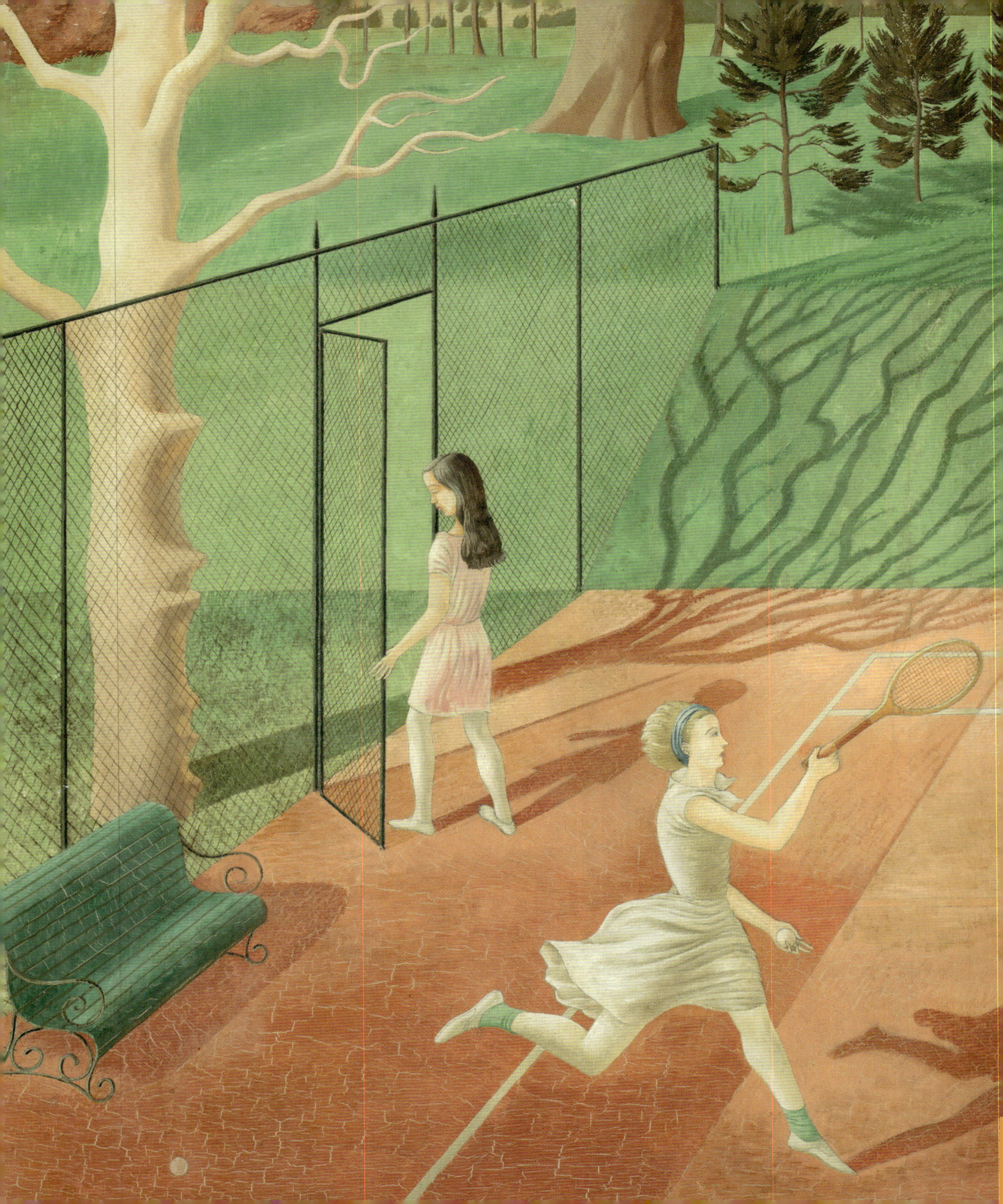

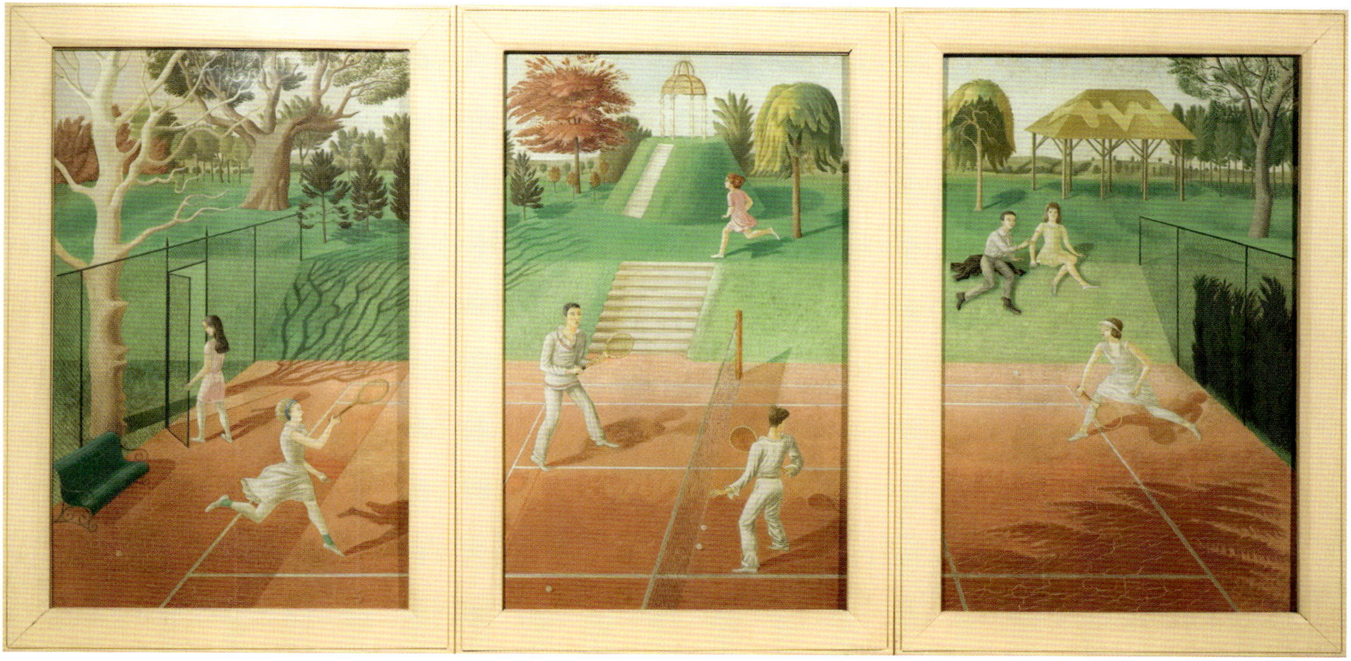

Eric Ravilious (1903-1942)
Tennis
tempera on three plywood panels, 1930
82.5 x 49.5, 82.5 x 58.5 and 82.5 x 49 cm
Presented by Sir Geoffrey and the Honourable Lady Fry, 1945
K1562-64

Along with his close friend Edward Bawden, Eric Ravilious studied under Paul Nash at the Royal College of Art. The older artist imbued a love of the English landscape in his pupils. Ravilious developed a quintessentially English take on Modernism with his gentle, naïve watercolour views of Sussex, his wood engravings and his designs for Wedgwood. 'I like definite shapes,' he once wrote, and his vision harked back to an ancient England with chalk figures carved in the landscape.

Ravilious visited Italy in 1925, travelling to Florence, Siena and Tuscany. On his return he taught at Eastbourne School of Art and the tennis court in this triptych is based on the Manor Gardens at Eastbourne. *Tennis* was commissioned to decorate the door of Sir Geoffrey Fry's Music Room in Portman Square, London. The action of the game runs across the three panels in a play on form and image. Ravilious rarely used oil and painted the panels in tempera in tribute to the frescoes he had seen in Italy. The delicate colours, flattened forms and marionette-like figures are reminiscent of the the figures of early Renaissance painting, although the spiky branches and foliage of the trees hint at the mysterious or surreal.

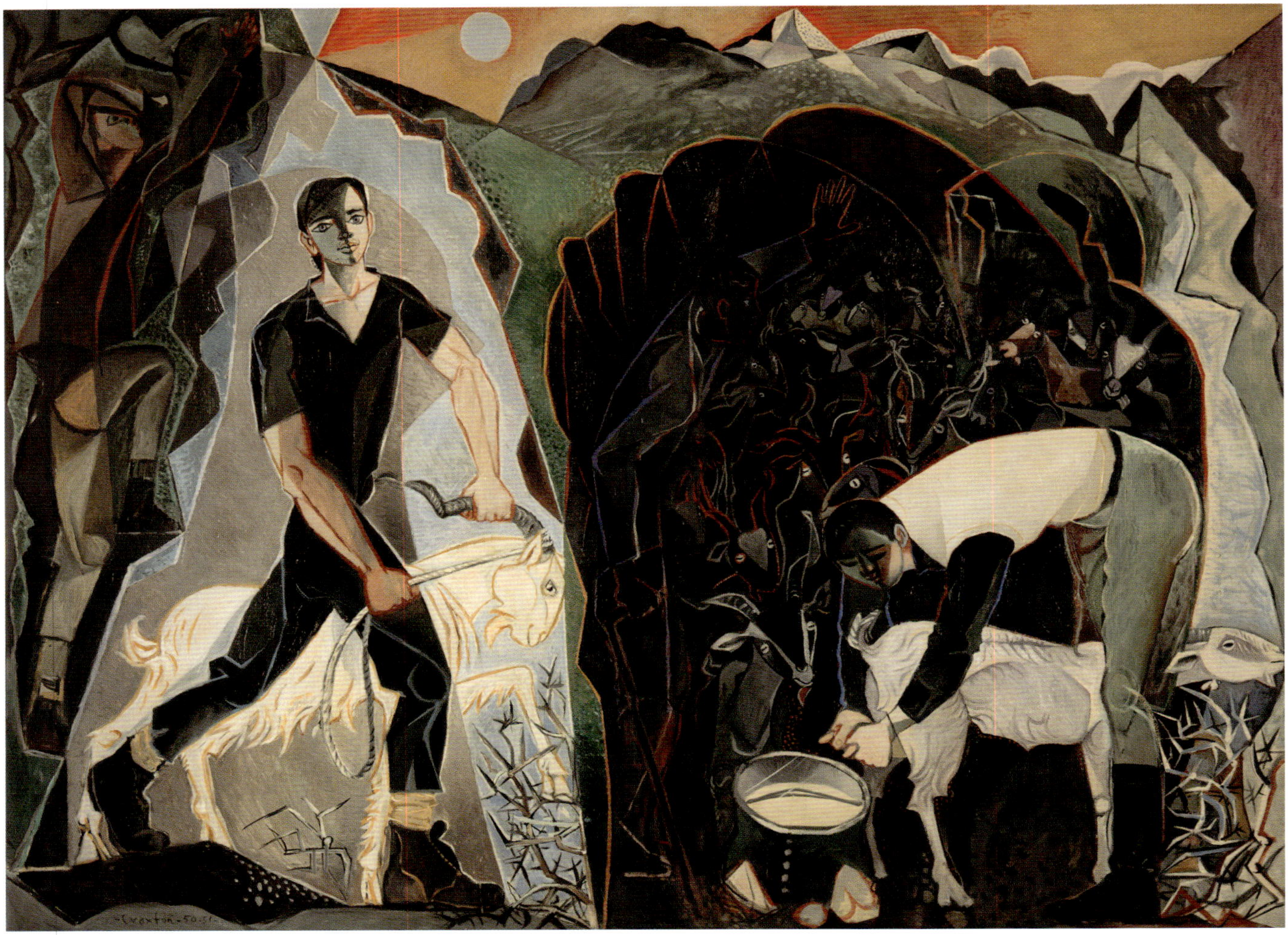

John Craxton (1922-2009)
Four figures in a mountain landscape
oil on canvas, 1950-51
160 x 213.3 cm
Purchased with the assistance of the Friends of Bristol Art Gallery, 1952
K2234

As a teenager John Craxton had seen *Guernica* when it was first painted by Picasso shortly after the German bombing of the Basque village in 1937. Not surprisingly he was transfixed by the power of Picasso's formal invention. Craxton had wanted to be an artist from early childhood and travelled to Paris for life drawing classes when still under the required age to paint from the nude in London. His early influences were William Blake and Samuel Palmer, visible in his pastoral drawings of poets in wooded landscapes published in Cyril Connolly's *Horizon* magazine.

During the war Craxton shared a studio in London with Lucian Freud ('artists of shame and compromise' they called themselves). In 1946 the pair discovered Greece, where goatherds and sailors soon replaced the poets of Craxton's earlier pastoral scenes.

By the 1940s Craxton had developed a kaleidoscopic visual language inspired by Cubism. Figures and landscape alike are rendered with strong, yet decorative lines and divided into coloured facets that give the imagery the chiselled appearance of a diamonds. Here the striding goatherd drags the stubborn animal by its horns to the cave where the other goats are herded for milking in the geometric mountain landscape.

Peter Lanyon (1918-1964)
High Moor
oil on canvas, 1962
182.9 x 177.8 cm
Purchased by the Friends of Bristol Art Gallery with the Dyer Bequest Fund, 1978
K4766

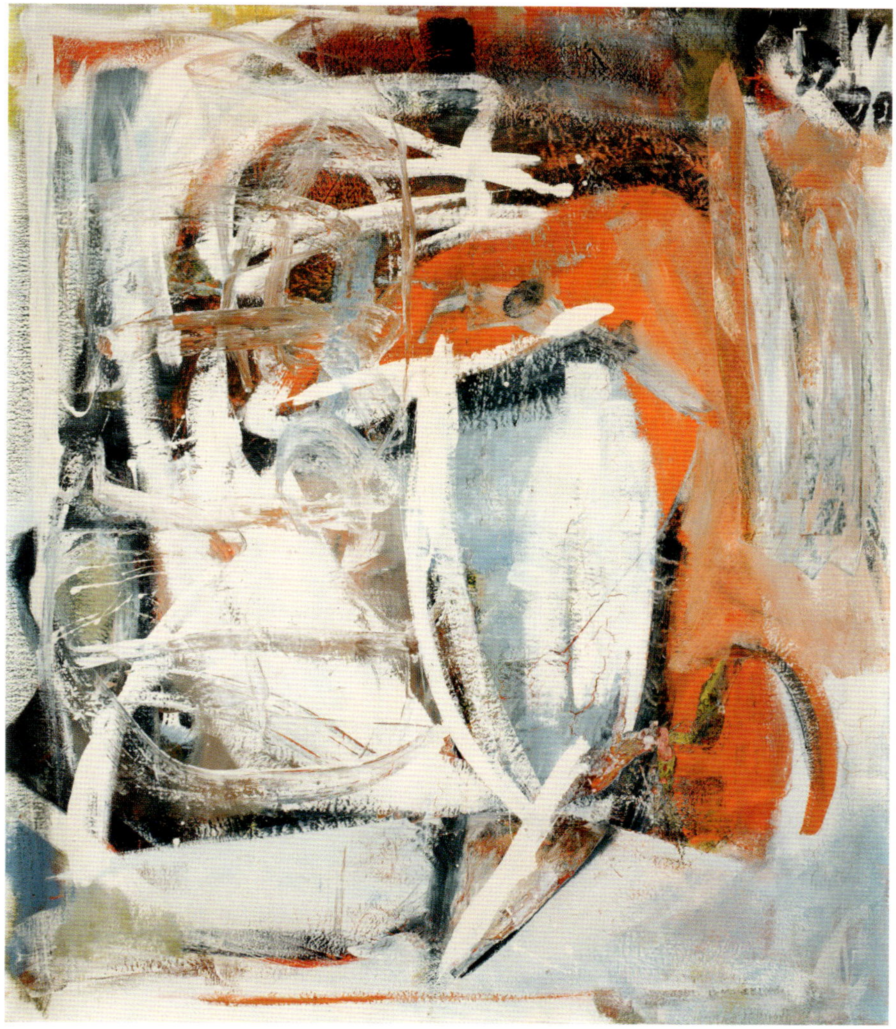

'I like to paint places where solids and fluid come together such as the meeting of sea and cliff, wind and rock, of human body and water.'

Peter Lanyon had always walked and cycled in his native Cornwall and in 1959 he took up gliding to 'get a more complete knowledge of the landscape'. Lanyon was taught by Ben Nicholson and Naum Gabo in St Ives and carried a reproduction of Gabo's Perspex sculpture *Spiral theme* with him during the war when he served as an aircraft mechanic in Egypt, Palestine and Italy. The effect of active service can be seen in the violence of paintings such as his *Crucifixion for St Just*. Lanyon compressed heavy layers of paint which he then attacked, creating a weathered surface texture that was redolent of the scars left on the Cornish landscape by the tin-mining.

Lanyon was an admirer of Asger Jorn and Karel Appel who founded the Danish, Belgian and Dutch collective CoBrA (named after the first letters of their capital cities, Copenhagen, Brussels, Amsterdam). In the 1950s Lanyon met and befriended the Abstract Expressionists Mark Rothko and Franz Kline. He showed work in New York from 1951, including a solo show at the Catherine Viviano Gallery in 1957. The densely-packed forms of the early 1950s gave way to the expansive gestures of *High Moor*, where the orange L-form seems to anchor the frenetic thermal circling in white. Although Lanyon admired the Abstract Expressionists he maintained that he always set out with a clear image in mind and a definite sense of place. His aim was to situate viewers within the environment he painted.

Challenging art: contemporary art

The pace of change seemed to accelerate in the 20th century as two World Wars and the financial crash of the 1920s triggered major political and social shifts which transformed the lives of millions of people in the West. Women secured the vote and gained entry to the workplace and education. Access to art education was also widened. In Britain, the post-war settlement, which included the creation of the National Health Service and the welfare state, fostered a belief in the ennobling and democratising power of culture. Organisations such as the Committee for the Encouragement of Music and the Arts (CEMA), the forerunner to the Arts Council, were established to encourage access to and participation in the arts.

Where the Enlightenment collectors and paternalist industrialists of the 18th and 19th centuries funded the construction of museums and art galleries, in the 20th century the state undertook responsibility for providing the cultural infrastructure as part of the social contract. The post-war broadening of the demographic of artists and audiences led to changing attitudes and a questioning of traditional forms of authority and the certainties of the past. A generation came of age which began to challenge the legitimacy of art itself.

This new generation had different frames of references. Pop artists reacted to the influence of mass culture – from advertising and television to rock and roll. Peter Blake took inspiration from naïve artisan folk art as well as Elvis and the Beatles. Bristol Museum & Art Gallery hosted Blake's first solo retrospective in 1969. With David Inshaw and others, Blake established the Brotherhood of Ruralists, who combined a Pre-Raphaelite attention to detail with an interest in dreams and a countercultural delight in the childlike.

Blake's contemporary, Howard Hodgkin, fused the personal and the abstract in his intimate portrayals of emotional situations, such as his recreation of an afternoon with friends, Robyn Denny and Katherine Reid.

The questioning of art by Conceptual artists was reflected in a new approach to the traditional British genre of landscape. The Bristol artist Richard Long situated his art beyond the space of the gallery, preferring to work directly with the landscape in an ephemeral way – arranging stones, branches, even blades of grass – that contrasted with the monumental memorial sculpture dominating civic centres up and down the country. The pastoralism of the 19th century has translated in the 20th and 21st centuries into a corresponding concern with the environment.

From its *avant garde* origins at the turn of the 20th century, artists' film has become an established way of working. Since the 1960s artists have used video to document performances, and also to animate or create narratives that question the forms of mainstream film and television. In *Lydda Airport* (2009) Emily Jacir uses animation to splice together archive imagery in a re-imagining of Palestine in the 1930s.

In our globalised and culturally homogenous world, a number of contemporary artists have returned to tradition as a way of invigorating particular cultures. Increasingly, art comments on its own conditions, as in the campaigner and dissident Chinese artist Ai Weiwei's inversion of Minimalism, *A ton of tea*. The fragrance of the massive block permeates the gallery and its wavy edges will gradually shift over time. The use of tea is a deceptively simple device that overturns Minimalism's rejection of content to make reference to a staple of Chinese trade.

The South Korean artist Do Ho Suh creates fabric installations that replicate homes he has lived in around the world, mirroring the transience and rootlessness of contemporary life. Based on the corridor of his New York brownstone crash pad, *New York City apartment/Bristol* shares the proportions and architectural details of the 1905 Bristol Art Gallery building. The flimsy architecture forms a ghostly link between histories and geographies, time and space, echoing the form and function of the museum. For centuries art has held up a mirror to the way we live, continually changing its form in the process. The art collection at Bristol Museum & Art Gallery offers an insight into this history and will continue to follow as artists pursue new and undiscovered paths.

Banksy (born 1974)
Paint pot angel
cast resin, with commercial paint pot and paint, on a wooden base, 2009
158.1 x 90.5 x 41.5 cm
Gift of the artist, 2009
K6300

The incognito artist Banksy burst onto the scene with his *Mild mild west* street painting of a teddy bear aiming a Molotov cocktail at a line of police officers. Spray-painted onto the side of a building in Bristol's Stokes Croft the image has become an alternative emblem of the city.

The daring of the street artist entered the museum world when Banksy smuggled a pebble inscribed with a shopping trolley – *The Peckham rock* – into an archaeology display at the British Museum. In a more political vein, he has painted images on the wall that divides the West Bank from Jerusalem and has recently opened a hotel, The Walled-Off, overlooking the wall.

Banksy combines a sharp eye for a strong image with an ability to respond swiftly (and secretly) to current events, a recent example being a painting on a wall in Dover of the European Union's stars of solidarity being chipped away by a workman up a ladder.

In *Banksy versus Bristol Museum* in 2009 his most ambitious prank was to transform the museum into a darkly humorous gallery of his own making. Subversive or quirky interventions appeared, as if overnight, in every display. *Paint pot angel* is one of those exhibits, an inversion of the kind of civic statue that might typically greet visitors in the entrance hall of a museum. It has been defaced with a pot of paint: the art equivalent of a custard pie.

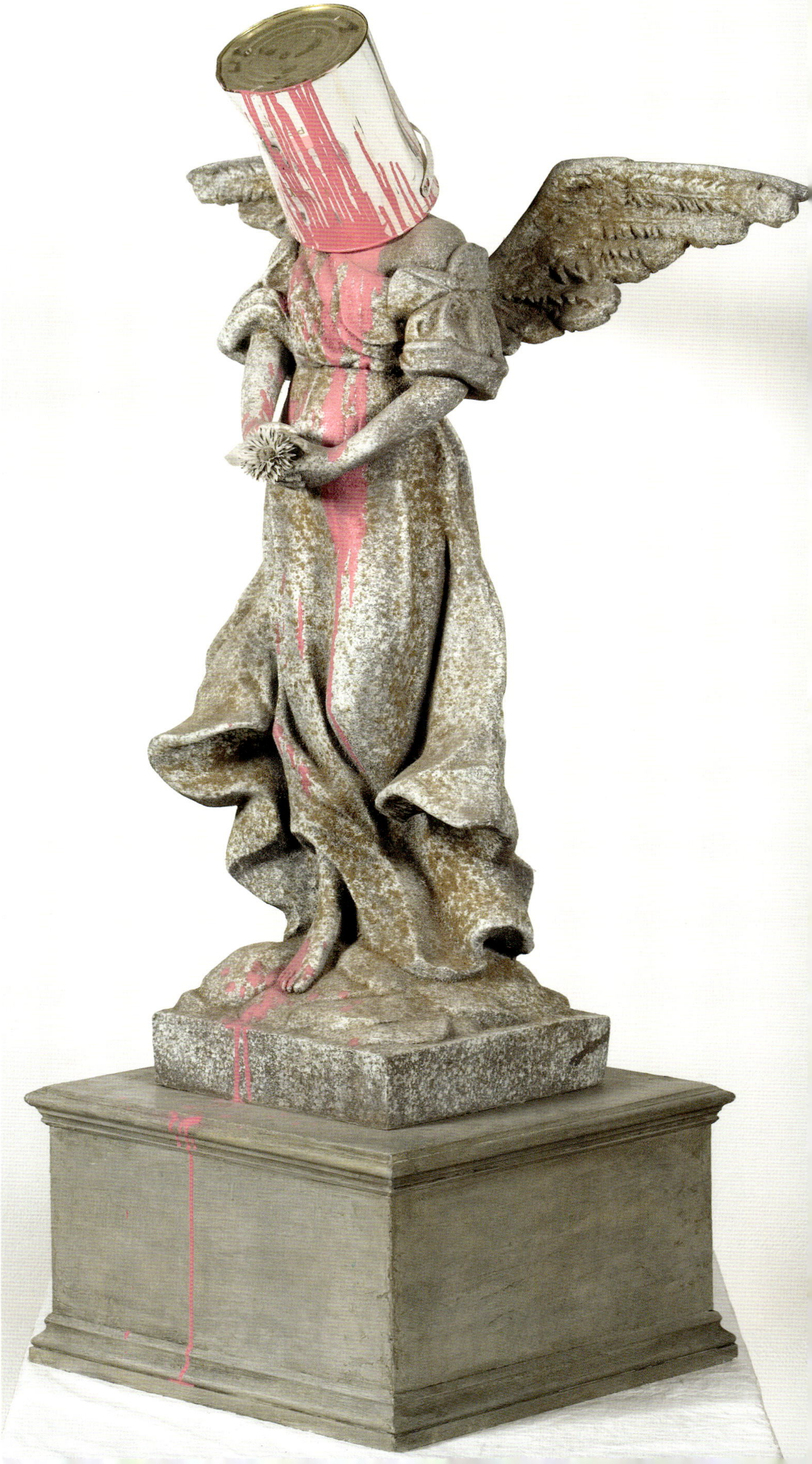

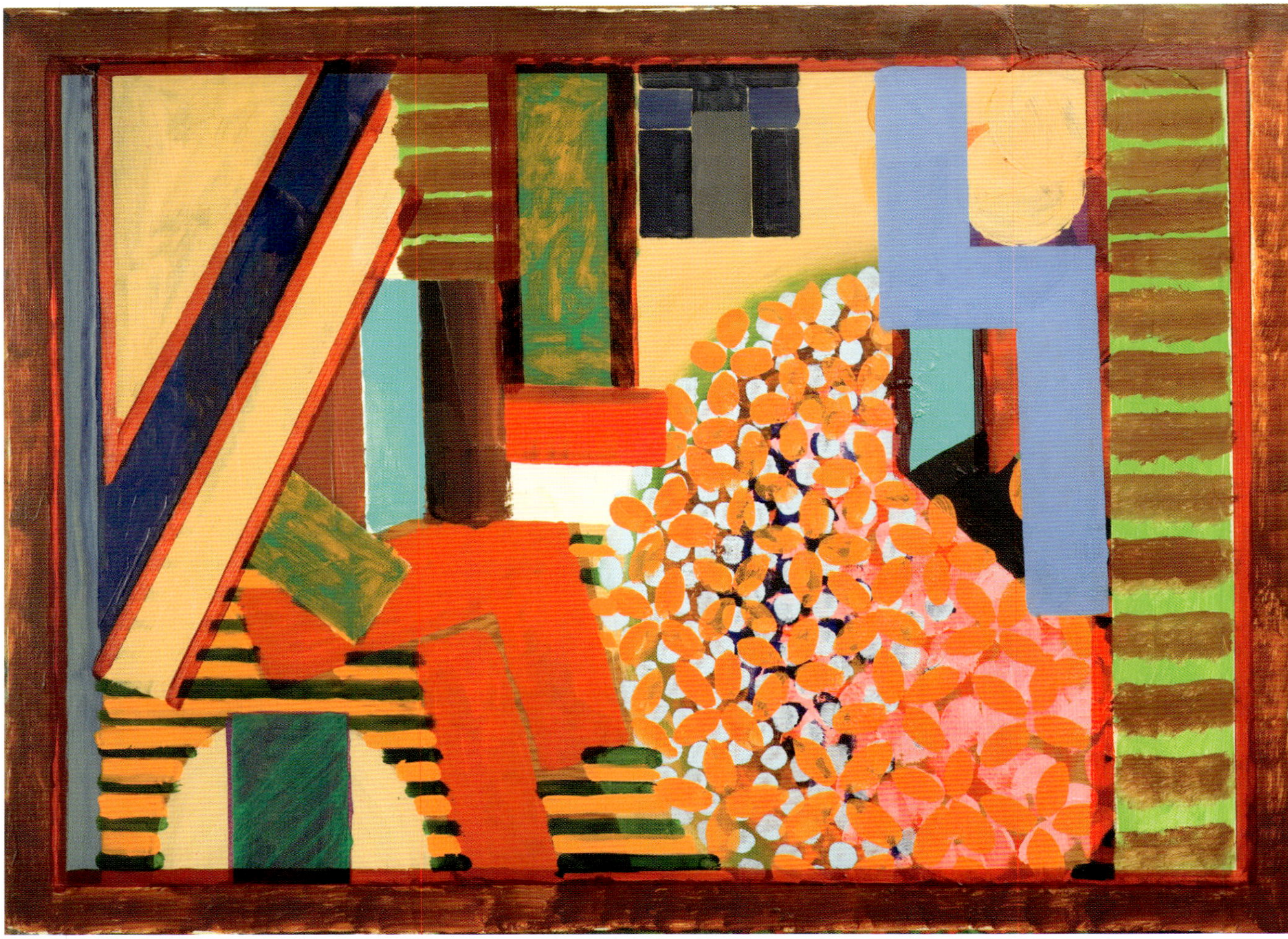

Sir Howard Hodgkin (1932-2017)
Robyn Denny and Katherine Reid
oil on panel, 1973-75
90.8 x 121.3 cm
Purchased with the assistance of the Gulbenkian Foundation, 1975
K4324

Howard Hodgkin called his paintings 'representational pictures of emotional situations'. His wartime experience as an evacuee in America gave him early exposure to Matisse and Fernand Léger at New York's Museum of Modern Art. He went on to study art at Corsham Court in Bath under Peter Lanyon and William Scott. While Scott's approach to abstraction rejected any notion of representation, Hodgkin's emotional approach was rooted in the idea of illustrating a subjective mood. Hodgkin's early work has been compared to the graphic forms of Pop Art.

This double portrait represents Hodgkin's response to his sitters, the artist Robyn Denny and the conservator Katherine Reid. A brown box-like structure frames boldly kinetic stripes that reveal Hodgkin's youthful admiration for the tubular figures of Léger. Layers of surface pattern that blur the depth of the image point to Hodgkin's interest in the interiors of Edouard Vuillard. What is also striking is the colour: the hot red and the warm orange and yellow are balanced by the chalky pink, blue and lilac and the cool green. Hodgkin visited India in 1964 and collected miniature paintings, as well as curating an exhibition *Six Indian Painters* with Geeta Kapur at the Tate in 1982.

Hodgkin's interests were wide-ranging but in the end his paintings remain very personal mood pieces.

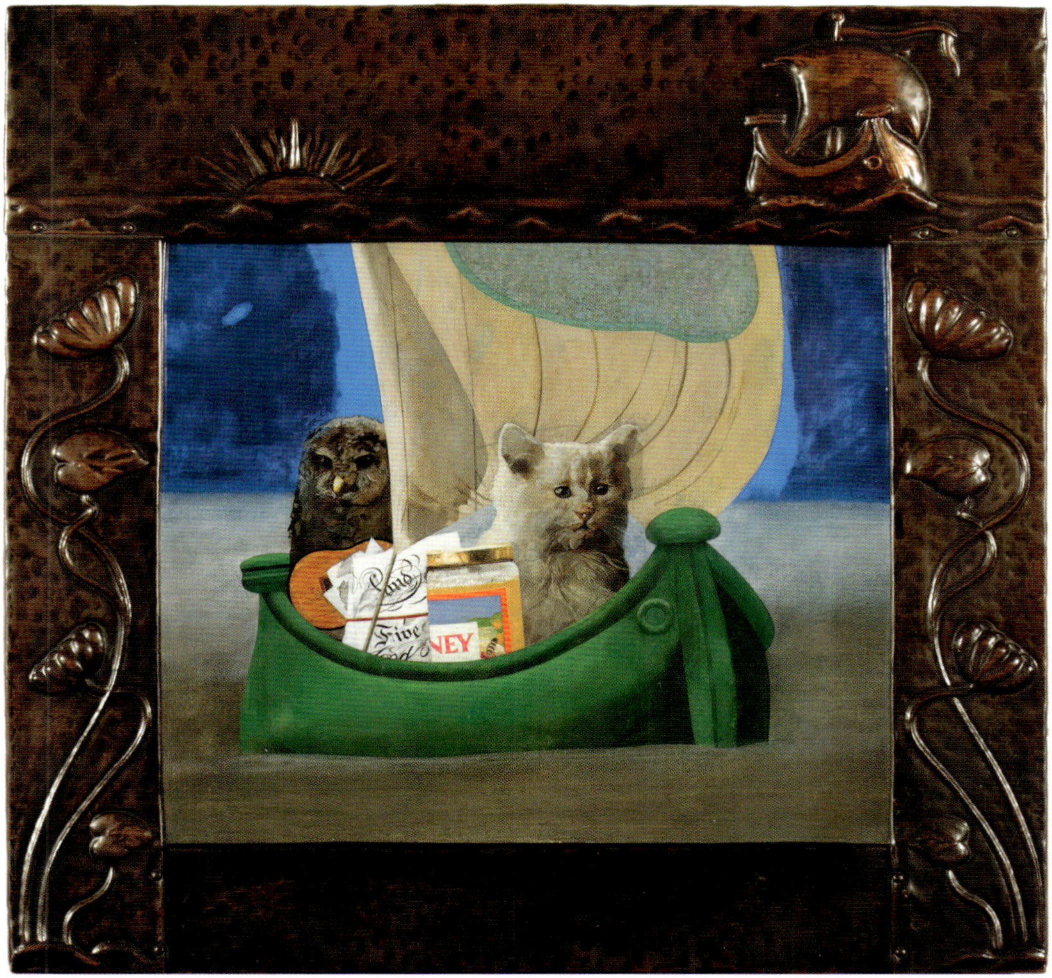

Sir Peter Blake (born 1932)
The owl and the pussycat
tempera on hardboard in copper frame, 1981-83
27.3 x 31.8 cm
Purchased from the artist, while in progress, with the assistance of the Victoria & Albert Museum Purchase Grant Fund, the Friends of Bristol Art Gallery and the Wills Fund, 1981
K5054

In 1969 Peter Blake moved with his wife Jann Haworth and their daughter to a disused railway station near Bath. Blake wholeheartedly embraced rural living. He and Jann established a new school and pioneered a progressive style of teaching. Parenthood inspired a love of the childlike and the couple collected Victorian children's books. Lewis Carroll became a major figure in Blake's imaginative sphere.

From early on in his career, Blake had incorporated three-dimensional items he'd collected into his work, such as children's toys and printers' trays. In this he was inspired by the artist Barbara Jones and her 1951 folk art show of everyday items, *Black Eyes and Lemonade*. By the 1970s Blake was using antique frames for his illustrations of fairies from *A Midsummer Night's Dream*. With David Inshaw he formed the Brotherhood of Ruralists. *The owl and the pussycat* is drawn from Edward Lear's poem of child-like wonder and nonsense logic. Blake sometimes copied his images from photographs, achieving an effect of heightened realism with his crisply-delineated patches of light and shade. He shows the kitten and owl setting sail in a boat matching the design on the *Art Nouveau* frame, with the five-pound note of the poem wrapped around the jar of honey.

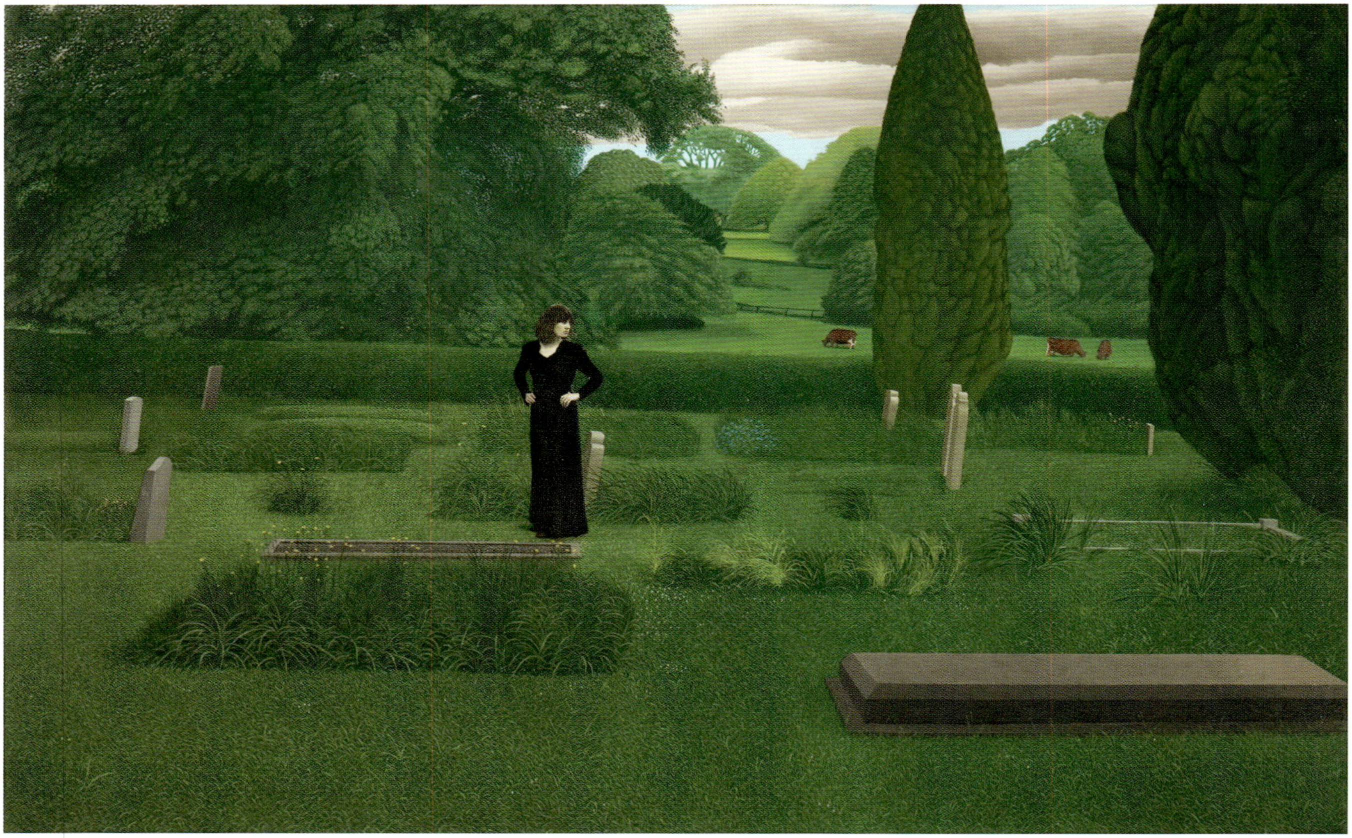

David Inshaw (born 1943)
Our days were a joy and our paths through flowers
oil on canvas, 1972
135.9 x 212.1 cm
Purchased, 1972
K4142

This was the first picture David Inshaw painted after moving to Devizes in Wiltshire in 1971. Inshaw's painting brings a photographic clarity to the themes of the English Romantic artists such as William Blake, Samuel Palmer, Rossetti and Ravilious. His landscapes are so minutely observed that it is almost possible to pick out a single blade of grass. Just as Pre-Raphaelite depictions of chivalric legend featured modern 19th-century sitters, Inshaw uses contemporary settings and models for his scenes of melancholy. He painted *Our days were a joy and our paths through flowers* for a solo show at Bristol's Arnolfini. The graveyard is in Shipley, Sussex. The title is a line from Thomas Hardy's poem, 'After a Journey' which imagines the ghost of Hardy's first wife, Emma Gifford, leading him along the couple's former haunts:

'Trust me, I mind not, though Life lours,
The bringing me here; nay, bring me here again!
I am just the same as when
Our days were a joy, and our paths through flowers.'

Inshaw gave the poem a pagan gloss, imagining an atmosphere where 'the spirits of the people buried in the churchyard liv[ed] on through the plants and the trees.' The woman in the centre of the painting was the student Gillian Matthews. The sense of stillness comes from the use of photography to capture her figure. Light and shade are rendered as flat tonal areas on Gillian's silhouette, the blackness of which contrasts with the lush green of the trees and grass.

Karl Weschke (1925-2005)
Leda and the swan
oil on canvas, 1985-86
183 x 137 cm
Purchased with the assistance of the Arnolfini Collection Trust, the Victoria & Albert Museum Purchase Grant Fund and the Friends of Bristol Art Gallery, 1994
K5706

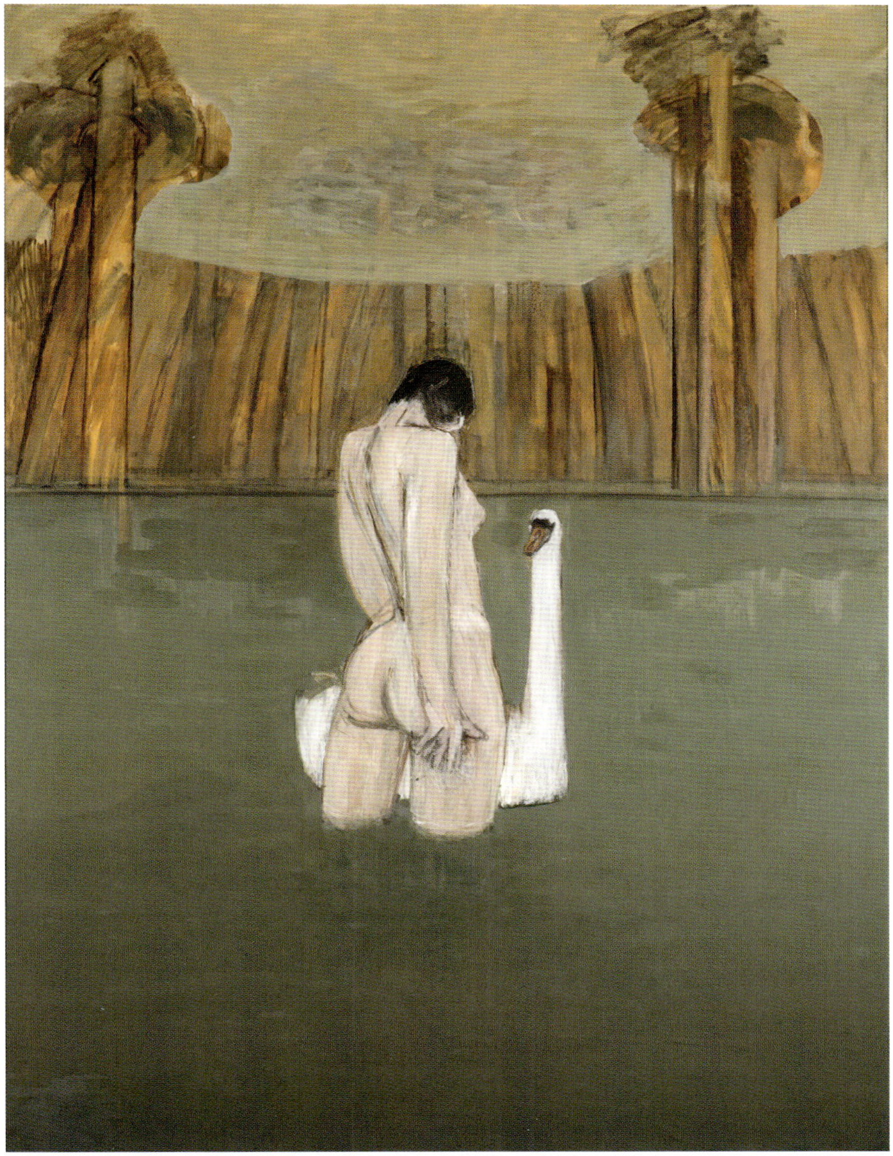

The German-born Karl Weschke came to England as a prisoner of war. After two years in POW camps he was transferred to an open prison in Cambridgeshire where he was drawn to art at extra-mural activities at the University. He settled in St Ives, Cornwall in 1955 where he stayed for the rest of his life.

Although Weschke was close to the St Ives artists his own painting was figurative. Earth tones of ochre and brown are expressively worked in scenes dominated by monumental figures.

Leda and the swan is a starkly sexual design. In an isolated setting a statuesque female figure stands in the grey waters of a lake and confronts a swan. In the classical myth Leda is impregnated by Zeus in the form of a swan. She gives birth to twins that hatch from eggs, one of whom becomes Helen of Troy: in his poem of the same name WB Yeats treated Leda's seduction as a portentous moment that led to the Trojan War. Whereas Yeats pictured Leda as passive ('helpless' and 'terrified') Weschke painted Leda approaching the swan, as aggressively sexual as he.

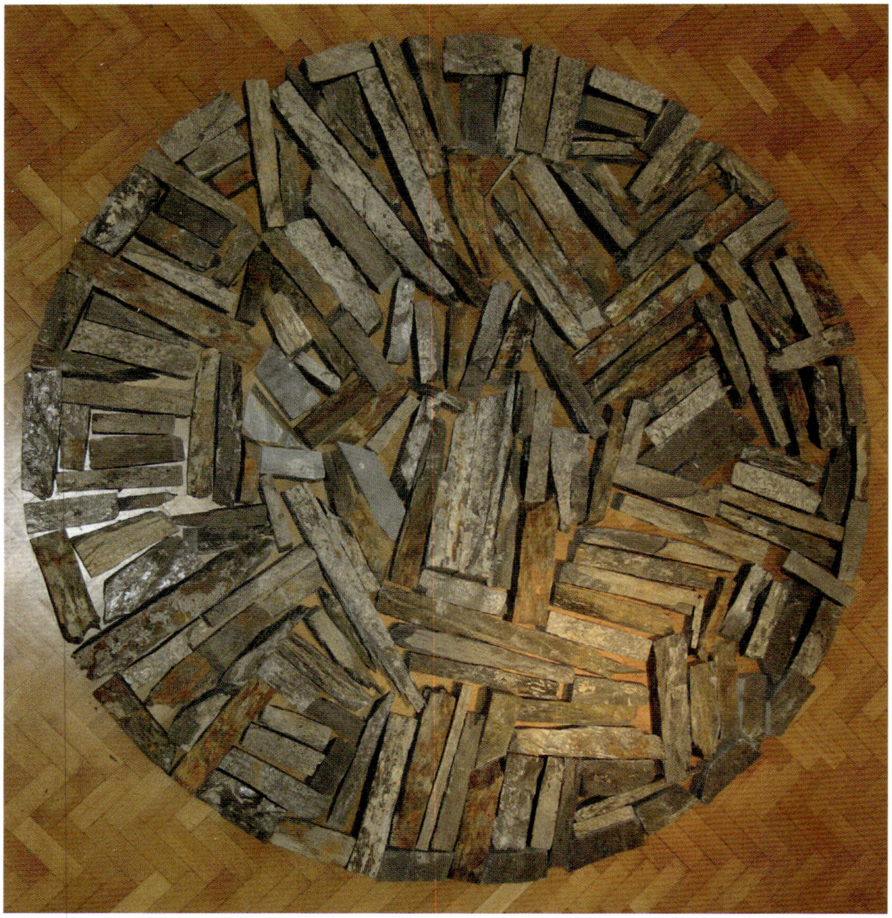

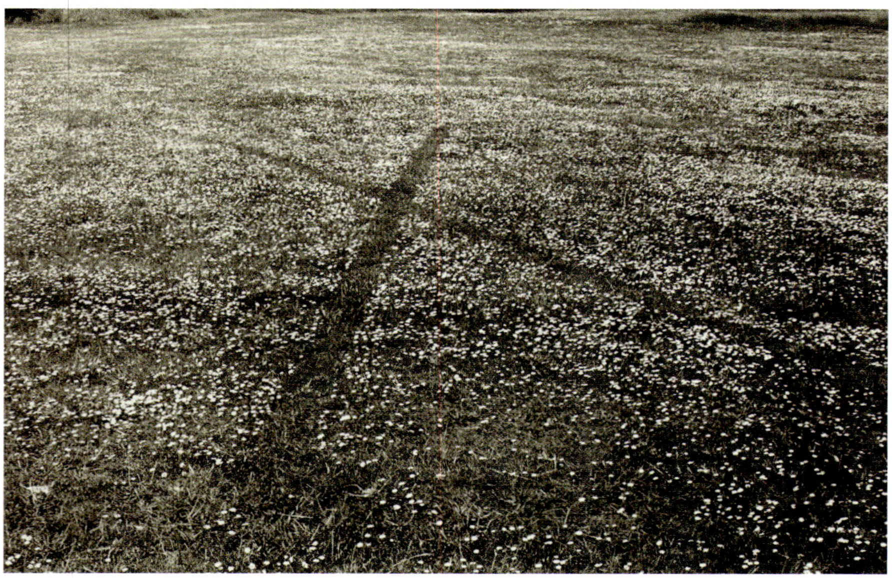

Richard Long (born 1945)
Delabole slate circle (Bristol)
slate, 1997
300 cm diameter
Purchased with the assistance of the Friends of Bristol Art Gallery and the MGC/Victoria & Albert Museum Purchase Grant Fund, 1998
K5866

England 1968
black and white photograph, 1968
48.9 x 74.9 cm
Gift, Arnolfini Collection Trust, 2000
K5941

'A walk marks time with an accumulation of footsteps. It defines the form of the land. Walking the roads and paths is to trace a portrait of the country.'

Richard Long's treatment of the landscape is an implicit rejection of the idea of the permanent monument. While a student at West of England College, Long formulated a non-interventionist way of working with the land that could take the form of gathered snow or a walk or an arrangement of stones on a path. *England 1968* is a record of a walk where Long traced the cross of England's flag into a field of daisies.

Long's floor-based sculptures bring his interventions into the gallery. The visitor is invited to walk around the slate circle, just as the artist walked in the landscape. At the same time, the line of a circle is an infinite form, a symbol that can be traced through archaeology to the earliest human creativity. Long's engagement with the landscape places him in a line of English artists from Turner to Paul Nash and Peter Lanyon.

Ai Weiwei (born 1957)
A ton of tea
compressed *pur eh* tea, 2007
100 x 100 x 100 cm
Presented by the Art Fund under Art Fund International, 2011
K6365

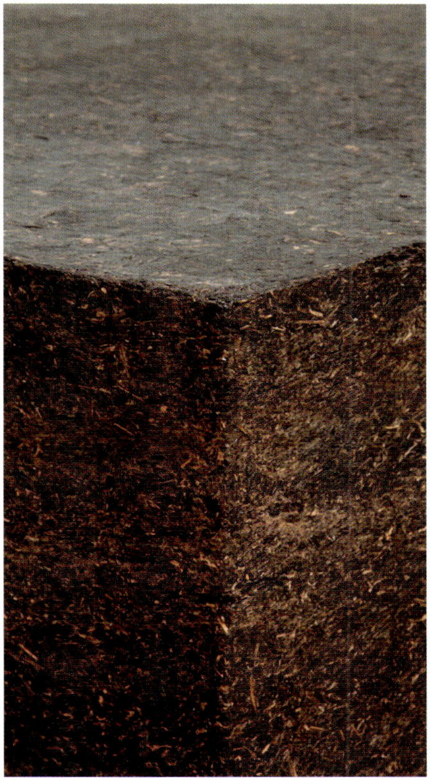

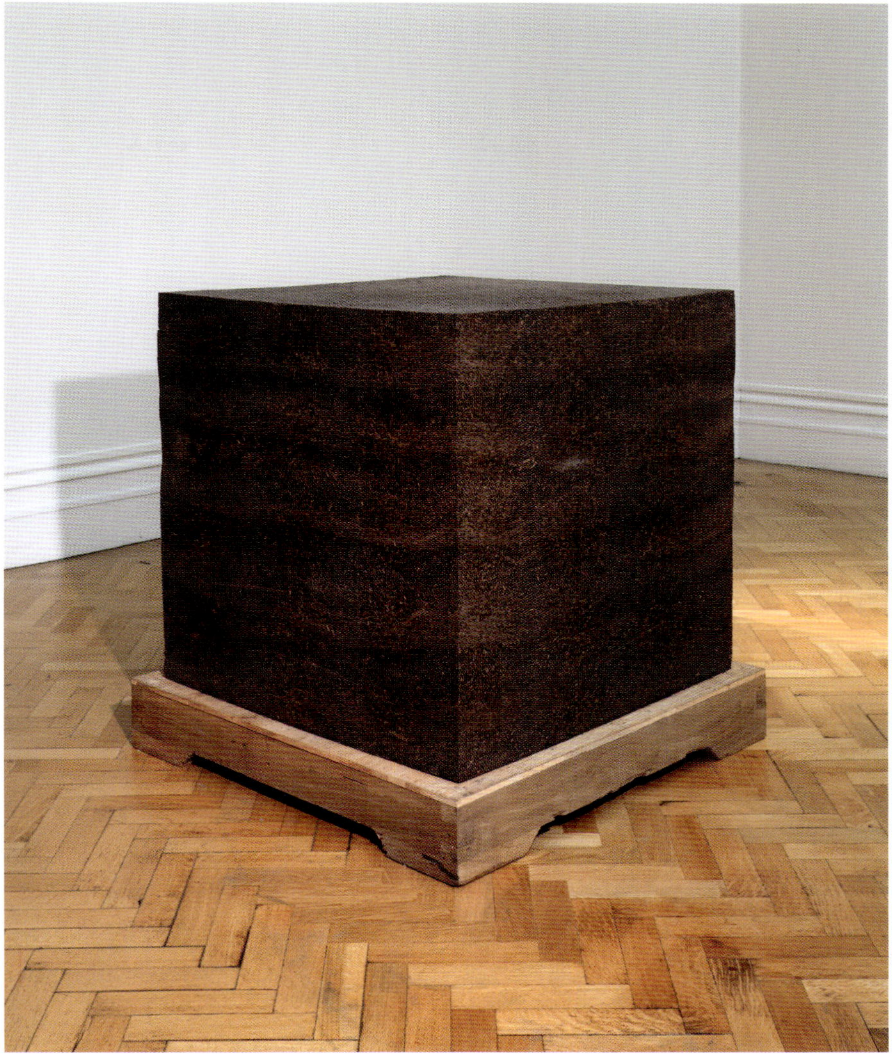

'My art always has something related to the ordinary.'

A ton of tea is a deceptively simple artwork by one of China's most renowned artists. The son of the poet Ai Qing, who was exiled under the Kuomintang and then again under Mao Zedong, Ai Weiwei has developed an international career as an architect, curator and artist. He has become known globally as a vociferous critic of the Chinese government.

With Xu Bing and Zhang Huan, Ai belongs to a generation of Chinese artists working after the Cultural Revolution who seized the chance to create 'experimental' (Conceptual) art. After his father was officially rehabilitated in 1978, Ai trained at the Beijing Film Academy where he became a member of the Stars group (*Xing xing*). Alienated by the political and aesthetic constraints of life in 1980s China Ai placed himself in exile in New York. While there he immersed himself in post-war American art, an influence that helped him to marry art theory with political content in his own work.

A ton of tea, a monumental cube of compressed tea, works both as a Minimalist gesture and a resonant artwork. The pared-down structure and commonplace material are a conscious reference to the American Minimalists' use of basic materials on a monumental scale. Yet for all the apparent simplicity of form and material, the humble substance of tea, China's oldest export, makes a symbolic reference to globalisation.

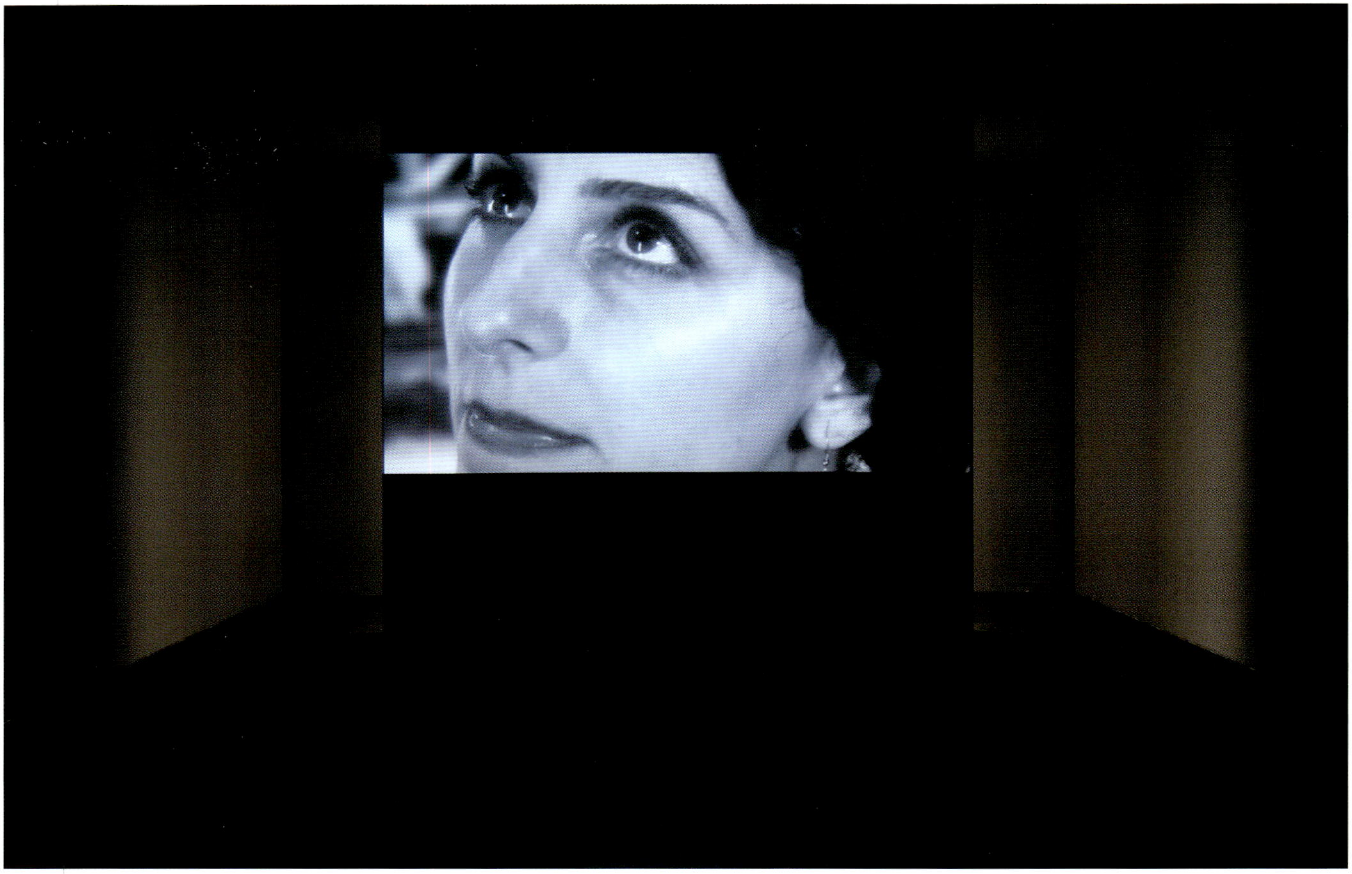

Emily Jacir (born 1970)
Lydda Airport
installation with single channel film and resin sculpture, 2009
5 minutes, 21 seconds
124 x 170 x 89 cm
Presented by the Art Fund under Art Fund International, 2014
K6428

'Lydda Airport *is a short animation film that takes place at Lydda Airport some time in the mid to late 1930s and I perform in it…One of the main characters in the piece is an airplane called Hannibal. It mysteriously disappeared in 1940 somewhere over the Gulf of Oman en route to Sharjah… In brief the work touches upon a lost promise and a moment of possibilities.'*

Emily Jacir's work, which includes video, photography, performance and interventions, subtly subverts social structures and frequently implicates the artist herself.

Lydda Airport was built in 1936 when Palestine was under the British Mandate. It was an important stop along the 'Empire Route' for the British national airline, Imperial Airways. In July 1948, the airport was captured by the Israeli Defence Force and eventually became Ben Gurion International Airport in 1974, when it was named after the first prime minister of Israel.

Lydda Airport is a black and white film composed using archival images. The story it relates took place in the 1930s, when a friend's father, Edmond Tamari, received a message that he should take a bouquet to Lydda Airport to welcome Amelia Earhart to Palestine. Earhart, the pioneering female pilot who disappeared over the Pacific on her journey around the world in 1937, never arrived. In the film Jacir plays the lonely figure waiting with the flowers. The Hannibal plane symbolises the glamour and modernity of that era of air travel. A pristine white model of the Art Deco airport building that accompanies the film contrasts with its dreamlike textures.

Do Ho Suh (born 1962)
New York City apartment, Bristol
polyester, 2014
298.3 x 168.5 x 977.5 cm
Commissioned with funding from the Art Fund under Art Fund International, Arts Council England/Victoria & Albert Museum Purchase Grant Fund and the Henry Moore Foundation, 2014
K6467

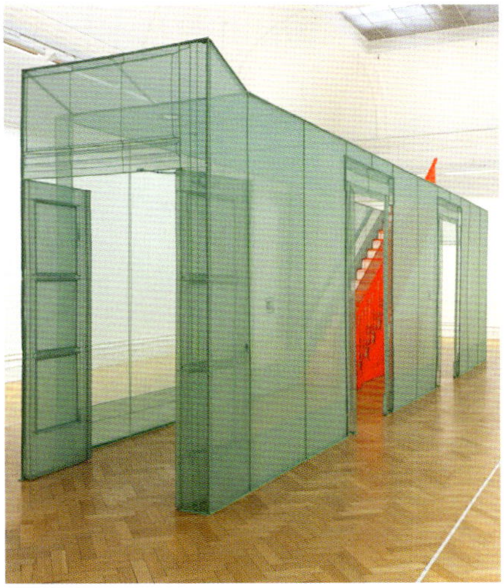

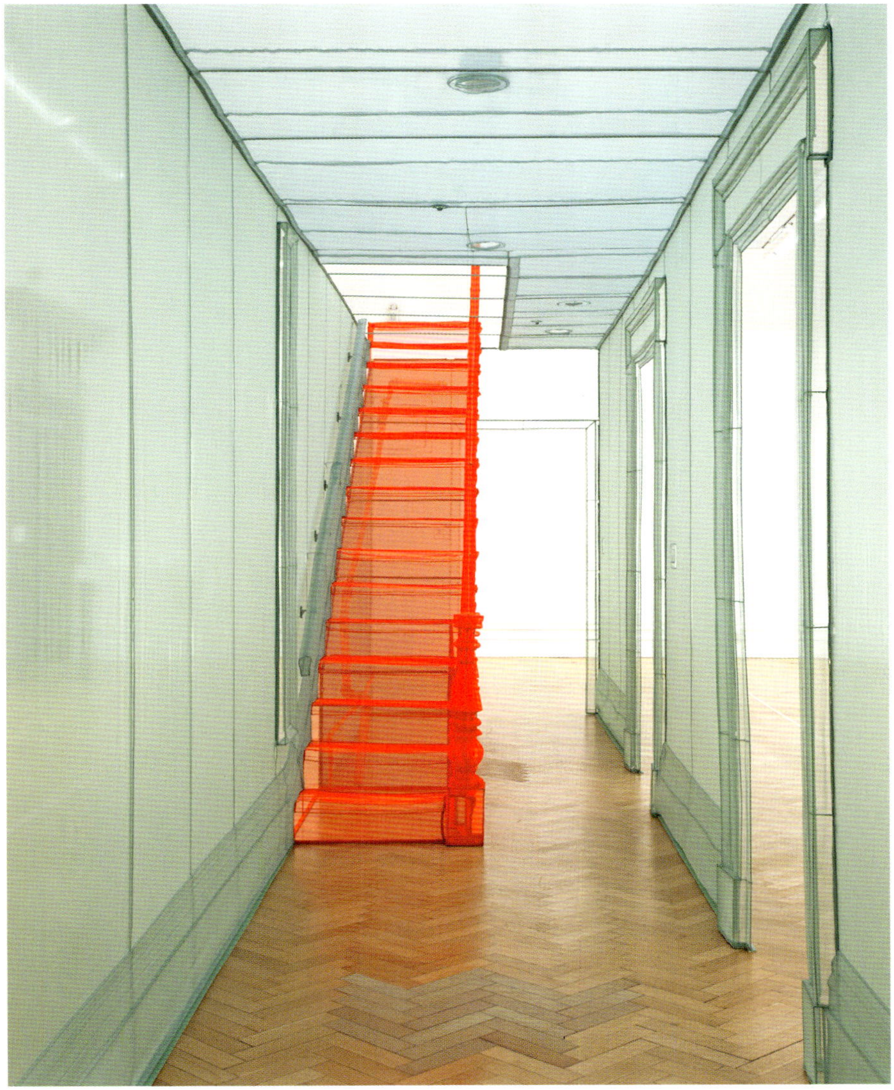

'I feel displaced, even in the house I grew up in'.

'Leaving South Korea for New York was one of the most difficult and important things I have done in my life... Indeed leaving home made me think about home for the first time.'

New York City apartment, Bristol is a fabric recreation of the corridor of 348 West 22nd Street, a brownstone building in Manhattan where the artist Do Ho Suh has rented a basement since 1997. The soft architectural structure acts a symbol of today's multi-cultural existence and the longing of the migrant for home.

Do Ho Suh moved from Seoul to study art in New England in 1997. The culture shock he experienced in the US continues to shape his work. The transparent fabric serves as a reminder of the contrast between the light screens of traditional Korean homes and the thick walls of European and North American houses. The tailoring is a play on words inspired by the Korean verb *jitda* which can mean to make clothing or to build a house. It is based on the artist's need to surround himself with something that is easily measurable and that can be related to his own body, like a garment. By fashioning his home in cloth Do Ho Suh has created an artefact that acts as a physical memory, an object that in theory can be packed up and carried away to the next place.

The floating cloth possesses a softness in contrast to the rigidity of New York's skyscrapers. Its transparency collapses the boundaries between public and private and in doing so conjures vulnerability.

Bristol Museum & Art Gallery – chronology

1808
Bristol Philosophical and Literary Society established.

1820
Foundation stone laid for museum building on Park Street (now Masonic Building), designed by CR Cockerell with frieze by EH Baily. Bristol Institution for the Advancement of Science and Art shared the building with the Society, the focus was on natural history but there was also an exhibition space for art, and an early piece in the collection was Baily's *Eve at the fountain.* Membership was by subscription.

1835
Bristol Corporation donated 100 guineas and a regular subscription.

1863
Bristol Institution merged with Bristol Library Society.

1872
Park Street building sold and museum relocated to Queen's Road building (now Brown's restaurant) designed by John Foster and Archibald Ponton, as Bristol Museum and Library Association.

1891
Museums and Gymnasiums Act enabled councils to levy funds for museums.

1893
Museum liabilities paid by Sir Charles Wathen and Corporation took ownership.

1899
£50,000 donation from Vincent Stuckey Lean paid for new library. Sir William Henry Wills donated £10,000 towards an Art Gallery, proceeding to offer further gifts of £10,000 towards building, in 1900, and ultimately in 1902, £40,000 to fund the whole building costs (this coincided with the amalgamation in 1901 of 13 British tobacco companies, led by Wills, into the Imperial Tobacco Company Ltd, raising the personal fortunes of the Wills family, which owned 68% of company shares, to £1,000,000).

1902
Foundations laid for a building designed by Wills's cousin Sir Frank William Wills.

1905
Art Gallery opened, with a speech by Professor Hubert von Herkomer *'...I say emphatically – keep the collection British!... The purchase of foreign pictures for a British gallery would only be logically advisable if the foreign pictures could teach the English school something... The British school of painting is not a myth; it is a reality!'*

1906
Library vacated museum site, for new building on College Green.

1919
Red Lodge purchased by the Wills family and private arts club the Bristol Savages and leased to the Corporation, with the Corporation taking control in 1948.

1925
A further donation of £75,000 from the Wills family, Sir George A Wills, enabled the expansion of the gallery, designed by John Bertram Wills, opening in 1930.

1936
Georgian House offered to the Corporation by Reverend Canon R Thorold Cole, opening in 1939.

1940
Bomb damage to museum and art gallery.

1945
Museum relocated to art gallery building, although the two were led by separate directors between 1944-1987.

1949
Blaise Castle Folk Museum opened.

1950-71
Extensive planning for a new museum on Wine Street, ultimately abandoned.

1978
Bristol Industrial Museum opened (redeveloped as M Shed in 2011).

2011
M Shed opened.

Significant art donors/ collections

William Jerdone Braikenridge, 1908 and various; topographical drawings of 1820s Bristol

Wills family, 1911

Heber Mardon, 1919, Old Master prints, and funding of the original print room

Lady Weston, 1908, 22 paintings by WJ Müller

Alfred de Pass, 1936, paintings, sculpture and applied art including Albotto, Etty and Ribot

FPM Schiller, 1946, 30 paintings and sculptures including those by Bellini and Cranach, furniture, carpets, Chinese art

National Art Collection Fund-administered Ernest Cook estate, 1955

Corporation annual purchase fund of £1000 rising to £15,000 between 1945-75

Arts Council England Victoria & Albert Museum Purchase Grant Fund

Art Fund (formerly the National Art Collections Fund)

The Friends of Bristol Art Gallery established 1948

Dyer Bequest of £4000, 1961

Gulbenkien match grant 1976-80 for contemporary art

Art Fund International 2007-2012 through the Art Fund - £1 million for international contemporary art

Acceptance in Lieu scheme

Index